The World of Wines

COLLIER BOOKS

A Division of Macmillan Publishing Co., Inc.

NEW YORK

COLLIER MACMILLAN PUBLISHERS

LONDON

CREIGHTON CHURCHILL

The World of Wines

SECOND REVISED EDITION

Maps by Ava Morgan

Macmillan Publishing Co., Inc.
866 Third Avenue, New York, N.Y. 10022
Collier Macmillan Canada Ltd.

Library of Congress Cataloging in Publication Data
Churchill, Creighton.
The world of wines.

Bibliography: p. 235
Includes index.
1. Wine and wine making. I. Title.
TP548.C54 1980   641.2'22   80-18612
ISBN 0-02-009460-4

Revised Collier Books Edition 1974
Second Revised Collier Books Edition 1980

PRINTED IN THE UNITED STATES OF AMERICA

Parts of the chapters on California and the storage of wine originally appeared in *Harper's* magazine, and the chapter on Portugal and Spain originally appeared in *Gourmet* magazine.

Wine, Woman, Baths—
By Art or Nature warme—
Us'd or Abus'd—do Man
Much good—or harme.

—CODE OF THE *Civitas Hippocratica*
  (MEDICAL SCHOOL OF SALERNO—10TH CENT.)

Contents

List of Maps and Charts

Tables

Preface

Many readers will want to know what changes have occurred in the world of wines since this book was first written almost twenty years ago. In one sense, very few. No one has invented a startlingly new wine, nor is anyone likely to; and except for a handful of hybrids and crosses usually yielding inferior wine, we still use the same grapes that grew in Burgundy, and on the Rhine, the Po, and the Danube since wines were first made in these places. Nor has the art of wine making radically changed: we still follow Nature's formula, giving Nature a little push or a nudge here and there, to slow it down or hurry it up a bit.

There have been temporal changes, of course, some for better, some for worse. French wines, especially Burgundies and the lesser châteaux of Bordeaux, have somehow fallen off. All but the most dedicated producers seem to have devised ways to circumvent the stringent laws and wine-making traditions of their country and to make half-acceptable wines to drink before their time. Overproduction and forcing the vine are not what Nature orders for the finest.

In much the same vein, Germany enacted laws in 1971 reducing the number of authorized vineyards from 20,000 to 2,500, at the same time erasing the identity of many of its greatest traditional vineyards—names that wine fanciers used to commit to memory. This has resulted in increased sales of wines, good or less good, often pooled under unfamiliar collective names. Prior to 1971, the German systems of labeling and identifying the quality of wines were by far the most truthful and comprehensive on earth, and no consumer ever asked that they be changed.

But these trends are happily not universal, and we can record improvements and changes for the better in wines from many other countries. Spain, for one, has at last awakened to the tastes of the rest of the world. Traditional Spanish wines used to be soaked in oak until the whites were the color of mustard and the reds hard as bricks. But today Spain exports canary-colored whites, often even fruity, and many a red that is soft and ready to drink by the time it reaches our shores. Italy has embarked on a program of reform and regulation for its vineyards and wineries—an almost Augean task for a country that once was known to color its common Chianti with oxblood and ship it in decorative little flasks with corks so short that the wine generally reached the consumer as vinegar. Italian wines—that is, the recognized classic ones—nowadays reflect quality and, most important of all, consistency. Good, inexpensive wines are also emerging from behind the Iron Curtain, notably Yugoslavia and Romania; and from two of our South American neighbors, Chile and Argentina, the latter having taken a generous leaf from the book of California wine-making technology.

Last but by no means least are the wines from our own West Coast. The progress of California wine making over the past twenty years (and more recently in Washington State and Oregon) is all but miraculous. Many of today's California wines are almost unrecognizable compared with those of two decades ago. This assessment includes all three categories of production: the large mass-producers, the medium-sized makers of the "premium wines," and the small wineries popularly known—we happen to think a bit disparagingly—as the "boutiques." Although our West Coast friends don't always like to hear it, the fact remains that the U.S. wine industry is still very much in its adolescence, not even a hundred and fifty years old. Compare this to Burgundy's two thousand years of settling down. This is the truly exciting aspect of what we like to call—borrowing a geopolitical term—the "developing" wines of the world. In the years ahead, these are the ones to watch.

CREIGHTON CHURCHILL

New York
June, 1980

Acknowledgments

Among the many whose advice and material assistance have so indelibly contributed to the preparation of these pages and the various revisions thanks and recognition must be given to Michel L. Dreyfus, Henri Malval, Warren B. Strauss, Peter M. F. Sichel, Charles M. Fournier, Konstantin Frank of New York; Otto E. Meyer, Robert Mondavi, Hanns J. Kornell, John Daniel, Jr., of California; Hubert Beauville, Mme. Emile La Planche of Paris; Guy Faiveley, Jacques Chevignard, Comte Georges de Vogüé, Robert Drouhin, Cyprian and Pierre Maufoux of Burgundy; Comte Bertrand du Vivier, Geoffroy deLuze of Bordeaux; Raymond Lillet of Podensac (Gironde); Michel Delas of Tournon-sur-Rhône; Dr. Richard Müller of Reil (Mosel); Fritz Rall of Worms; Dr. Helmut Becker of Geisenheim; Franz Karl Schmitt of Nierstein; Dr. Ludwig von Bassermann-Jordan of Deidesheim, Germany; Ferando de Terenas Latino, Antonio Julio Pereira, Fernando Van Z. Guedes, Antonio C. Sarmento of Portugal; Fernando Calleja of Madrid, Diego Ochagavia, Jésus M. Satún, Pedro López de Heredia of the Rioja, Spain; Lazlo Terelmes of Budapest.

The World of Wines

CHAPTER 1

Wine—What Is It?

What is wine? What are the best wines? How did wine come to be?
We hear these questions every day—and little wonder. How many liquids there are that come in a bottle today labeled wine.

Perhaps we should answer the last question first, since it can be little
more than speculation. For although wine is an integral part of the history of man, it is also deeply buried in man's history.

Wine is certainly as ancient as the Bible—however ancient that may
be. It is mentioned several hundred times in that book, in which the
framers of our religion generally appear to have approved of it, though
they often took pains to urge its temperate use. One of Noah's first acts
was to plant a vineyard, according to legend in Illyria, now eastern
Yugoslavia. And we are all familiar with the miracle at Cana, when
Jesus is said to have transformed water into wine for the guests at a
wedding. Paul of Tarsus, thought to have been a Greek physician, is
the author of the phrase "Take a little wine for thy stomach's sake."

Elsewhere in the Middle East, wine was made in Egypt and in Persia
by very much the same methods as are employed today in Europe, California and elsewhere—except that our modern techniques of fermentation, aging and preserving wine are more efficient and, as a result, we
drink far more potable table wines than our forebears did. The wines

[1]

of old were coarse and hard, and the ancients usually watered them when they drank them.

Wine, properly speaking, is made from what are known as wine grapes, which—although closely related—are not the same variety of grape as table or eating grapes. The wine grape, botanically called *Vitis vinifera*, is smaller, more acid in taste and far less palatable than the table grape (*Vitis labrusca*)—and though the latter also makes wines of sorts, most wine drinkers of the world do not associate their taste with that of wine.

History naturally does not record what special or single type of the several hundred forms of *Vitis vinifera* was used to make the first wine, but the variety appears to have first appeared in the Middle East—and like so many of the good things that man eats or drinks today, wine was undoubtedly not invented, but came about by accident. One might say that nature must have clearly ordained that man drink wine, because every necessary ingredient of wine is packaged, so to speak, by nature herself, and may be found in the ripe wine grape or in the surrounding air. Man has almost never needed to do more than supervise nature's simple receipt, although modern vintners—seeking to outdo nature's formula or to compensate for local deficiencies—often supplement natural grape juice with cultured yeasts, tannin, acids and sometimes sugar.

When the mature grape is crushed (the ancient tradition of using bare feet still exists in a few parts of the world today), the yeasts, ever-present in the atmosphere, commence feeding on the sugar in the juice, and in turn convert part of this juice to alcohol. What is needed, essentially, is sweet fruit juice—and the appropriate yeasts. This fermentation or chemical conversion can also occur with a peach or a cherry or even a dandelion blossom—but usually these fruit wines that we know today have had sugar added after fermentation and have been fortified with more alcohol than they acquired by natural fermentation. Thus they technically fall into the category of cordials or liqueurs, or else what the French call *apéritifs*, drinks best consumed before or after meals. Nature's yeasts are capable of producing only a certain amount of alcohol, and natural wine from the wine grape, which rarely contains more than 14 per cent alcohol (and usually less), almost always seems to be best with food. The exceptions are wines such as Sherry, Port and Madeira, which are all fortified with extra alcohol, and happen to be as delightful and appropriate with certain foods as without them.

What wines seem to go best with what foods is a subject we will cover in Chapter 11—but in the meantime the best advice to be given any wine drinker is this: If you don't like a particular wine when you try it, don't give up—try another! There are literally hundreds of different varieties, enough to match varying tastes, so that some wine will surely suit nearly every one of us, provided we are persistent enough to find it. Just as some people become sick the first hour at sea and swear on the Bible never to travel again if God will only deliver them safely back to dry land, the mistake many of us make is to decide, at the first try, that we just don't like wine. Yet there are sweet wines, dry wines, strong and less strong wines, sparkling, red, white and pink (*rosé*) wines—and they are all quite different. Once you have found one you like you will discover, in turn, that your taste often will grow to others—and often in a most surprising fashion.

Whereas wine consumption in established European nations remains almost static, this is not the case with the English-speaking nations of the New World, especially the United States. Even though, per capita, we drink about one-fifteenth of what France or Italy drinks, our thirst and enthusiasm and interest are all rising rapidly—and our country has become the marketing target, for better or worse, of virtually every wine-producing nation on earth. Exorbitant prices asked by the classic wine makers of Europe have, to be sure, led to an influx of inferior and/or overpriced imported wines (which the eager wine drinker will soon ferret out); yet, on the brighter side of the picture, our own wines, especially those of California, Oregon and Washington, show an improvement in character and quality each year, and our shelves are also bedecked with a galaxy of imports never before imagined. Thus the experimental wine drinker has an almost infinite choice: California, France, Italy, New York State, Portugal, Spain, Israel, Austria, Australia and dozens of others.

Wines fit with food—and one is always making the pleasant discovery that certain wines fit better with certain foods than others. The right wine never fails to enhance the right food, and vice versa. Yet wine is also a generally healthful but mild food in itself, and we should not forget it has been an integral part of the diet for peoples of many lands for uncountable generations. Even today peasants of some European nations thrive on a simple fare of bread, cheese—and wine. They have their meat on Sundays. Wine whets the appetite and aids digestion, and because the roots of the wine grape often penetrate the subsoil deeper than the roots of the trees of the forest, the grape contains many

THE VINEYARDS OF
Europe
and North Africa

Morgan

5'

NETHER-
LANDS
terdam
R.RHEIN
(RHINE)

Bonn

G E R M A N Y

R. DONAU (DANUBE)

Vienna

Bern
SWITZERLAND

A U S T R I A

Budapest

R O M A N I A

R. PO

Belgrade

Bucharest

CORSICA

Y
U
G
O
S
L
A
V
I
A

Sofia
B U L G A R I A

R. TIBER

I
T
A
L
Y

Rome

G
R
E
E
C
E

SARDINIA

SICILY

Athens

R
R
A
N
E
A
N

TUNISIA

Tunis

S E A

10'

15'

20'

25'

trace minerals and other properties that we do not ordinarily get in our day-to-day diet.

One will be glad to learn, too, that wine's caloric content is low—not even comparable, in fact, to a drink of whiskey or a cocktail. Its benefits are what we might term "side benefits." In addition to stimulating appetite and digestion, wine nourishes a brief, rosy, but harmless viewpoint which is very different from the oftentimes unfortunate effect of hard liquor; and there is entirely sound medical evidence that it reduces the cholesterol content of the blood—an important factor in heart ailments. Contrary to popular opinion, it does not produce gout. And though you may have heard that it is bad for the liver, the fact is, because wines go so well with foods, many people, especially Europeans, are tempted to consume far more rich food than is good for them—washing it down with good wine to aid the lagging digestion and thus creating a vicious cycle of gluttony. The French, for example, are always talking about their "bad livers," usually blaming it on wine, and many an overstuffed Frenchman annually puts in time at one of his country's spas or watering spots, such as Vichy or Évian, where the water one drinks reputedly helps the liver. Yet it always seems to be overlooked that all these spas have skilled medical staffs in attendance whose function it is to put the patient on a strict regimen which does not necessarily always exclude wine.

What are the best wines? Since the avowed purpose of this book is to discuss wines of the countries that may be available to U. S. drinkers, the reader may be puzzled to observe that more than one-third of these pages is devoted to the wines of France and Germany—which, taken together, actually produce only a fraction of the world's wines. The point to be emphasized is that the production of good wine—leaving out the comparatively minute human factor—fundamentally depends on a subtle combination of three vital elements: (1) soil, (2) a wine grape or grapes appropriate to this same soil and (3) climate. Without all three of these elements present—in fact, in almost perfect harmony—good and great wines are simply not made by man, however hard he tries. Although the wine grape is cultivated in many parts of the world, there is a marked difference among the types and qualities of wines from different climatic zones and from different soils. Over the years, the soils and climates of France and southern Germany have proved to be the best for wines. Even if the only evidence were the preponderance of French and German wine terms used by others—California "Rhine wine," Chilean "Burgundy," Australian "Claret"—it could still be said that France and Germany have set the traditional standard for the world. None of which means one should minimize the importance of Italy or Spain or our West Coast—especially in a day of high prices and at a time when few great wines are allowed to age to any degree approaching true perfection.

In terms of climate, there exist on all the continents certain definite northern and southern limits, beyond which the wine grape either does not produce profitably or else makes a wine so coarse and unpalatable that no one nowadays cares much about drinking it. In Europe this geographical range extends roughly from the 30th to the 50th parallel, north of which almost no wine is produced—with the exception of a little bulge of celebrated vineyards along the Rhine and Moselle rivers in Germany and a handful of distinctly experimental ones in southern England. Algeria and Israel, close to the southernmost boundary of the European zone, produce wines that are hardly rated at all by connoisseurs, although Algerian wines were for a long time the source or at least the basis for blends of most of the common wines (*ordinaires*) drunk in France. Farther south, as long ago as 5000 B.C., the wine grape was raised along the Nile in Egypt—until it was found that wines brought down from Greece were better. The Romans, in turn, drank Greek and what are now Italian, Portuguese and Spanish wines until Gaul was developed—after which their most prized vintages came from their Gallic outposts, now France and Germany.

Thus history has shown that, in addition to the consideration of soils, man has progressively found the wines of northern countries more delicate and desirable—greater, as the term goes—than those of the south, which tend to be coarser and less subtle. This is very amply illustrated on our own continent on the West Coast, the largest wine-producing area in North America, where the wines from the northernmost limit of the wine-growing zone—the regions north and south of San Francisco Bay, extending north to Oregon and Washington—are traditionally thought to be the best. In warmer parts of the south, California wines increasingly resemble the bland and comparatively less delicate products of other warm, sunny lands, such as southern Italy and Algeria. Mexican wines, the southernmost product of our North American continent, are nothing anyone usually wants to bring home. And below the equator nature's same rule holds: the wines of Chile and Argentina definitely outshine those of Peru and Brazil; Australia and Africa likewise make their best wines in the colder parts of their wine-producing zones, those closest to the South Pole.

Even people who have drunk wines for years are often sorely perplexed by their names and their numbers, and particularly by the specialized language on the labels. In the United States alone we see hundreds of wines from dozens of different countries, and with all of them the nomenclature of their labels—not to mention the pronunciations—affords grounds for confusion, and often seems to have little or no logic. Yet it is not quite so difficult or discouraging as it might appear, once one catches on to certain fundamental patterns. A wine almost invariably derives its name from one of three sources: either the name of the principal grape from which it is made (the case with most of the best Californian, Alsatian or South American wines); the geographical area from which it comes (Chablis, Champagne, Chianti); or, in the case of the traditionally finest wines, mostly European, a particular vineyard or parcel of soil (Château Haut-Brion, Clos de Vougeot, Schloß Johannisberg).

There are some irritating exceptions, of course, most of which we discuss in detail in later chapters. One of the arch crimes of producers of nearly all wine-producing countries is the fallacious use of names stolen from other parts of the world—"type names," or what are known as "generics." For example, the sweet, luscious dessert wine called Sauternes is made only in a region of southwestern France, but because of its worldwide fame, United States, Australian and many other producers copy the name, even though there is no similarity whatever in the wines. Burgundy is also a term bootlegged the world over. Another case is Champagne, which in France itself may legally be called Champagne only if it is produced in the so-called Champagne district from certain prescribed grapes.[1] But the name Champagne has been purloined by United States wineries and many others to enhance almost anything white or pink with a fizzle. Yet another type of hoax involves the wine known as Liebfraumilch, the most popular of all exported German wines. Liebfraumilch (Milk of the Holy Virgin) is

[1]Other French sparkling wines must be labeled *mousseux*. And although some few nations adhere to the request of the French and avoid the term Champagne, it is a matter of record that France saw to it, in the Versailles Treaty, that no German sparkling wine would ever be called Champagne. German sparklings are called *Sekt*.

regrettably a name that may be legally attached to almost any wine from a large, even though demarcated, section of the Rhineland. Thus it is a common (and highly profitable) practice to use it for any and all wine not meriting a more specific or noble title. Some producers hope, too, that many a wine drinker will believe that Liebfraumilch, which is made by the thousands of gallons, springs from a celebrated, tiny vineyard (itself the source of excellent wine) within the city of Worms, belonging to a church known as the Liebfrauenkirche.

Obviously, were one to decide to become an expert on wines, which would involve knowing all the best wines, one would begin by learning the names (and the tastes) of those wines from all the most famous plots of soil on which the wine grape has traditionally flourished over the last thousand years or so. For the great majority of us, this would require far too much travel and homework, not to mention a rather staggering expense. As we shall see, there are many shortcuts to a knowledge and appreciation of wines that do not require the labors of an expert. But it is still well to remember—for those who would ask the question "Can some wines really be so *much* better than others?"—that the finest of them do indeed come from the appropriate grapes cultivated on time-tested soil, ground that has the ideal chemical properties for the wine grape, the best exposure to the sun and just the right amount of rainfall, as well as protection from winds and frosts. There are not too many of these ideal spots on the face of the earth: this is why fine wines have always brought high prices. Yet there is the redeeming truth that most people who pursue even a mild interest in wines sooner or later acquire an ability to recognize the qualities of the best. Even though they may never have tasted the actual best, they become singularly equipped to distinguish the sheep from the goats. A great majority of them will have begun as the average man must do: by finding one or two wines he likes, sticking to his taste for them as long as the taste lasts—and, of course, continually experimenting.

CHAPTER 2

Wines of France

The Versatile Wineland

In the pre-Christian world the Greeks were the active colonizers and developers of the *Vitis vinifera*, or wine grape. They were followed by the Romans, who were in turn succeeded—beginning in the Middle Ages and continuing virtually into our own day—by the Church. We shall have more to say about the Church's role over the centuries in fostering the wine grape: there is almost no wine-producing portion of the world, including our own California, which is in this respect not heavily in the Church's debt.

The first known plantings of the wine grape in France took place about 600 B.C. at a Greek colony on the Mediterranean, near what is now Marseille. Many oenologists (the scientists of viniculture) are nowadays convinced that the *vinifera* grew naturally in most of Europe below the 50th parallel, and that the subsequent burgeoning of the wine grape in this part of the world was not so much a matter of colonizing as of developing what was already there. The Romans loved their wines, and knew how to make them; they also needed them for the comfort and courage of their legions in distant lands. With their arrival on the scene, the culture of the wine grape soon spread up the Rhône

Valley and westward and northward to other parts of France and the Moselle. Even in the days of Julius Caesar, the wines of Gaul were being talked about in Rome—and under Roman domination the industry showed such promise that about a hundred years later the Roman emperor Domitian took steps to suppress it, one reason given being a fear that these Gallic wines might blanket the fame of Rome's own traditional vineyards. Another and more logical reason was that Rome wanted more grain planted to feed the legions and the expanding populations of the colonies. In any event, the somewhat naïve command went out from Rome to destroy all the vineyards in Gaul. Happily, the ban was all but ignored—and from that day on, France was well on her way to becoming the indisputable queen of all the wine-producing nations on earth. Nor is there, even today, a shred of evidence that her preeminence in the world of wines ever will vanish or fade. As we have noted, great wines derive in large part from soils and climates—and within her perimeter France has not only a wide variety but also nearly all the proven best.

France is smaller than Texas, with a population of about six times that of the Lone Star State—and nearly everyone in France drinks wine. The annual consumption for each French man, woman and child is somewhat more than thirty gallons—which amounts to nearly a pint a day.[1] This is not to say that every French child drinks a pint of wine daily, although many French children still do drink wine, usually watered, instead of milk. Their fathers think nothing of consuming a bottle of it as the standard accompaniment to each of the day's two major meals. The French, like so many European peoples, consider wine to be as much a food as a beverage. France devotes about three and a half million acres (one-third of her acreage in wheat) to the production of one and a half billion gallons of wine—and as though this shouldn't be enough to take care of the national thirst, she imports another million gallons or so. Formerly this latter supply came largely from Algeria; now it comes from Portugal, Spain, Greece, Tunisia, Morocco and Corsica. Only in Italy—half the size of France, but producing almost half as much wine again as France itself—is the industry more important to the national economy.

[1] By contrast, the average American still drinks about two gallons a year.

French Labels and Vintages

In both the United States and England the great majority of truly
fine imported wines are German and French, and this situation will no
doubt continue—even with a rising spiral of prices and an ever-increas-
ing demand. But it must be emphasized that these imported French
wines are not the ones which the French people ordinarily drink themselves on a daily basis. France has always been a frugal nation, and her
citizens would not dream of drinking their best wines—except on very
special occasions—when they can reap a nice profit on them abroad.
Thus the ordinary Frenchman drinks a comparatively unsavory, coarse
blend of his country's inferior wines, often put together with Italian,
Greek or Iberian wines as a base—and sends most of his choice products to West Germany, Belgium, England, Switzerland and the United
States, in roughly that order. Significantly, the United States pays the
highest bill—meaning, of course, she buys more of the best.

France's wine exports are a mere trickle compared to her immense
production and prodigious national consumption, and most of these
common wines of France, the *ordinaires*, rarely see a bottle or a label—
and are thus of no concern to us here.

One often hears that the way to become knowledgeable about wines
is to learn to read a label. In general, this is sound advice—except that
in the case of French wines the matter of becoming an infallible expert
in the field of labels may require the devotion of a good part of a life-
time. No country in the world, even method-minded Germany, has
stricter or more sensible regulations about the production of its wines
than France—and correspondingly looser and more illogical laws about
its labels. French law prescribes the type of wine grapes to be used on
a specific piece of soil, the maximum production per acre (a factor in
a wine's quality), the minimum alcoholic content of the wine and the
exacting methods by which the vines of each locality are to be pruned
each year. Even setting the exact day when the grapes may be picked
in the autumn is carefully regimented by local authorities. Out of a
hundred or so wine grapes in popular use in France today, usually only
one or two are authorized for a given piece of soil or for a region that
is rarely larger than an average county in the United States. These
officially sanctioned grapes are the ones tradition has proven to be the
best suited for the soil and climate—and only the Lord can help a
French wine grower caught deviating from the official formula. By

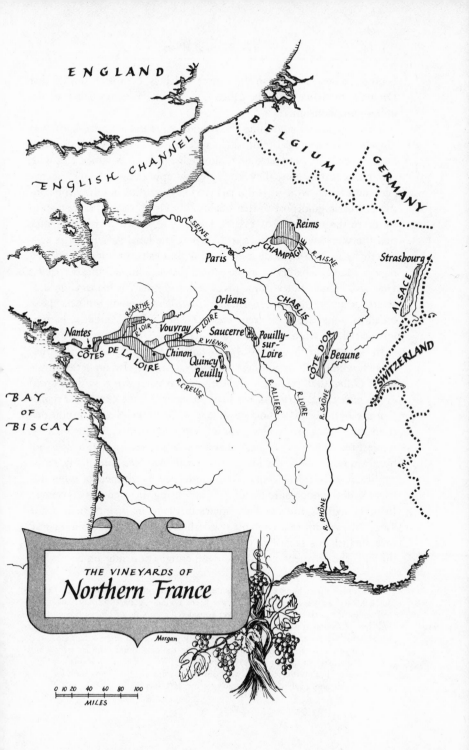

ENGLAND

BELGIUM

GERMANY

ENGLISH CHANNEL

R. SEINE

Reims

CHAMPAGNE

Paris

R. AISNE

Strasbourg

Orléans

CHABLIS

ALSACE

R. SARTHE

R. LOIR

Vouvray

R. LOIRE

Saucerre

Pouilly-
sur-
Loire

Nantes

CÔTES DE LA LOIRE

Chinon

R. VIENNE

Quincy
Reuilly

CÔTE D'OR

Beaune

SWITZERLAND

BAY
OF
BISCAY

R. CREUSE

R. ALLIERS

R. LOIRE

R. SAÔNE

R. RHÔNE

THE VINEYARDS OF
Northern France

Morgan

0 10 20 40 60 80 100
MILES

contrast, when it comes to the matter of labels, one often wishes that
Divine Providence could be called upon to intervene on behalf of the
unknowing consumer.

The regulations governing the French wine industry are known as
Appellations Contrôlées (controlled appellations)—two words of prime
importance to anyone seeking a knowledge of French wines, for, with
few minor exceptions, they must by law appear on the label of any
genuine French wine of real quality.[2] They are thus not only the consumer's basic guidepost to that quality, but also his skeleton key, so to
speak, to the mysteries of French labels. These two words guarantee
that the wine actually comes from where the label specifies it does—
whether this be a large district, such as Bordeaux; or a more confined
region, such as Chablis; or in the case of the very finest wines, a specific
vineyard. Hence, unless some producer or vintner has managed to out-
smart the authorities, an *Appellation Contrôlée* wine will not be a cheap
blend of wines from different localities, nor will it contain a base of
vinous red ink from Spain or North Africa.

In addition to the words *Appellation Contrôlée*, labels of the finer
French wines will usually bear the vineyard name, and on occasion the
terms *Grand Cru*[3] (variously indicating great vineyard, growth or crop)
or *Premier* (first) *Cru*. As we shall see later, *Grand Cru* and *Premier
Cru* are both terms authorized in *certain* of France's vinicultural districts for wines from vineyards of superior quality. Unfortunately,
while French law prescribes what shall be put on a label, it does not
by any means specify a limit as to what may *not*, and many terms
applicable to one district are often bootlegged by vintners of other districts with the hope of misleading or confusing the innocent consumer.
In other words, the laws have spikes in them for malpractices in the
vineyards, yet afford a veritable featherbed for anyone who might seek
to embellish his labels! It is for this purpose—the reader's guidance
through the frequent pitfalls of conflicting, confusing or downright

[2]The only important exception is Champagne, a name officially controlled and a guarantee in itself. Labels of certain other lesser French wines—generally country or provin-
cial wines not in the classic tradition yet considered deserving of official recognition—
will bear a second appellation, the initials *V.D.Q.S.* (*Vins Délimités de Qualité Supérieure*), which freely translated means wines of a superior quality from a delimited area.

[3]The consumer should be especially alerted to the confusingly similar term *Grand
Vin*, apt to appear on the label of any French bottle. An archaic term of quality, *Grand
Vin* nowadays has no official status whatsoever. Probably the best translation for *grand*,
as used in this unofficial, often promotional sense, is "super."

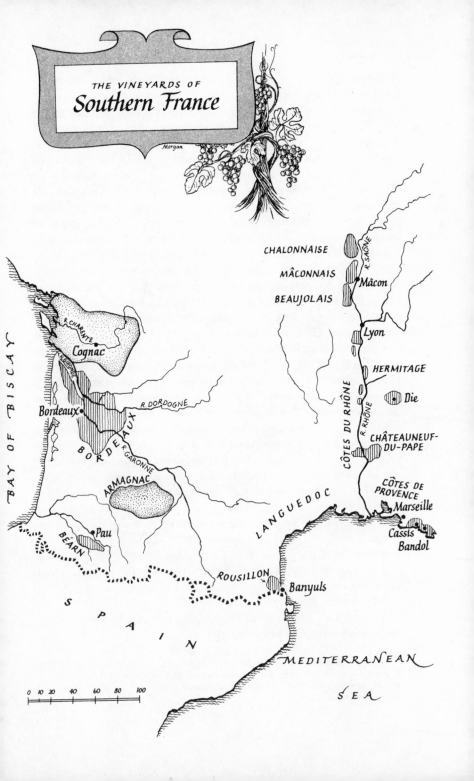

THE VINEYARDS OF
Southern France

Morgan

BAY OF BISCAY

R. CHARENTE
Cognac
R. GIRONDE
R. DORDOGNE
Bordeaux
BORDEAUX
R. GARONNE
ARMAGNAC
Pau
BÉARN

SPAIN

CHALONNAISE
MÂCONNAIS
BEAUJOLAIS
Mâcon
R. SAÔNE

Lyon

HERMITAGE
CÔTES DU RHÔNE
Die
R. RHÔNE
CHÂTEAUNEUF-
DU-PAPE

CÔTES DE
PROVENCE
Marseille
LANGUEDOC
Cassis
Bandol

ROUSSILLON
Banyuls

MEDITERRANEAN

SEA

0 10 20 40 60 80 100

dishonest terms on French labels—that many of the tables which follow have been prepared.

Another example of the Frenchman's method of persuading the buyer that his wines are better than the next man's is to print the word *Monopole* on the label. This grandiosely implies a monopoly on a certain formula, vineyard or *cru*, and the reader should be forewarned that what counts more than any merchant's monopoly on anything is what the wine is like when the cork is pulled. Perhaps the best possible rule of thumb to be given about French labels as a whole is this maxim: the simpler the label, the more genuine the wine is apt to be. Just as a truly beautiful woman requires a modicum of lipstick and makeup, so with a wine. To a sincere, hard-working wine producer of any land, "packaging"—especially the types and forms often imposed on him by demanding importers and agents—is anathema. And except for certain traditional, local shapes and sizes one should beware of exotically shaped bottles that look more appropriate to perfume or other things than to wine. Cultivate a healthy suspicion of ornate or indecorous labels, of ribbons and medallions, of extraneous objects dangling from the bottle's neck, of the word *Grand* attached to nearly anything but *Cru*, of *Monopoles*, of names in quotes or catchy trade names.[4] French law requires that all coined names or trade names be accompanied by the words *marque déposée* (registered trademark). But many a French vintner somehow manages either to omit the term or to print it in pinpoint type in a place where the eye will be sure to miss it. One of the best examples of an honest French label known to the writer is that of one of the several owners of the tiny white-wine vineyard of Montrachet in Burgundy, traditionally one of France's greatest. Printed in simple, readable type, it provides all the components of information that the consumer should need, and nothing more, in the following order:

The name of the vineyard: *Le Montrachet;*

The term *Appellation Contrôlée*, certifying that the vineyard is officially recognized as a *Grand Cru;*[5]

The year the wine was made;

The vintner's name and address (a guarantee that he stands behind the wine's quality and authenticity).

---

[4]One of hundreds of examples is *Nectarosé* (rosy nectar), a wine which could far better be presented to the consumer (and reflect more creditably on the integrity of the supplier) simply for what it is: *Rosé d'Anjou*—a standard *rosé* wine from the Loire Valley.

[5]See section on Burgundy.

Why further adorn a born princess?

A French wine without a year on its label is generally a wine that is a blend of two or more years—or else it is a wine of a year of such lowly repute that the vintner has decided he can perhaps sell it better without disclosing its birth date. Wine years, good or bad, are known as "vintages"—or sometimes "vintage years"—and, as we have mentioned, most of the world's finest wines come from the northernmost countries of the wine belt, parts of the world where the weather can be treacherously variable. In 1956 and 1960, for example, the vineyards of France and Germany were not favored by nature, and the wines were almost universally inferior. In poor vintage years the vines have perhaps not flowered in time for the grapes to ripen under the hot suns of the long August and September days; or maybe there was too much rain at a time when it was not needed. Thus the grapes do not contain enough natural sugar to create the necessary alcohol and the wine is proportionately too acidic. In some places no wine is made at all; in others, what wine there is goes to the blenders of "regional" or "district" wines—wines that may, or need not, be sold with the year on the label, depending upon the success of the blend.

Good and bad years often vary according to locality. Thus as part of each of the following sections on the various French wine districts, the reader will find specific recommendations for the vintage years, in addition to a summary (see page 234) giving the general characteristics of recent vintages. But it should be emphasized that these are intended to serve as only a general guide. Vintage charts and other recommendations can give only an over-all picture at best, and like all other statistics, they have their outstanding exceptions. Ordinarily no reputable producer or vintner will put his name and label on a bottle of wine stemming from a very poor year. On the other hand, it can happen through some quirk of nature, or by extra skill or luck, that a French producer will make an excellent wine (or contrive a superior blend) in an off year. Under these circumstances, he is prouder than ever to market the wine under his own name, instead of dumping it less profitably on the blenders.[6] Such off-year wines are always good bargains. And their discovery usually constitutes an invaluable link in the chain of

[6]This high-minded practice of the best French vintners, sacrificing their poorer wines to protect their reputations, often results, paradoxically, in better regional blends (wines labeled simply Bordeaux, Médoc, Côtes-du-Rhône) for a poor year than a good year. In a "great" or a very good year, every vineyard owner wants to market his own wines under his own label—leaving the blenders with only the poorest to pick from.

one's private search for the names of honest foreign vintners and domestic importers.

Summary

Although a familiarity with labels goes hand in hand with an appreciation of the best in French wines, French practices in labeling unfortunately do not always provide for either clarity or consistency. Two convenient rules of thumb: (1) look for the words *Appellation Contrôlée* (or the initials *V.D.Q.S.*) on a label, both of which are a guarantee of an authentic wine, and (2) remember that, within reason, the simpler, less complicated or ornate the label (or bottle), the better the quality of the wine is apt to be. An honestly made French wine needs only to be described on its label in terms of four elements: the name of the vineyard or locality, the official appellation, the year and the vintner's name and address. Overembellishments usually spell trouble.

Never be a slave to the vintage charts. French vintages vary from very bad to very great as a result of quirks of weather. But fine wines are often made by good producers or blenders in certain localities in off years, constituting excellent bargains.

"Regional" blends from poor years are frequently of better quality than comparable blends from the great ones.

Remember that the good and great wines of France, bringing high and perhaps even higher prices, tend to be put on the market far sooner than formerly. This particularly applies to red wines. To drink an expensive good or great red wine before it has been afforded adequate bottle age is a waste of money and a potential disillusionment. (See separate chapters for minimal ages.)

Bordeaux: Hub of the Wine World

The vineyard district of Bordeaux, which takes its name from France's fourth-largest city, is a vast and enormously productive agricultural area lying in the southwestern corner of France, near the Spanish border. It is France's largest producing district of fine wines, and its most prolific: the home of the great red clarets and the white sweet Sauternes—considered by many connoisseurs to be the two finest wines in the world—and of many another wine hardly less well known.

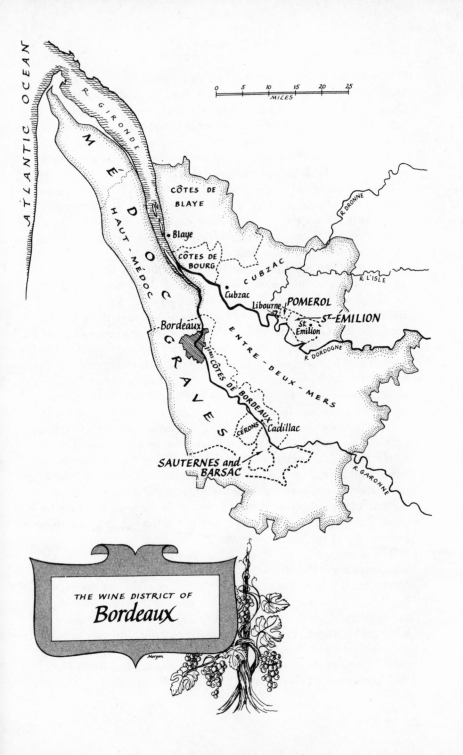

ATLANTIC OCEAN

R. GIRONDE

MÉDOC

HAUT-MÉDOC

CÔTES DE BLAYE

• Blaye

CÔTES DE BOURG

CUBZAC

• Cubzac

R. DRONNE

R. L'ISLE

Libourne

POMEROL

St-EMILION

St. Emilion

GRAVES

Bordeaux

ENTRE - DEUX - MERS

R. DORDOGNE

1res CÔTES DE BORDEAUX

CÉRONS

Cadillac

SAUTERNES and BARSAC

R. GARONNE

0   5   10   15   20   25
MILES

THE WINE DISTRICT OF
Bordeaux

Morgan

The Bordeaux area is drained by two rivers, the Garonne and the Dordogne, which join about eighty miles from the sea to form the tidal Gironde. The ancient city lies on the Garonne, within ample reach of high tide, just above the confluence of the two streams. It is one of France's busiest ports—and distinctly a wine port. A good part of its citizenry lives and sells and tastes and drinks wines from morning until night. Along the length of the city's famed Quai des Chartrons are some of the oldest and most celebrated wine houses in the world, establishments of bottlers and blenders and shippers, most of whose ancestors have been engaged in the international wine trade for several hundred years. To say that these people are proud of their tradition would be a naïve understatement.

The great low-lying peninsula that shields the city from the temperamental waters of the Bay of Biscay and the Atlantic Ocean is loosely called "the Graves." *Graves* means gravel or a gravel bank—and in that very particular part of the peninsula where the wines are literally called Graves, the roots of the vines sometimes penetrate thirty feet or more of gravel to obtain the necessary moisture and nourishment. This Graves region would be an American building contractor's dream—but let it not be thought that any Bordeaux vineyard owner would part, for any recompense in the world, with one shovelful of his precious gravelly soil for so menial a purpose as a concrete footing or a concrete block. In some parts of the Bordeaux wine district certain wine makers, out of a dedicated sentiment for land and wine that we would find hard to understand in the New World, have themselves buried in their vineyards. Here are perhaps the most unique graves on earth; a lone tombstone stands untended amid the waving vines, with no little strips of lawn or flowered plots to be lovingly cared for by those left behind. Obviously the soil is far too precious for such foolishness.

The wines of Graves, which lies to the west and south of the city, are about equally divided between reds and whites (see map, page 19). Most vineyards make both. The reds, the best of which are to be numbered among France's finest, tend to be dark, with much body and a strong flavor. A good red Graves is almost always slow to mature. The whites of the region are dry, tasting more alcoholic than they actually are, with a peculiar "rusty" flavor that defeats any real elegance. With the exception of the champion of them all, Château Haut-Brion Blanc, they cannot be numbered among the most distinguished of France.

Popular in their own land (one seems to run across them most frequently in French dining cars), comparatively few of them are exported.

North of the city we find the region of Médoc, the source of some of the most aristocratic and delicate red wines of the world—of which we shall say more later when we discuss what are known as the château-bottled wines of this particular region. To the south are the regions of Sauternes and Cérons. These latter areas produce white wines exclusively, most of which tend to be very sweet, what the French call *liquoreux,* perhaps best translated as "luscious." Two other famed regions of Bordeaux are St.-Émilion and Pomerol, which (although they lie on higher ground across the Dordogne River) also have some soils that are predominantly gravel. St.-Émilion and Pomerol produce powerfully fragrant red wines that are now in great demand, bringing increasingly high prices.

Although the five regions mentioned above are the classic ones for Bordeaux, there are many other parts of the district that are responsible for good wines, both red and white, many of which are beginning to appear on foreign markets. Between the two rivers, for example, is a great pie-sliced area known as Entre-Deux-Mers (Between Two Seas). Entre-Deux-Mers produces mild, dry white wines which—though not necessarily great, and not often seen outside of France—are both drinkable and comparatively inexpensive. Other "unknowns" gradually emerging from obscurity are the also relatively inexpensive reds from the Premières Côtes de Bordeaux, from Bourg and Blaye on the right bank of the turbulent Gironde, as well as ones from a nearby region with the quaint name of Cubzaguais—this latter at the moment meriting only the appellation of Bordeaux (see District Wines—Table A).

In terms of labeling and identification, each of these regions, as well as the greater Bordeaux district itself, has its own authorized system of *Appellations Contrôlées,* the official term we have already mentioned as being the consumer's basic guarantee of authenticity. What must be emphasized here, however, is the fact that the Bordeaux district embraces nearly three dozen *Appellations Contrôlées,* all based theoretically on a sliding scale of quality—embodying the general principle that the smaller the defined geographical area, the finer the wine. Hence wines (or blends) that are authorized to use the term *Appellation Contrôlée Bordeaux* only—the lowest in terms of quality—are not apt to be of great value. Better wines, stemming from smaller geographical areas of Bordeaux, carry regional appellations (*Appellation Contrôlée Graves*), and in the case of the finest the name of the commune (township), vineyard or château is added.[7]

Contrary to what one might think, a château in Bordeaux rarely means a castle or manor house or an "estate," but simply an officially demarcated plantation of vines, with the buildings and equipment necessary to the production, storage and bottling of wine. With the finest wines of Bordeaux (unlike many other parts of France), it is customary to make and bottle the wine at the vineyard itself, leading to the use of the term *Mise en bouteilles au Château* (château-bottled)—a term which is usually both burned into the cork and printed on the label. Without words to this effect, a château-bottled wine may be a fake, something an unscrupulous vintner has managed to put together in the privacy of his own cellar.[8]

The Blends or Common Wines

Throughout the Bordeaux district, where every nook and cranny of wine-producing land is a treasure trove, there are more than three thousand officially authorized châteaux—far too many, else undeserving, to be listed in a volume of this nature. In the twin regions of St.-Émilion and Pomerol alone, for example, there are more than a thousand vineyards. Fewer than half of these vineyards ever produce wines that are considered marketable with a château-bottled label; the balance, usually of quite mediocre quality, is sold in bulk to one of the numerous shippers in the cities of Bordeaux or Libourne, the port of the Dordogne, where it is blended with another wine or wines, usually (but not always) of the same year, and from vineyards of the same region. Thus it is sold under what is known as a regional labeling with its own appropriate *Appellation Contrôlée*.

When these regional blends have been produced on the superior soils of the five classic regions—Haut-Médoc (upper Médoc, that part nearer to the city of Bordeaux), Graves, Sauternes (which includes wines sometimes labeled Barsac and sometimes not!), St.-Émilion and

[7]Occasionally *Clos* or *Domaine* is substituted for *Château*.

[8]One should be especially wary of wines labeled *Mise en bouteilles dans mes caves* (or *dans nos chais*)—bottled in our cellars. Hoping that the consumer will be so unsophisticated as to assume that the cellars *must* be at the vineyard itself, many a Bordeaux shipper has in this way profitably rid himself of inferior admixtures and vintages.

Pomerol—and their labels bear the names of honest and reliable merchants—they will almost always be of excellent value. This is especially valid today in view of the exorbitant prices being asked for the château-bottled wines with illustrious names. Again it must be emphasized that one of these regional wines is apt to be far better than any wine simply labeled *Appellation Contrôlée Bordeaux*—for under the law the latter *may* derive from any part of the entire Bordeaux district, and will in all probability be a blend of inferior wines that cannot be marketed otherwise. Since the quality (and labeling) of French wines is so inseparable from geography, one may be sure that if a wine of a good year has been produced on famous soil—whether it be a region, a subdivision of it or a specific vineyard—the vintner will have certainly seen to it that the label bears the highest allowable geographical appellation.

One of the more obvious reasons for blending wines is to stretch the qualities of a good one to improve a less good one. The origin of the Bordeaux blends, which also involves the derivation of the word "claret"—a term commonly used, especially in England, for Bordeaux reds—has amusing aspects. In the twelfth century an English prince, Henry Plantagenet, descended from William the Conqueror, married Eleanor, the daughter of the French Duke of Aquitaine. When he succeeded to the throne he became not only King of England but also ruler (by virtue of the marriage) of a large part of southwestern France, including the Sénéchausée, or incorporated domain, of the city of Bordeaux.

In those days, wine was rarely found far from its place of origin. People habitually drank local wines—just as they contented themselves with meat from their own farms and fish from the nearby sea or streams. Transportation by land was both hazardous and expensive; each little walled town on the way demanded its toll, each turn of the road harbored a possible plundering brigand. Furthermore, the alcoholic content of much wine of that day was usually too low to warrant long, arduous land journeys, for even the strongest wine—unless, like Madeira or Sherry, it be fortified with spirits—can be joggled and shaken to the limit of its tolerance.

Thus, when wine moved at all, it usually followed the waterways. Alsatian and Rhine wines floated down the Rhine to the cities of northern Germany and thence across the Channel to England; the popes at

Avignon were fortunate in being able to glut themselves on the rich reds of Burgundy, which came down the Saône and Rhône. The court in Paris was less fortunate. It had to be satisfied with tart and undistinguished wines from local vineyards, or with those of Champagne (in that day a still and very dry wine) and Chablis, arriving by the Seine. Just as today many of us will drive fifty miles and back to have a good dinner and go to the theater, in that day the rich and noble were impelled to journey hundreds of miles to drink the best wines, and frequently did. Even as late as the seventeenth century, a French king traveled all the way from Paris to St.-Émilion to sample the famous red wine he had never tasted—triumphantly pronouncing it *un doux nectar* (a soft nectar).

Once the tidal port of Bordeaux had become, under the Plantagenets, a part of the great seafaring nation of Britons, a fresh and vast outlet for Bordeaux wines was opened. The English had known a few wines— those of Champagne, the whites from Alsace and Germany, which had come to them across the Channel. The voyage from Bordeaux was not too long; the wines were cheap and strong and warming during the long damp winters, and made a fine variant for ale and mead. At first they had liked the whites of England's newest province, but it was not long before they were demanding the stout red wines, of which travelers increasingly talked. The only drawback—from the viewpoint of the Bordelais—was that the supply of good red wine was limited. The superior wine the English demanded—the darkest and strongest—was in that day made only in certain parts of the Graves peninsula and on the highlands across the Dordogne. Throughout the rest of the territory under the control of the Sénéchausée of Bordeaux there was plenty of wine to be had, except that it was either white or—in the case of the reds—weak and insipid, and of a distinctly inferior nature.

History has not recorded the identity of the Frenchmen who originally hit upon the practical idea of exploiting the English with a blend of the good and the less good, somehow persuading the gullible islanders that a fine red Graves, rendered milder and lighter by having been mixed with something else, would be an even more desirable drink than the original. All innovations, of course, need a name—preferably an arresting name, one which entices and excites the consumer and makes him think he's getting something new and different. The French called their new blend *clairet* (literally: something lighter than something else), and by virtue of some touch of marketing genius, the implication of *clairet* came also to imply something *better*. So successfully did this vogue for these new "lighter" wines catch on, that not only did *clairet* become a British national drink but, even in Bordeaux itself, it got out of hand. Soon many owners of red-wine vineyards, not to be outdone by the blenders, took to planting white-wine grapes of their own and making their own *clairets*.[9]

Excessive blending, either for honest purposes or otherwise, always goes hand in hand with a demand exceeding the supply. Although following the three-hundred-odd years of the English occupation of Bordeaux, the market for *clairet* considerably diminished (though the term "claret" for red Bordeaux survives to this day), and the Bordelais settled down to shipping great wine once again, a situation of much the same nature arose in Burgundy in the first few decades of this century. In this instance, the world's demand for a bottle labeled *Burgundy* suddenly became so great that adulteration and falsification proved to be—except with a very few producers—positively irresistible. It was to combat this insidious practice that the French government finally stepped into the breach and created the Institut National des Appellations d'Origine—a task force to legalize, control and police the country's wine industry. This was the agency responsible for the *Appellations Contrôlées* laws and which—to protect the consumer—eventually graded and classified all the best wines of France.

In the case of Bordeaux, as will be seen in Table A, the wines are divided into three geographical categories: (1) district wines, (2) regional wines and (3) château-bottled wines. If, in using this table, the reader continues to keep in mind the overall principle that the smaller the geographical area classified with an *Appellation Contrôlée*, the better the wine is considered to be, he should experience little trouble in assessing the potential quality of any Bordeaux wine from its label.

The Château Wines

In Bordeaux the traditionally great pieces of land are called "châteaux," a term, as we have said, having little or nothing to do with the presence of a castle or a country house. A few handsome and sometimes historic dwellings are connected with Bordeaux vineyards, but they are the exception, not the rule.

[9]This may well explain the survival of so many white wines remaining in the Graves vineyards, which have always produced red wines of far better quality.

TABLE A
Appellations Contrôlées of Bordeaux

BORDEAUX DISTRICT WINES
Red, White or *Rosé*

APPELLATION CONTRÔLÉE BORDEAUX   From anywhere in the Bordeaux district. May be a blend. Sometimes labeled with trade or *monopole* names. (A Bordeaux *Supérieur* must by law have a slightly higher alcoholic content.)

REGIONAL WINES OF THE FIVE CLASSIC REGIONS
Red Wines

APPELLATION CONTRÔLÉE MÉDOC (or HAUT-MÉDOC)   Though all the finest come from Haut-Médoc, appellation is often shortened to MÉDOC.* Inner subdivisions:

MOULIS	LISTRAC
PAUILLAC	ST.-JULIEN
MARGAUX	ST.-ESTÈPHE

APPELLATION CONTRÔLÉE GRAVES

APPELLATION CONTRÔLÉE POMEROL   Subdivision bordering Pomerol:

Lalande de Pomerol

APPELLATION CONTRÔLÉE ST.-ÉMILION   Subdivisions bordering St.-Émilion, authorized to hyphenate their names with St.-Émilion:

Lussac	*Montagne*
Puisseguin	*St.-Georges*
Parsac	*Sables*

White Wines

APPELLATION CONTRÔLÉE GRAVES †

APPELLATION CONTRÔLÉE SAUTERNES ‡   Subdivision of Sauternes with option to use its own *Appellation Contrôlée:*

BARSAC

OTHER REGIONS OF BORDEAUX ENTITLED TO THEIR OWN *APPELLATIONS CONTRÔLÉES*

Côtes de Bourg or Bourg (red)	Entre-Deux-Mers (white)
Blaye (red)	Côtes-de-Bordeaux-St.-Macaire (white)

T A B L E A Continued
Appellations Contrôlées of Bordeaux

Néac (red)
Côtes de Fronsac (red)
Côtes Canon-Fronsac (red)
Cérons (white)

Graves de Vayres (white)
Loupiac (white)
Ste.-Croix-du-Mont (white)

Premières Côtes de Bordeaux (red and white)
Ste.-Foy-de-Bordeaux (red and white)

CHÂTEAU WINES (*CRUS CLASSÉS*)
[See Table B]
The traditionally finest are labeled as from:

MÉDOC or HAUT-MÉDOC (MOULIS, PAUILLAC, MARGAUX, LISTRAC, ST.-JULIEN, ST.-ESTÈPHE)

GRAVES ST.-ÉMILION
POMEROL SAUTERNES (BARSAC)

*White and *rosé* wines of Haut-Médoc are entitled only to *Appellation Contrôlée Bordeaux.*

† A Graves *Supérieure*, like a Bordeaux *Supérieur*, requires a slightly higher alcoholic content.

‡ Both the terms *Haut-Sauternes* and *Haut-Barsac* on a label are entirely meaningless. Likewise *Grand* (*Grand* Médoc, *Grand* St.-Julien, etc.).

Note: Bottles of Bordeaux wines, sometimes seen bearing a seal with the initials ADEB (Association pour le Développment de l' Exportation du Vin de Bordeaux) indicate that the wine has been voluntarily submitted to a panel of Bordeaux experts before export. As a rule, this may be considered a mark of added quality.

A list of the best-known château wines of Bordeaux may be found in Table B. These are known as the *Crus Classés* (Classified Growths), and in the case of seventy-odd top vineyards of Haut-Médoc[10] and about twenty of Sauternes, the gradings are based on an official classification that traces back to 1855. This classification, done at the request of Napoleon III, endures to this day, despite periodic efforts to change it. The committee appointed for the task—a job that no one appears to have had the courage to tackle as a whole since—paid little attention to personal preferences, but based its judgments wholly on economics, choosing the wines from the Médoc and Sauternes that had brought

[10]Only the red wine of Château Haut-Brion was included.

the best prices over the preceding ten years or so. Because of the high sums it brought on the market, the committee also included the wines of Graves' Château Haut-Brion. It remains a mystery why the leading vineyards of St.-Èmilion and Pomerol were given no consideration at the time. Several—especially Pomerol's Château Pétrus, and Château Ausone and Château Cheval Blanc in St.-Émilion—were certainly eligible. The omission may have been attributable to the long-standing rivalry, traceable to the days of the English occupation, when the city's merchants each year contrived to block shipments of wines from beyond the Dordogne, until inventories of peninsula wines—Médocs, Graves and Sauternes—in which they themselves had vested interests, were used up.

In the 1855 classification the Médoc wines were divided into five principal categories or *crus*, beginning with four *premiers crus*, fifteen *deuxièmes*, fourteen *troisièmes*, eleven *quatrièmes* and seventeen *cinq-uièmes*. (Later, seven *crus exceptionnels*, as well as a number of vine-yards rated as *crus bourgeois supérieures* were added.) As one can imag-ine, this division into seven separate classes has been a source of contention ever since the classification was first made. Certainly the most publicized case was that of Château Mouton-Rothschild, placed at the head of the list of *deuxièmes crus* instead of among the *premiers*, which latter list included only Châteaux Margaux, Latour, Lafite-Rothschild and Haut-Brion. The owners of the two Rothschild châ-teaux were cousins, members of the celebrated banking family; and to the owner of Mouton-Rothschild, omission from the top classification was intolerable. Henceforth his labels bore the motto *Premier ne puis; seconde ne daigne; Mouton suis!* ("I can't be first; I won't be second; I am Mouton!"). The wines of Mouton-Rothschild have improved since 1855—as has their price many times over. Seemingly today the matter of where Mouton stands on any list is academic, though the present owner (a Rothschild descendant) finally succeeded, in 1973, in having his wine included in the official first category.

Like the owners of Mouton-Rothschild, nearly every Bordelais has his own version of how the list should be rewritten, and usually thinks his own wine has been erroneously classified. Since 1855 several of the original sixty-odd châteaux have gone out of existence, some names changed, and the wines of many, by virtue of changes in management, have also changed in quality. Our advice to the reader is to forget the official list (except perhaps for the first five châteaux) and approach all sixty-odd wines as one would the members of a large clan. Assessment of individual and comparative quality is then in order. In Table B we have given the official list, along with notations indicating which châteaux, in the judgment of experts, should be placed in higher classifications. Maybe one should also remember that many of the experts are owners with their own private fish to fry.

The Médoc

Before exploring the so-called Médoc, the source of some of France's greatest red wines, a few matters of terminology must be cleared away. That district of Bordeaux that stretches northward for some eighty miles, from the city to the Pointe de Graves at the peninsula's end, is loosely known as the Médoc. Until fairly recently its northern half was called Bas-Médoc (Lower Médoc) and the half nearer to the city, Haut-Médoc (Upper Médoc). Some years ago the Bas-Médoc, where the vineyard land is distinctly inferior, took it into its head that the term "Bas" was degrading, inhibiting the sale of the wines. As a result, it was agreed that Bas-Médoc should thereafter be called Médoc, with Haut-Médoc remaining as such. Regrettably, vintners when labeling their wines do not necessarily follow suit. All the great châteaux are to be found in Haut-Médoc; yet one will often see labels on which the distinction is not made. The term Médoc is also carelessly used, in print and in spoken word, to mean either the whole peninsula or, most confusingly of all, just Haut-Médoc.

Another confusion arises with labels of many a château that omits the *Appellation Contrôlée* of Médoc (or Haut-Médoc) and uses one of six authorized subregional names. The wine of Château Latour, for example, a *premier cru*, is entitled to that of its commune, Pauillac; it is also a Haut-Médoc; also a Médoc; also a Bordeaux. It could use any of the four, but it logically chooses Pauillac, the most prestigious. Château Margaux, subregionally a Margaux, on the other hand, has been known to label its wines with the appellation of Haut-Médoc.

Proceeding northward from the city, the six commune names of the "inner" classifications are Margaux, Moulis, Listrac, St.-Julien, Pauillac and St.-Estèphe. Except for only one or two châteaux (those situated in Listrac and Moulis), most of the great vineyards are to be found along a thirty-mile stretch of road near the river, on the ancient route from the city to the Pointe de Graves. As one travels northward, several significant geological characteristics may be observed. The best vineyards are on the highest land—land that is none too high, but still more so than its surroundings. One will observe, too, that the soils of the greatest vineyards are filled with white pebbles. Where the land drops lower, the pebbles disappear. These pebbles have the effect of reflecting the sun's heat by day and holding it by night. According to geologists, they were dropped by a glacier—the same glacier that also scraped away all the alluvial topsoil, creating the perfect conditions for the wine grape. Fertile topsoils are not indicated for the *Vitis vinifera:* it needs deep, well-drained banks of gravel or pebbles for its roots to explore for moisture and nourishment.

What one may not observe, however, is the subtle difference of soils that renders the wines softer and lighter at one end of the thirty-mile stretch, and harsher but longer-lived at the other. The wines of Margaux and its neighbor Cantenac, for example, are known for their finesse and velvety qualities. Those of Pauillac and St.-Estèphe, on the other hand, are by contrast high in tannin, hard in their youth and slow to mature. These differences are attributable to sparse admixtures of clay and chalk versus sand among the pebbles or gravel, along with variations in iron content. The soil of Margaux contains more iron and sand; that of Pauillac, more clay.

Another factor in the variation of the wines involves the grapes and the formulas used by each individual château. Under the *Appellations Contrôlées* regulations, red wines of Médoc may be made from six different red grapes. These are principally the Cabernet sauvignon and the Cabernet franc, with lesser ingredients of Merlot, Malbec, Petit Verdot and Carmenère. Of the six, the Cabernet sauvignon—the universal "claret" grape found today from the Black Sea to Australia—is the basic ingredient, especially in the Médoc. In the blends of châteaux such as Latour and Mouton-Rothschild it may run as high as 90 percent. With others it may share the honors with its cousin, the Cabernet franc. The Cabernets are also shy producers and give hard wines. Thus a certain proportion of the "softer" Merlot often shares in the blend, also bringing about faster maturity. Even so, a great Médoc requires a minimum of fifteen years of bottle age.

Château Margaux, the principal château of its commune, whose *premier cru* wines are considered by many to be the most delicate and refined of the Médoc—the word "feminine" is frequently used—lays claim to the most imposing building on the peninsula. With a massive colonnaded portico and elaborate outbuildings, it sits incongruously amid its expanse of vineyards. The château also produces a relatively undistinguished but good white, Pavillon Blanc du Château Margaux. Across the road is Château Lascombes, at the present writing a definitely overrated *deuxième cru,* a contrast illustrative of how varying managements produce varying wines, even between two neighboring vineyards once classified one tiny step apart in 1855.

For almost ten miles beyond Margaux one sees no more pebbly soil, and few vines. Then suddenly, around a sharp bend, one comes upon perhaps the most famous of the so-called St.-Julien group, Château Beychevelle, a handsome, well-kept country house surrounded by spacious gardens commanding a superb view of the Gironde. The name Beychevelle dates from the sixteenth century. Its proprietor of that day was the Duc d'Épernon, Grand Admiral of France under Henri III, and passing ships on the Gironde habitually lowered their sails in salute—the term *baissevoile* being later colloquialized to Beychevelle. The château's production of nearly twenty thousand cases a year is considerably higher than that of the average château of the Médoc, and its wines are enormously popular in both England and the United States. In the opinion of nearly all the experts, Bordelais or otherwise, here is an instance where the committee of 1855 erred. Beychevelle, a *quatrième cru,* is a wine of great body, fragrance and individuality—yet the reader should be wary: of all the wines of the Médoc, it is among the slowest to mature.

Other celebrated vineyards in the St.-Julien group include a foursome of famous châteaux: Léoville-Las-Cases, Léoville-Poyferré, Léoville-Barton and Langoa-Barton. The first three are *deuxièmes crus,* the last a *troisième;* all four produce wines of high quality. Also in the same group are Châteaux Gruaud-Larose and Talbot, both the property of one of Bordeaux's most respected shippers, M. Jean Cordier. These, too, are wines made with consummate skill; that of Gruaud-Larose in particular being rich and full, with a deep color. By itself, Gruaud-Larose would suffice to make any commune famous.

Pauillac's most noted vineyard is the aristocratic Château Latour, a *premier cru.* Its lonely tower was once used by Pauillac to defend itself against ocean-going pirates. Few vineyards of the Médoc are as meticulously maintained as those of Latour; and the preponderance of egg-sized pebbles speaks for itself. One notices, also, a large proportion of ancient, gnarled vines. At Château Latour the vines are allowed to grow to a ripe old age, instead of being pulled out and new vines replanted when the peak of production has passed. Traditionally fine wines are made from old, long-established plants; but the older a vine grows, the less it produces. Latour's wines are heavy and full-bodied: one must afford to wait many years for them to mature. Next to Latour, on either side of the road, are the twin vineyards of Pichon-Longueville, one named for the Baron de Pichon, the other for the Comtesse de Lalande—former owners. Both vineyards are *deuxièmes crus*, producing wines of quality, although they are not as much in demand as many of their neighbors. In any new classification, they would probably lose face.

Beyond Latour is Château Pontet-Canet, whose ubiquitous bottles are a familar sight in almost any wine shop. Pontet-Canet is a *cinquième cru*. Its wines—in our opinion sometimes good, sometimes not quite so good. Adjacent are two giants: Château Lafite-Rothschild and Château Mouton-Rothschild. The château at Lafite, a saffron-colored, large country house, commands the highest land in Pauillac. Purchased in the middle of the last century by a Rothschild for what would today be the equivalent of $1,500,000, the vineyards consist of approximately one hundred and fifty acres planted to the two Cabernets, the Merlot and the Petit Verdot. In great years Lafite's wines can be the most elegant of all, and its owners, Rothschild descendants, spare no expense in keeping them that way. After those of Château Latour, its vineyards are the most carefully tended of the Médoc. Only the very best is labeled as Château Lafite-Rothschild—wine from the most mature vines. When coming from younger vines it is called Moulins de Carruades, a less expensive but nonetheless superb wine.

The northernmost commune of Haut-Médoc, St.-Estèphe, contains two important *deuxièmes crus* and one outstanding *troisième:* Châteaux Cos-d'Estournel and Montrose, and Château Calon-Ségur. St. Estèphes are the "hardest" wines of Haut-Médoc—partly the result of a larger proportion of clay in the soil, and also attributable to the practice of using more juice of the Cabernet sauvignon in the blends. St. Estèphes are anything but "feminine" wines. Château Cos-d'Estournel's wines are among the most distinctive of the region—as fruity and redolent as the roses the landowners in the Médoc cultivate along the roads and lanes.

The last great vineyard of St.-Estèphe is Château Calon-Ségur, almost at the border of Haut-Médoc and Médoc (Bas-Médoc). This is a *troisième cru* that most experts would raise to the status of a *deuxième*.

The same feelings were evidently held by its eighteenth-century owner, the Marquis de Ségur, then also proprietor of Châteaux Lafite and Latour. "I make wines at Lafite and Latour," the marquis is quoted as having said, "but my heart is at Calon." Today's owners make an unfortunate commercial use of the quote by embellishing Calon-Ségur's label with a pinkish heart. Calon-Ségur is virile and powerful. Bottles born as long ago as fifty years are only attaining their peak today.

Graves

West and south of the city of Bordeaux is the red- and white-wine region of Graves; and twenty miles or so up the Garonne, one finds the sweet-white-wine region of Sauternes. Thirty years ago wines of these regions merited a far larger place in the sun than today. Graves produces both red and white wines, but the whites are losing in popularity, and the reds, with few exceptions, are no longer in as much demand as their peers of the Médoc and St.-Émilion. Similarly, the sweet Sauternes and Barsacs, once so important to Bordeaux's wine trade, have had to bow to a changing world. The custom of serving them in their appropriate role, as wines with desserts, has faded, and with the exception of Château d'Yquem, the best known, few châteaux in Sauternes and Barsac are free of economic headaches.

Some of the finest vineyards of Graves have been overrun by the expanding city. One such, the most famous of all, is the *premier cru* Château Haut-Brion, whose vines are entirely engulfed by busy suburbs. The château has a distinguished history. It once belonged to Talleyrand, who took a supply of its wines, accompanied by France's most able chef, to the Congress of Vienna, considerably furthering his diplomatic negotiations. Haut-Brion's vintages were publicized at an early date in England, where Samuel Pepys drank them at a London tavern. With the influence of its present owner, the family of Clarence Dillon, once U.S. Secretary of the Treasury and Ambassador to France, a large part of the château's production now comes to the United States. The red wines of the château and its neighbors have a pronounced richness and fullness—often called "earthiness." Château Haut-Brion also makes a small quantity of white wine, Haut-Brion Blanc, thought by many to be the finest of Graves: whether one cares for it or not, it is a wine of extraordinary character.

Also in the suburbs (in fact, just down the street) are three other excellent vineyards hyphenating Haut-Brion to their names: La Mission-Haut-Brion, La Tour-Haut-Brion and Laville-Haut-Brion. Laville produces white wines only, La Tour red, and La Mission both, its white, confusingly, being labeled under the name of Laville. Among those few vineyards of Bordeaux with past Church affiliations, the Mission was at one time the property of an order founded by St. Vincent de Paul. The Saint now stands in the chapel at the Mission, lending validity to the legend that his desertion of heaven to glut himself on the wines of Haut-Brion resulted in his being turned to stone by the Almighty.

Another red-wine vineyard of Graves, Château Pape-Clément, has a history that is hardly legendary. It was planted in the fourteenth century by Bertrand de Goth, the archbishop of Bordeaux who circumvented conventional channels and succeeded in having himself elected pope. Pope Clément moved the papacy to Avignon, where he must have had a strong hand in developing the Rhône vineyards of Châteauneuf-du-Pape. After his investiture Clément gave his vineyards to the Church in Bordeaux. It was of the wine of Château Pape-Clément that Cardinal Richelieu is supposed to have said, "If God did not intend man to drink, why did He make it this good?"

The countryside of Graves, in contrast to that of the Médoc, is hilly, dotted with patches of woodland and crisscrossed by small streams. The châteaux themselves, too, have their distinct charms. Château Olivier is a thirteenth-century building surrounded by a moat—an architectural gem as pristine as its clear, dry white wine. Another is the fourteenth-century Château Carbonnieux, originally owned by Benedictine monks. The name Carbonnieux involves a colorful story. During the regime of the Benedictines, a sultan of Turkey somehow acquired an unorthodox taste for white Graves. Alcohol was, of course, forbidden in Islam; but through the complicity of the Benedictines in Constantinople, the sultan was able to receive wines labeled "Eau Minérale Carbonnieux." Château Carbonnieux's red, made in small quantity, actually rates higher than its white.

Sauternes

The most celebrated white château wines of Bordeaux are the sweet Sauternes and Barsacs, the most famous of which is Château d'Yquem, a wine that in the original classification of Bordeaux wines in 1855 was singled out for the highest possible of titles, *Premier Grand Cru* (First

Great Growth). These *liquoreaux* wines made in Sauternes, Barsac[11] and nearby Cérons—comparable to the sweet German *Beerenauslesen* and the syrupy Hungarian Tokay—owe their particular character to the presence of an indigenous mold or yeast known as the *Botrytis cinerea*, called by the French the *pourriture noble* (noble rot). Again a part of nature's "packaging" of the wine grape, the *pourriture noble* manifests itself—though only in certain wine-producing parts of the world—as a grayish film that covers the skin of the grape when the latter has almost completely matured.[12] This extraordinary little organism grows tiny roots that pierce the skin, feeding on the liquid within and thus appreciably reducing the water content of the grape. In consequence, those grapes which have been attacked by it possess an abnormally high percentage of sugar—far more than is necessary for the natural yeasts to bring the wine to its maximum alcoholic limit—and the ensuing wine is thus left with a considerable quantity of residual sugar. These *liquoreux* wines also have unusual body or thickness, for along with more sugar, they contain a higher proportion of glycerine and other elements than a dry wine does. And there is a subtle "nutty" flavor about them, imparted by the *pourriture noble* itself. Most people prefer to drink them at the end of a meal, with desserts.

At the Château d'Yquem, an imposing and turreted country establishment that is deserving of the name, there is a legendary tale of how, many generations ago, this vineyard—which, like its neighbors, once made only dry wine—came to produce sweet. In that day the grapes were never harvested without the express permission of the lord of the manor—and in the case of the Château d'Yquem, the lord happened at the time to be a gay blade who apparently preferred the salons and cotillions of Paris to the boredom of his country seat.

One particular autumn, as all the neighboring vineyards commenced the *vendange*, or harvest, the grapes of the Château d'Yquem had to be left on the vines. Frantic appeals were sent to Paris; one thinks of the old peasants wringing their hands, of the priest initiating special prayers. But to no avail: the young noble had found an undeniable attraction—or possibly two. Finally, weeks later, a cloud of dust appeared on the road, the young lord clattered into the courtyard and gave the seem-

---

[11]One of five communes of the Sauternes region, Barsac wines may be legally labeled as themselves, or alternately as Sauternes—an arrangement that in poor years works to the distinct advantage of the Barsac growers.

[12]The white wines of Sauternes, as with all Bordeaux whites, are a blend of three white grapes, the Sémillon, the Sauvignon (both sources of California dry white wines) and the Muscadelle.

ingly futile order. In those days orders were orders—even if given by
a love-smitten young madman. The peasants moved obediently to the
vineyards and commenced the seemingly futile task of picking the rotten grapes—and thus was born the greatest sweet wine of all France!
Nowadays the grapes in Sauternes are no longer harvested in such a
hurry, but bunch by bunch—or even one by one with scissors—as they
reach the desired degree of sticky sweetness brought about by the pred-
atory *pourriture.*

In the middle of the last century, a sweet-toothed brother of one of
the czars paid twenty thousand francs (the equivalent of $10,000) for
four small casks of Château d'Yquem, but wine drinkers these days
seem not to have either the time or the taste for sweet dessert wines,
especially the expensive imported ones. Some of the vineyards of Sauternes and Barsac are returning once again to the production of dry
wines—those made from grapes before the *pourriture* has settled on
them. This renders them comparable to—though not necessarily any
better than—the white wines of nearby Graves, which have always
been dry. The whites of Graves are, in the opinion of most connoisseurs, a rather undistinguished lot—as a certain writer of the last century aptly put it: "Not very well endowed." At best one must be skeptical about the future of all French *liquoreux* wines, and we should
mention a few outstanding ones while they are still available. Two
often seen on shelves or lists are Châteaux Climens and Coutet, both
Barsacs, where a chalky soil endows the wines with a sharper character.
Two others are Châteaux Rieussec and La Tour-Blanche, labeled
Sauternes.

All Bordeaux whites are ready to drink when they are two or three
years old, although the sweeter ones will improve slightly in the bottle
over a period of ten or fifteen years. The consumer should be warned,
however, that there is always a danger that with too much age these
latter will become what is known as *maderizé,* a form of oxidation to
which all wines—whether sweet or dry—are susceptible after a certain
time. The term *maderizé* is an entirely literal one: white wine turns the
color of Madeira, and takes on a bitter, acrid taste. The best rule of
thumb: drink most French white wines when relatively young.

St.-Émilion and Pomerol

Twenty miles to the east of the city, beyond the two rivers and the
swallow-tailed Entre-Deux-Mers, lie those highland vineyards that

have been known for their wines since Roman times. Most of the best vineyards are situated on a plateau overlooking the Dordogne Valley: an area shared with St.-Émilion proper by the little commune of Pomerol, and another section called Graves-St.-Émilion—again indicating a predominantly gravelly soil. Yet another region includes five communes (see Table B) that hyphenate their names with St.-Émilion, but do not produce wines of anything like the same quality. The region as a whole is the largest wine producer in Bordeaux. Principally red wines are made here; the white wines are entitled only to the lowly appellation of Bordeaux.

Vines were certainly grown on the St.-Émilion plateau long before they appeared in the Médoc; but there remains some question whether they preceded vineyards in Graves and Sauternes. To the Romans, in any event, St.-Émilions were the best. They were praised by the poet and fourth consul Ausonius (who also appreciated Moselles); and they were also undoubtedly the first wines of this part of France to reach England. King John, who gave the town of St.-Émilion a charter in 1199, reputedly could never get enough of its wines; a century later Edward I created what was certainly the first *Appellation Contrôlée* in Europe, an ordinance requiring that every cask of St.-Émilion be marked with the town's coat of arms. Edward, obviously, wanted no substitutes.

In that day wines of these vineyards were shipped from Libourne, the port near the mouth of the Dordogne. This competition of trade was logically resented by the Bordelais, who eventually had their revenge during the reign of Henri III. Among other privileges, Henry allowed Bordeaux (the city) to trade with England with markedly reduced taxes; it was also given its own charter, and the privilege of electing its own mayor and its own government, called the Sénéchaussée. Such was the beginning of the great Bordeaux wine estates, and the monopoly of the wine trade by the antecedents of what are now the great Bordeaux houses. It also meant a long eclipse for Libourne. Wines of the highlands and Gascony to the east were perforce channeled through Bordeaux, but their casks waited on the quays of the city until all those of the Bordeaux burghers had been sold and shipped. Obviously, when they finally reached England, they were approaching a state of sad deterioration.

Just outside Libourne the "wine road" starts to climb gently into the country of Pomerol. Possibly it is only because of the comparison to the flat peninsula of Médoc and Graves, yet one finds these highland vineyards have a refreshing airiness about them, a sense of being a bit closer to heaven. One is soon in the thick of the best, for St.-Émilion, and especially Pomerol, are filled with innumerable small estates, all packed closely together, many of them infinitely small producers. Château Pétrus, the "king of Pomerols," is on your right; barely a stone's throw away are l'Évangile and Vieux-Château-Certan. Across an unmarked border is one of St.-Émilion's two best, Cheval Blanc, an undistinguished group of buildings, typical of all the rambling farmhouses generally associated with the names of the famous châteaux. Cheval Blanc was once the site of an ancient inn of the same name. Needless to say, all its wines are red—contrary to the writings of a well-known English writer, who somehow managed to construe that since *blanc* means white, so must be the wine.

The soil of this countryside is gravelly and stony, alternately mixed with light dosages of chalk and clay. It produces rich, dark wines with the softness of velvet and lovely fruitlike bouquets, characteristics that have led them to be described as the "Burgundies of Bordeaux." Comparable to Burgundies, they mature early: a Château Pétrus is usually at its peak within ten years—at about the same time a very great Pauillac or a St.-Julien might still be tasting like so much warmed-over yesterday's tea. St.-Emilions mature less rapidly than Pomerols, but the difference is largely academic. What differentiates all of them from the Médocs and Graves is the formula of grapes: in St.-Émilion and Pomerol the predominant grape is the soft Merlot; its principal partner is called the Bouchet, a Cabernet cousin. Recent vintages at Château Pétrus, for example, have tended to be almost 100 per cent Merlot.

Although it is not a country for great wines, one should not overlook wines from Lalande de Pomerol, or the villages of St.-Georges, Montagne and Lussac—this last commune having the highest elevation of all the vineyards in the Bordeaux district. All three, along with nearby Puisseguin and Parsac, hyphenate their appellations with St.-Émilion. Generally speaking, their wines do not compare with their distinguished neighbors (though some from St.-Georges often possess much merit). And in days of high prices and unavailability of the "greats," Pomerols and St.-Émilions of lesser fame are to be highly recommended—provided one can acquire them with a little age, say four or five years, and is able to lower one's sights a bit. Certainly of all the minor red wines of Bordeaux, they come closest to the compromise which the average consumer must nowadays make. Cuttings from Bordeaux have been carried all over the world and grown in every type of soil and under every conceivable condition, but at no other place on the face of the globe has any vintner ever been able to surpass, or even duplicate with any crowning success, that exact character and flavor of the wines from the soils of the Graves peninsula, St.-Émilion and Pomerol.

St.-Émilion itself is a charming medieval town. On its outskirts vines grow amid the ruins of an ancient church, and almost within earshot of the town hall are the Clos Fourtet and Château Canon, two of St.-Émilion's finest. Just below the town is Château Ausone, thought to be the site of the villa where Ausonius retired in order to be near the source of his favorite wines.

Within the last few decades (many of the finest red and, as we have pointed out, the best of the sweet white wines of Bordeaux are sometimes capable of this span of years) the best vintages have been 1959, 1961, 1962, 1964, 1966, 1967, 1970, 1971, 1973, 1975 and 1976.

Summary

The words *Appellation Contrôlée* must appear on all wines of Bordeaux labeled in three general grades, in this ascending order of excellence: (1) *Bordeaux*, which may be a wine (or blend) from any part of the entire district; (2) regional or subregional, the best coming from Haut-Médoc and Sauternes (and their subdivisions), Graves, St.-Émilion and Pomerol; and (3) château wines, stemming from officially recognized and classified vineyards.[13]

Of the reds, Haut-Médoc produces the finest (the aristocracy), those of Graves are somewhat heavier and coarser, the St.-Émilions and Pomerols are lighter and more flowery, more like red Burgundies.

Graves whites are dry, often lacking in distinguished tastes; the classic Sauternes and Barsacs are sweet wines to drink with desserts.

Other, less expensive, red wines to watch for are minor château wines from communes hyphenated with St.-Émilion and Pomerol, also ones from Bourg, Blaye and the Premières Côtes de Bordeaux.

Among dry whites, try labels from Entre-Deux-Mers, Premières Côtes de Bordeaux, Graves de Vayre.

[13]One should remember that, to be authentic, each of their labels must not only bear the *Appellation Contrôlée* of the appropriate, authorized regional or subdivisional area (see Table A), but also the vineyard name (*Château, Clos, Domaine, etc.*).

Many of the classic sweet white wines of Bordeaux (Sauternes, Barsac) are still within the price range of the average consumer.

TABLE B
Château Wines of Bordeaux

CLASSIFIED RED WINES (*CRUS CLASSÉS*) OF HAUT-MÉDOC

[Based on 1855 classification]

1. (*Premiers Crus*)

Château Lafite-Rothschild
Château Margaux

Château Latour
Château Haut-Brion (Graves)

Château Mouton-Rothschild

2. (*Deuxièmes Crus*)

Château Rausan-Ségla
Château Rauzan Gassies
Château Durfort-Vivens
Château Lascombes
Château Gruaud-Larose
Châueau Brane-Cantenac
Château Pichon-Longueville (Baron de Pichon)

Château Léoville-Las-Cases
Château Léoville-Poyferré
Château Léoville-Barton
Château Cos-d'Estournel
Château Ducru-Beaucaillou
Château Montrose
Château Pichon-Longueville (Comtesse de Lalande)

3. (*Troisièmes Crus*)

Château Cantenac-Brown
Château Palmer
Château La Lagune
*Château Calon-Ségur
Château Ferrière
Château Marquis-d'Alesme-Becker

Château Giscours
Château Kirwan
Château d'Issan
Château Lagrange
Château Langoa-Barton
Château Boyd-Cantenac

Château Malescot-St.-Exupéry

4. (*Quatrièmes Crus*)

Château St.-Pierre-Savaistre
*Château Branaire-Ducru
Château Duhart-Milon-Rothschild
Château Pouget
Château Lafon-Rochet

*Château Talbot
Château La Tour-Carnet
*Château Beychevelle
Château Prieuré-Lichine
Château Marquis-de-Terme

*Considered by most experts to be deserving of a higher classification.

TABLE B Continued
Château Wines of Bordeaux

5. (*Cinquièmes Crus*)

Château Pontet-Canet
*Château Batailley
*Château Grand-Puy-Lacoste
*Château Grand-Puy-Ducasse
*Château Lynch-Bages
Château Lynch-Moussas
Château Camensac
Château Cos-Labory
Château Clerc-Milon

Château Dauzac
*Château Mouton-Baronne Philippe
Château Le (du) Tertre
Château Haut-Bages-Libéral
Château Pédesclaux
Château Belgrave
Château Croizet-Bages
*Château Cantemerle
*Château Haut-Batailley

6. (*Crus Exceptionnels et Bourgeois*)

Château Villegeorge
*Château Angludet
Château La Couronne
Château Moulin-Riche
*Château Capbern
*Château Dutruch-Lambert
*Château Fourcas-Dupré
*Château Le Boscq
*Château Meyney
*Château Les-Ormes-de-Pez
*Château Paveil-de-Luze

*Château Chasse-Spleen
*Château Poujeaux-Theil
Château Bel-Air-Marquis-d'Aligre
*Château Fourcas-Hostein
*Cru Gressier-Grand-Poujeaux
*Château Lanessan
*Château de Pez
*Château Phélan-Ségur
*Château La Tour-de-Mons
*Château Sénéjac
*Château Gloria

CLASSIFIED GROWTHS OF GRAVES
(*Crus Classés*)

Red Wines
[Classified in 1953]

Château Bouscaut
Château Carbonnieux
Château Smith-Haut-Lafitte
Château La Mission-Haut-Brion
Château La Tour-Haut-Brion
Château Haut-Brion

Château Fieuzal
Château Malartic-Lagravière
Château Haut-Bailly
Domaine de Chevalier
Château Olivier
Château La Tour-Martillac

Château Pape-Clément

White Wines
[Classified in 1959]

Château Haut-Brion

Château Couhins

TABLE B Continued
Château Wines of Bordeaux

Château Bouscaut   Château Carbonnieux
Domaine de Chevalier   Château Olivier
Château Malartic-Lagravière   Château La Tour-Martillac
Château Laville-Haut-Brion

CLASSIFIED GROWTHS OF SAUTERNES AND BARSAC
[Classified in 1855]

1. (*Grand Premier Cru*)

Château d'Yquem

2. (*Premiers Crus*)

Château La Tour-Blanche   Château Rabaud-Sigalas
Château Lafaurie-Peyraguey   Clos Haut-Peyraguey
Château de Suduiraut   Château Rayne-Vigneau
Château Climens   Château Coutet
Château Rieussec   Château Guiraud
Château Rabaud-Promis

3. (*Deuxièmes Crus*)

Château Myrat   Château Doisy-Daëne
Château Doisy-Védrines   Château d'Arche
Château Filhot   Château Broustet
Château Nairac   Château Caillou
Château Suau   Château de Malle
Château Romer   Château Lamothe

CLASSIFIED GROWTHS OF ST.-ÉMILION
[Classified in 1953]

1. (*Premiers Grands Crus Classés*)

Château Ausone   Château Trottevieille
Château Beauséjour   Château Cheval Blanc
Château Canon   Château Belair
Château Figeac   Clos Fourtet
Château Magdelaine   Château La Gaffelière
Château Pavie

TABLE B Continued
Château Wines of Bordeaux

2. (*Grands Crus Classés*)

Note: Many St.-Émilion vineyards are awarded a *Grand Cru* status in certain years only by vote of an official tasting committee.

Château l'Angélus
Château Bellevue
Château Cadet-Bon
Château Canon-la-Gaffelière
Château Chapelle Madeleine
Château Corbin
Château Coutet
Château Curé Bon
Château Fonroque
Château Grand-Barrail-Lamarzelle
Château Grand-Corbin-Despagne
Château Grand Pontet
Château Guadet-St.-Julien
Clos des Jacobins
Château La Clotte
Château La Couspaude
Château Larcis-Ducasse
Château Lamarzelle
Château Chauvin
Château Corbin-Michotte
Château Croque-Michotte
Château Fonplégade
Château Franc-Mayne
Château Grand-Corbin-Figeac
Château Grand-Mayne
Château Grandes Murailles
Château Jean Faure
Château La Carte
Château La Cluzière
Château La Dominique

Château Laroze
Château La Tour-du-Pin-Figeac
Château Le Châtelet
Château Le Prieuré
Château Moulin-du-Cadet
Château Pavie-Macquin
Château Petit-Faurie-de-Souchard
Château Ripeau
Château St.-Georges-Côte-Pavie
Clos St.-Martin
Château Trimoulet
Château Troplong-Mondot
Château Yon-Figeac
Château Balestard-la-Tonnelle
Château Bergat
Château Cadet-Piola
Château Cap-de-Mourlin
Château Larmande
Château Lasserre
Château La Tour-Figeac
Château Le Couvent
Château Mauvezin
Château Pavie-Decesse
Château Pavillon-Cadet
Château Petit-Faurie-de-Soutard
Château Sansonnet
Château Soutard
Château Tertre-Daugay
Château Trois-Moulins
Château Villemaurine

Clos La Madeleine

TABLE B Continued
Château Wines of Bordeaux

PRINCIPAL RED WINES OF POMEROL
[Unofficial classification by the Pomerol Wine Growers Syndicate]

1. (*Grands Premiers Crus*)

Château Pétrus   Château Certan
              Vieux-Château-Certan

2. (*Premiers Crus*)

Cru l'Évangile   Château Nénin
Château Beauregard   Château Petit-Village
Château Clinet   Le Clos Lacombe
Château Lafleur   Le Clos (Domaine) de l'Église
Château La Commanderie   Clos du Clocher
Château Gazin   (Château) Certan-Sauteloup
Château Le-Gay-La-Fleur   Château Trotanoy
                 Château Guillot

Burgundy: *Wines of an Ancient Dukedom*

No real wine lover could praise the wines of Bordeaux without including, in the same breath, those of Burgundy. The wines of these two districts, quite different in character, are without doubt the finest in France. Of this there has never been any question.

Burgundy produces both red and white wines, but many people think of Burgundy only as a red wine—as they think of Burgundy as a red color with a slightly purplish tinge. It is true that the traditionally great vineyards of Burgundy, many of which have existed since Roman times, are predominantly devoted to red rather than to white wines—but when one thinks of fabulous ruby-colored wines such as Chambertin and Clos de Vougeot, one should never discount the charm and power of a rare white vintage of Corton-Charlemagne and Montrachet, or Chablis or Meursault.

Closely packed into a tight little ribbon, the greatest vineyards of Burgundy stretch southward for approximately thirty miles from the city of Dijon, almost in the center of France. This is Burgundy proper, known as the Côte d'Or, in the fifteenth century the epicenter of a little duchy which, during the aggressive reign of its aptly named ruler, Charles the Bold, came near to becoming the start of the French nation. Today Dijon might well hold the position of Paris, except that, like all power seekers, Charles spread himself too thin, drove his people into too many debilitating wars and was eventually unseated by Louis XI, a crafty little man from the west who planned his wars and ran his country while riding around on a donkey and quietly chatting with the common people.

Nowadays Burgundy (Bourgogne) is more a name than a place. Viniculturally speaking, the term is used for almost all the wines made in central France, beginning about one hundred miles south of Paris, to the Rhône. This includes the region of Chablis in the north, the home of very dry white wines—classics with seafoods; the Côte d'Or itself, producing both reds and whites; and the scattered vineyards known as Southern Burgundy, split into three regions called the Côte Chalonnaise, the Mâconnais and the Beaujolais.

There are so many vinicultural differences between Bordeaux and Burgundy that it seems best to begin by disposing of the major ones. To begin with, whereas the wines of Bordeaux are blends or mixtures of several grapes, a fine Burgundy is invariably made from one prescribed grape alone. In fact, in all of greater Burgundy, only three grapes are officially authorized for the better wines. These are the white Chardonnay (often called the Pinot Chardonnay, especially in California), the red Pinot noir and the Gamay, the grape responsible for the delicious, fruity red wines of Beaujolais.

Again in contrast to Bordeaux, where the vineyards (châteaux) are relatively large (except perhaps in St.-Émilion and Pomerol) and usually owned by a single individual, Burgundian vineyards are minuscule in size—sometimes only a few acres—and oftentimes subdivided among dozens of owners. Many of these owners may have only a few rows of vines. Originally parts of larger tracts belonging, in many instances, to the Church, their subdivision took place during the French Revolution, when for *le bien national* (the national good) the property of the Church and of the high and mighty was confiscated by the state and divided among the masses. The châteaux of Bordeaux miraculously escaped this fate; but in Burgundy and many other parts of France, *le bien national* created anything but an ideal situation for making consistently good wines. Nowadays the owner of a few rows

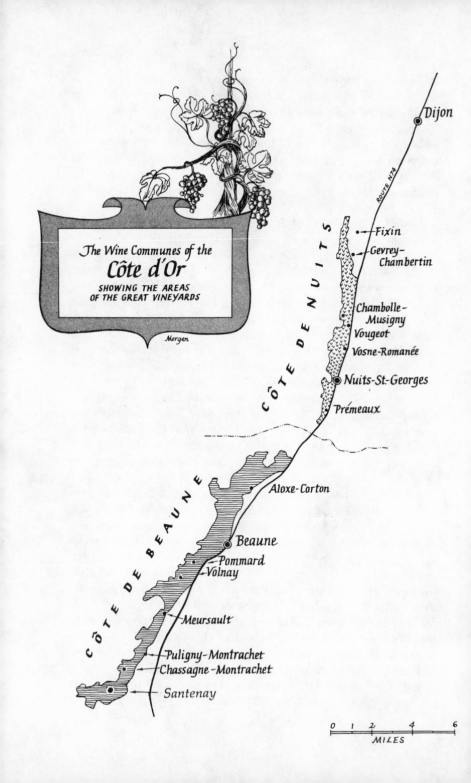

The Wine Communes of the
Côte d'Or

SHOWING THE AREAS
OF THE GREAT VINEYARDS

Morgen

Dijon

ROUTE N74

CÔTE DE NUITS

Fixin

Gevrey-
Chambertin

Chambolle-
Musigny

Vougeot

Vosne-Romanée

Nuits-St-Georges

Prémeaux

Aloxe-Corton

CÔTE DE BEAUNE

Beaune

Pommard

Volnay

Meursault

Puligny-Montrachet

Chassagne-Montrachet

Santenay

0   1   2   4   6
MILES

of vines in a great and famous vineyard of the Côte d'Or may make his wine very differently from the owner of the next few rows; yet the vineyard name on the label—the wine drinker's logical guide to quality among Burgundies—remains the same.

Once again, unlike the usual practice in Bordeaux, Burgundian vintners usually make their wines away from the vineyard, in the privacy of their own cellars in the villages or towns. Obviously the government inspectors cannot be everywhere at the same time—and Burgundies may be among the most variable wines in the world for this reason.

These cellar-bottled wines of Burgundy are often known as "estate-bottled," and their labels will generally bear words such as *Mise en bouteille au domaine* or *Mise à la propriété* (bottled on the property). The point to be emphasized is that "estate-bottled" is by no means comparable to the Bordeaux term "château-bottled," and no real insurance of a wine's quality. Even if all the wine did come from grapes of the *domaine* or estate of the owner of the cellar (the theoretical law behind the term), there is no true guarantee that the mixture will not be a hodgepodge of good and bad. Given the name of the vineyard, the wine drinker must also know the names of reputable producers and importers, or be guided by a conscientious and knowledgeable dealer. For this reason—although the reader will readily understand that it is impossible to give all the names of all the good producers and bottlers in Burgundy—Table F, somewhat farther along in these pages, has been prepared as a partial list of reputable producers and shippers (*négociants*) for the Côte d'Or itself.

Chablis

The white, delicate and extremely dry "flinty" wines of Chablis (the northernmost region of modern Burgundy) have for many generations been the world's favorite accompaniment to seafood. They are all made in a small region lying about a hundred miles southeast of Paris, the best being grown on chalky slopes drained by a placid little stream, the Serein—the French word for serene. It was by virtue of this little stream, which turns into the larger Yonne, and thence into the Seine, that the wines of Chablis were among the first to reach the French court. A few of them must even have been allowed to slip through Paris and make their way across the Channel, for it is a matter of record that, as early as 1212, King John of England was negotiating for a supply of his own. In fact, Chablis vies with the still wines of Champagne for the place of being the first French wine to be exported in any quantity.

As has so often been the case with the great wines of the world, it is to the Church that the basic credit must be given for Chablis. History reveals a group of Cistercian monks busily experimenting around the vineyards of Chablis and its two adjacent towns, Auxerre and Tonnerre, in the early part of the twelfth century, trying out one grape after another, searching diligently for the best soils and exposures. They were not long in settling on the Pinot Chardonnay, which they called the Beaunois—after the town of Beaune in the Côte d'Or, from which they themselves had evidently come.

While there is ample evidence that over the centuries wines of many localities have radically changed, usually for the better, in Chablis the Cistercians evidently established, some eight hundred years ago, a lasting prototype. A description of the wine of Chablis written by a traveling monk in 1280 is, remarkably, almost as valid today as it was then: "A white wine, sometimes golden, which has aroma and body, an exquisite, generous savor, and fills the heart with joyous assurance." Had he added the word "dry" and perhaps noted that Chablis's light greenish goldenness is (to use the words of another thirteenth-century account) like "the color of spring water in sunlight"—one could not better describe it.

Chablis is produced under the most trying circumstances, and unfortunately, so great is the world's demand for it (estimated at about ten times the supply) that a vast quantity of wine so labeled is either adulterated with other wines, or not Chablis at all. Taken together, all the vineyards producing wine within the two top grades allowed by the *Appellations Contrôlées* of Chablis amount to considerably less than a thousand acres. Thus good Chablis is logically both rare and expensive. Recent promotional rumblings in Chablis entail the expansion of outlying vineyards (those entitled to appellations of *Chablis* and *Petit Chablis*), but unfortunately it does not bode well for better wines in quantity. There is just one small pocket of soil that makes great wines; and the area as a whole has always been beset by adversities. Among others, the region itself—though well south of the northernmost growing limit for the wine grape—about every five years out of ten is plagued by killing frosts or other ravages of nature. And as though this were not enough, the chalky sloping land does not adapt itself to mechanization, and there is a perennial shortage of labor.

Nonetheless, always bearing their expense in mind, it must be said that wines from any of the *Grand Cru* or *Premier Cru* vineyards, all of superior quality, may be numbered among the finest and driest wines of France. There is nothing better with oysters, clams or even the menial halibut. But the reader must be warned that the wines of the two lower appellations—*Chablis* and *Petit Chablis*—may well be weak and acidic, and will more often than not constitute a bitter disappointment, especially in view of the price one must pay. Before buying them, one should look well to the name of the producer and to the reputation of the importer—and perhaps end by settling for another type of dry wine.

The name Chablis, too, holds the somewhat questionable title of having been appropriated, more than any other European white wine, by almost every white-wine-producing country of the world. It is well always to remember that there is no relationship. Only on the chalky banks of the Serein—part of the geological Kimmeridgian stratum which manifests itself again in the Cliffs of Dover—does the Chardonnay grape produce this flawless type of white Burgundy, and then only in the best vineyards and at the hands of the best producers. Most imitation Chablis is anything but "bone dry." Spanish "Chablis," for example, may be a fairly acceptable wine, but it no more resembles its French namesake than bourbon is reminiscent of crème de menthe. New York State and Australian "Chablis" are even more nondescript. California "Chablis" (never made from the Chardonnay) is something that is best described as merely white and light. This is not to say it cannot be pleasant, and very often far more potable than a bad version of its French namesake. Finally, there is no such wine (in France) as a pink Chablis.

Table C gives the eight *Grands Crus* (Great Growths) and the twenty-four *Premier Crus* (First Growths) of Chablis, each category being entitled to its own authorized *Appellation Contrôlée*. As we have mentioned, within the two lower official classifications (*Chablis* and *Petit Chablis*) one should choose carefully: the name of a reliable grower is of paramount importance. A *Premier Cru* Chablis without a vineyard name on the label will not necessarily be a poor wine: often-times scarcity or other legitimate factors force a shipper to bottle the wines of two vineyards as one. In these circumstances, under the law, he may not give the wine a recondite geographical title.

As we have mentioned, most French white wines need but a year or two in the bottle. But a great Chablis *can* live a long time. For this reason, our list includes the best vintages of the past twenty-odd years: 1955, 1958, 1959, 1961, 1962, 1966, 1969, 1970, 1973, 1974, 1976. The Chablis region is perhaps the sole exception to our caution that slavery to vintage charts is a form of abject foolishness. Chablis of a poor year may be a bitter disappointment.

TABLE C
The Two First *Crus* of Chablis

Grands Crus

Blanchots	*La Moutonne
Bougros	Les Preuses
Les Clos	Valmur
Grenouilles	Vaudésir

Premiers Crus

Beauroy (Boroy)	Mont de Milieu
Beugnon(s)	Montée de Tonnerre
Butteaux	Montmains
Chapelots	Pied d'Aloup
Châtains	Séchet (Seché)
Côte de Fontennay	Troême (Troêne)
Côte de Léchet	Vaillons
Les Forêts	Vaupulent
Fourchaume	Vaucoupin
Les Fourneaux	Vaulorent
Les Lys	Vosgros
Melinots	Vogiros (Vaugiraud)

*The *Grand Cru* vineyard of La Moutonne has for some years been under a cloud of disputes within its family management and contentions with the Institut des Appellations d'Origine. When bottles under its own name have appeared, or appear again, it is to be recommended as one of the finest.

Just south of Dijon, a city gastronomically famous for its powerful mustard, hams and Cassis, a syrupy liqueur made from black currants which, when mixed with white wine, makes the popular *apéritif* called Kir, there begins the little region called the Côte d'Or—the Slope of Gold. Its glamorous name should provoke the image of some sparkling cove on the Riviera, or perhaps a buttercup-carpeted valley high in the

Alps—but such is simply not the case. The Slope of Gold is, in truth, an undeniably drear, unassuming range of low hills, paralleled (and certainly not enhanced) by a trunk railroad and the busy highway (and the not-too-distant Autoroute) from Paris to the Mediterranean. Its predominantly clay and limestone soil was once filled with rocks and boulders, and far too poor for growing much of anything but the wine grape; its little villages—whose famous names are seen in wineshops the world over—are by no means among the most charming of France.

The vineyards themselves are slightly elevated above the valley floor, exposed to the southeast and protected by hills to the west, and concentrated into a narrow ribbon of land that is barely thirty miles long and less than half a mile wide at its broadest. Midway between Dijon and the ancient fortress city of Beaune, this undulating little ribbon almost completely vanishes, like some underground river. An ugly quarry appears, the countryside takes on an almost commercial aspect and the ribbon is hardly seen again for almost two miles. North of this break, the Côte d'Or has the subdivisional name of the Côte de Nuits; the southern half, containing the city of Beaune, is known as the Côte de Beaune.

The wines of the Côte de Nuits, which include the greatest Burgundies, are nearly all red. They are sturdier and tend to live longer than those of the Côte de Beaune. Although the term is almost never seen on a label, the twenty-odd finest have been awarded the official title of *Grand Cru*,[14] these latter carrying the right to use on labels the words *Appellation Contrôlée* as applied specifically to the vineyard itself (see Table D). The next-best wines are known as *Premiers Crus*. Their labels bear not only the vineyard name (supplemented sometimes with the term *Premier Cru*),[15] but also the *Appellation Contrôlée* of the town or commune from which they come.

Unfortunately, a hidden danger lurks in many of these communal names of the Côte d'Or, which the unknowing reader should be aware of for his own protection. Toward the end of the last century—doubtless for the purpose of selling more inferior wine—many of the communes of the Côte d'Or adopted the practice of hyphenating the name

[14]Previous to the advent of the *Appellations Contrôlées*, the finest vineyards of the Côte d'Or were called *Têtes de Cuvée*, meaning the best in a commune. The term is sometimes still seen on labels.

[15]As in Chablis, a Côte d'Or label bearing the words *Premier Cru* without a vineyard name means a blend of wines from *Premiers Crus* vineyards.

of the commune with that of its most famous vineyard. Thus, for example, Gevrey (the commune) was married to Chambertin (its most celebrated vineyard), and officially became Gevrey-Chambertin. Chambolle took on the name of its most illustrious wine, Musigny, to become thenceforth the commune of Chambolle-Musigny. And since the great white vineyard of the Côte de Beaune, Montrachet, was spread between the two communes of Puligny and Chassagne, both claimed it. Today they are Puligny-Montrachet and Chassagne-Montrachet, respectively.

This practice, comparable to calling *all* Milwaukee beer Milwaukee-Schlitz, has no doubt been an economic boon to the Côte d'Or; but the wine drinker should not forget that a bottle labeled simply Chassagne-Montrachet or Gevrey-Chambertin is only a wine—and often a quite common one—from any vineyard within one of these two communes respectively; or a blend of wines from two or more vineyards within the same commune. In any case, it will certainly not be a true Chambertin or a bona fide Montrachet, nor one of those other several vineyards that are officially entitled to hyphenate their names with those of the greatest (see below and Table D).

Going south from Dijon, the first cluster of vineyards one meets are those of Gevrey-Chambertin. These include the famed Chambertin and its twin, the Clos de Bèze, and the other seven nearby vineyards whose wines are so excellent that they are authorized to hyphenate their names with the parent *Grand Cru* vineyard of Chambertin and also use their own individual *Appellations Contrôlées*. We repeat: do not fall into the trap of confusing them with a communal wine named simply Gevrey-Chambertin. Chambertin, so goes the traditional story, was once a field planted with turnips, adjacent to the great tract belonging to the Abbey de Bèze. So excellent were the wines of the Abbey that a rival religious order finally could bear it no longer, and subsidized the peasant owner of the turnip patch to rip up his crop and plant vines. This peasant was named Bertin—thus the vineyard acquired the name of Champ de Bertin (Bertin's field).

Wines of the Chambertin cluster are dark and heavy, with a reputation for aging comparable to the Médocs of Bordeaux, although this is not par for the average red Burgundy. Over the years the Chambertins have been the favorites of many an illustrious person. Napoleon is said to have allowed nothing else on his table, and to have taken an ample supply to Russia with him during the ill-fated campaign of 1812. As we have already warned, each of these *Grands Crus* vineyards, like most of the Côte d'Or, is divided among many growers, resulting in wines of variable quality. When made by a conscientious producer, there are few finer red Burgundies; yet even the more poorly made ones are hard to find, and expensive. Alternately, we recommend the *Grands Crus* wines of the adjacent commune, Morey-St. Denis, the best of which are Clos de Tart, Clos de la Roche and the Clos St.-Denis; as well as the other excellent *Premiers Crus* wines listed in Table D.

All Burgundies from the Côte d'Or are noted for their almost overpowering fragrances—aromas that carry overtones of more than just wine. Some people relate these overtones to raspberries, violets and even truffles—and in the case of the white Montrachet, the term often used by Burgundians is "beeswax." The red wines of the next three communes—Chambolle-Musigny, Vougeot and Vosne-Romanée—are the most fragrant of the whole Côte d'Or. Red Musigny[16] is indeed redolent of raspberries; nor does it take a veteran to spot the fragrance of violets wafting from a glass of well-made Clos de Vougeot.

Almost the entire commune of Vougeot is taken up by the hundred-and-thirty-acre Clos, one of the Côte d'Or's largest vineyards. Planted in the twelfth century by Cistercian monks, whose noble monastery still stands amid the rows of vines as the headquarters of a promotional organization of Burgundian vintners (the Confrérie des Chevaliers du Tastevin), no wines on the whole Côte d'Or have been more praised in days gone by than the flowery ones of this vineyard. Its glories have been sung by Stendhal and Voltaire, by popes and kings and generals; in fact, to this day the vineyard is still honored by passing regiments, for whom it has become customary to halt and present arms. Regrettably, *le bien national* wrought more than just the usual harm to the Clos de Vougeot, for even this sacrosanct ground was not spared the revolutionary auctioneer's hammer; and the Clos is now divided among literally dozens of owners, many of whom simply fall back or capitalize on its famous name. Thus the wine drinker should look carefully for the name of a reputable producer, shipper or *négociant* on a label of Clos de Vougeot. A small section of the Clos is devoted to the production of an excellent though rare white wine—Clos Blanc de Vougeot, happily the monopoly of a superior vintner.

[16]This vineyard is also the source of one of France's finest and rarest white wines, Musigny Blanc.

Whereas the lore of the Clos de Vougeot captures the inherent sentiment of the entire French nation, the most glamorous vineyards of the Côte d'Or are to be found in the next commune of Vosne-Romanée. Though in our opinion its wines are nowadays considerably overrated and certainly shockingly overpriced, the fact remains that the tiny four-acre vineyard of Romanée-Conti has probably been coveted over the years by more powerful and colorful personalities than any other plot of land on the surface of the earth. Originally the site of a Roman camp (hence the name Romanée), this little vineyard and its four *Grands Crus* neighbors—La Romanée, La Tâche, Richebourg and Romanée-St.-Vivant (once all simply known as Romanée)—have been squabbled over and jockeyed for by more princes and kings (including their mistresses), churchmen, diplomats and fortune seekers than bears recounting. A comparatively recent owner in this long line, the Prince de Conti, once an adviser to Louis XV, sagely saw to it that the most precious four-acre section of the original Romanée should forever perpetuate his name. Having stolen the vineyard from under the very nose of Madame de Pompadour, the king's mistress, he promptly hyphenated its name to his. Today Romanée-Conti is safely in the hands of a conservative syndicate.

All the wines of Vosne-Romanée are fragrant and light-colored, with a unique softness. A phrase coined for them two hundred years ago by one of the Prince de Conti's friends requires no amendment: "Bottled velvet and satin." Yet the wines of this commune are not as well made today as they once were, and almost comparable quality may be found, at far more reasonable prices, from the adjacent commune of Flagey-Échézeaux, the latter being such a vicious tongue twister to the average foreigner that it is held responsible for the relatively small popularity of its wines outside of France. One may take comfort, however, in the probability that one's wine dealer won't know how to pronounce the word, either.

Rather inexplicably, none of the excellent vineyards of the two southernmost communes of the Côte de Nuits—Nuits-St. Georges and Prémeaux[17]—were given official *Grand Cru* status, even though many of them are numbered among the finest red Burgundies—the best having been traditional *Têtes de Cuvée*. The vineyards here are perhaps the oldest of the Côte d'Or, and their grapes have a way of ripening earlier,

[17]Both are entitled to the *Appellation Contrôlée* of Nuits-St.-Georges, although one often sees the term Nuits-St.-Georges-Prémeaux.

thus containing more natural sugar than those of many other parts of the region. The resulting wines have an unusual degree of mellowness. This quirk of nature also often renders them less subject to the sanctioned, though not always enhancing, practice known as *chaptalization*—the adding, especially in a poor year, of sufficient sugar to the fermenting grapes to attain the required amount of alcohol. In addition to this mellowness, these are also wines of verve and vitality.

Between the two communes there are almost four dozen *Premiers Crus* vineyards, nearly all of which are of outstanding excellence. Among the best in Nuits-St.-Georges are Les St.-Georges, Les Cailles, Les Vaucrains and Les Porrets; in Prémeaux, the Clos de la Maréchale, Les Didiers and Les Corvées. Nor is a mere communal Nuits-St.-Georges something to be overlooked if it comes from a good vintner.

The first commune for great wines on the Côte de Beaune is Aloxe-Corton, the source of the red Corton (often seen as Le Corton), as well as the equally prized Corton-Charlemagne, a distinguished though nowadays expensive dry white wine. The Emperor Charlemagne once owned this vineyard, which should be indicative of its traditional greatness; Voltaire (known for his parsimony) is said to have been so fond of the heavy-bodied red Corton that he drank if himself while providing ordinary Beaujolais for his guests. As will be observed in Table D, many vineyards of the commune, such as Les Bressandes and Le Clos du Roi, hyphenate their names with the great Corton—an authorized mark of added quality. Another of Corton's excellent reds is the wine called Château Grancey or Corton-Grancey, which, though an officially unclassified wine, is produced by one of the Côte d'Or's outstanding growers, Louis Latour (see Table F).

South of Aloxe-Corton lies the largest commune of the Côte d'Or—Beaune.[18] Here, a bit like a boa constrictor which has just swallowed a rabbit, our thin ribbon of vineyards has acquired an unproportionate bulge. In the bulge's center lies the medieval city of Beaune itself, the lovely wine capital of the Côte d'Or, flanked by walls and bastions nowadays used as wine cellars. Perhaps the best one-word description of the wines of Beaune is "uncomplicated." One will find them earthy—and many people refer to them as "men's wines," meaning they may be consumed in gulps and swallows, without lingering too

[18]With one exception, an outstandingly fragrant wine called Clos des Mouches Blanc, all the fine wines of Beaune are red.

long over refinements and flowery aromas. Beaunes are favorites with
the Burgundians themselves, who have a traditional saying: "There are
no bad wines in Beaune." There are also no truly great ones. But like
the communal wines of Nuits-St.-Georges to the north, the blends of
this commune generally rank a notch or two above many of their communal neighbors—though in this connection it is well to remember
that *Appellation Contrôlée Beaune* on a label indicates a far better standard than a *Côte-de-Beaune* or a *Côte-de-Beaune-Villages*. These latter
special appellations apply to wines from vineyards further afield than
Beaune itself, and wines so labeled may more often than not be only a
step or two away in quality from *ordinaires*. Many producers seem,
somehow, to adulterate them with non-Burgundy.

The city of Beaune, as picturesque as any in France, houses a celebrated semi-charitable institution, the Hospice de Beaune, a hospital
and almshouse that functions in a lovely fifteenth-century Gothic
building, and is supported almost entirely by the proceeds of its vineyards. Founded in 1443 by Nicolas Rollin, Chancellor of the Duchy of
Burgundy, and his wife, Guigone de Salins, over the years it has
become the recipient of several dozen vineyards scattered across the
Côte de Beaune. Along with other duties, Rollin was the tax collector
thereabouts, which led to the facetious remark of the then king of
France to the effect that, since Rollin had taken so much money away
from so many people, it was only proper and fitting that he return some
of it.

The wines of the Hospice, known as *Cuvées*, are named after the
donor of each particular vineyard and carry the *Appellation Contrôlée*
of the commune in which they are produced. None of them are *Grand
Crus*, and though not all of equal quality, their production is at least
under a single supervision, a rare and happy circumstance in the Côte
d'Or. Some of the best vineyards of the Hospice—owning both reds
and whites—are Nicolas Rollin, Guigone de Salins, Dr. Peste and Gau-
vain. Every mid-November the whole *côte* turns out for a three-day
wine *fête* centered on one of the most dramatic auctions in France. This
is when the casks of the Hospice are sold, one by one, to the highest
bidder. The bidding on each cask ends not by the fall of any auctioneer's hammer, but when a flickering taper has burnt to its end. Wine
buyers from all over the world attend, and careful attention is given to
the prices paid, since they are always indicative of the prices Burgundies will bring for that particular year.

Below Beaune are the twin communes of Volnay and Pommard, producing red wines that are usually light in color, tending to be more tart and fruity than other reds of the Côte d'Or. The fame of Volnay and Pommard is purported to have spread because their names—like their delightful potable wines—slip so smoothly across the tongue and therefore present no pronunciation problem to the foreigner. A more plausible explanation involves the fact that in the seventeenth century this little section of the Côte d'Or was one of the strongholds of the Protestant Huguenots. Following the revocation of the Edict of Nantes, many citizens of Pommard and Volnay were forced to flee France. Wherever they settled, they sent for their native wines, and soon the outside world, too, came to appreciate the virtues of these simple, unassuming vintages.

Until the advent of the *Appellations Contrôlées* laws in 1936, perhaps only Chablis—among French wines—was more tampered with or adulterated than Pommards and Volnays. As we have mentioned, tampering or extreme practices of blending are nearly always the result of a demand exceeding a supply—and it so happens that the wines of both Pommard and Volnay were the first Burgundies to attain popular world appeal, thus creating an inordinate demand. Yet there was another, unrelated factor to cause a shortage, one that pertained not only to Burgundy but also to all the wines of the Old World. In the 1870s and 1880s an American vine louse, or aphid, brought to England on experimental cuttings, accidentally leaped the Channel and spread through the vineyards of France, and thence throughout the rest of Europe. Only two spots on the entire continent, in fact, the remote Rioja district of Spain and the deep, sandy Colares vineyards on the coast of Portugal, were not seriously affected—and even the good fortune of the Rioja lasted only a few decades. Known as the *phylloxera,* this insidious little organism, which attacked the roots of the vines and thus could not be reached or affected by chemicals or any known insecticides, had its origin among the native grapes of the eastern United States, which over the years had become resistant to it. Its effect on the other side of the Atlantic was almost catastrophic. The vines withered and died like insects under DDT. Wine production all over Europe fell to a mere trickle, and it was many years before the problem was solved by importing impervious wild-grape roots from the upper Mississippi-Missouri watershed to be used as grafting stock.

With the introduction of new root stock, European vineyards were on the road to revival—but at this juncture the vintners of the Côte d'Or and many other parts of France made a serious error. Instead of grafting with their traditional Pinot noir, many of them gave in to temptation and used another red Burgundian grape called the Gamay— hardier than the Pinot and a comparatively prolific producer. On certain soils, such as in the Beaujolais region of Southern Burgundy, the Gamay makes delicious (though hardly great) wine,—but not the Burgundy that the world knew and demanded from the Côte d'Or at the turn of the century. Between the *phylloxera* and the Gamay the shortage of true Burgundy reached a low from which it did not recover for almost sixty years. Finally banned by the Institut National des Appellations d'Origine from all the best vineyards, the juices of the Gamay are now to be found only in Beaujolais and in pedestrian regional Burgundies with the *Appellations Contrôlées* of *Bourgogne Ordinaire* and *Bourgogne Passe-Tout-Grains*, both authorized blends of the Pinot noir and the Gamay.[19]

The southernmost vineyards of the Côte de Beaune are predominantly devoted to white wines, and situated chiefly in the communes of Meursault, Puligny-Montrachet and Chassagne-Montrachet. As mentioned, the great Montrachet vineyard is shared by both the latter communes. Along with Bordeaux's Château d'Yquem, the wine of this eighteen-acre plot (owned by many owners) is one of the most highly prized whites of France. Fairly dry, with a highly distinctive flavor and bouquet all its own, it is the color of gold and, needless to say, extremely difficult to come by. Comparable to Bordeaux's giant, white Haut-Brion Blanc, even though one may not like it one will hardly fail to understand why over the ages the great and the powerful have always coveted and praised it. Rabelais called it "divine"; Dumas once said that it should be drunk "only while kneeling." When well made, Montrachet is the quintessence of the Chardonnay. The acknowledged best comes from that part of this tiny vineyard owned by the Marquis de Laguiche, and will be so labeled. Wines from four neighboring *Grands Crus* vineyards allowed to hypenate their names to Montrachet (see Table D) are of nearly the same quality, less scarce and easier on the pocketbook. Also to be recommended are the *Premiers Crus* vineyards of these three communes.

[19]The Gamay also has a white counterpart, the Aligoté, used (with or without the Chardonnay) for a wine officially classified as *Bourgogne Aligoté*. At its best, the wine called Aligoté is not a very palatable drink. The best vineyards of the Côte d'Or are restricted to one white grape only, the Chardonnay.

The white wines from the commune of Meursault, to the north, are stronger in taste, less delicate, usually a little less dry than the Montrachets. Not too many of them are seen away from their own land, though their popularity in France itself is extremely high. Among the best are Les Perrières (or Clos des Perrières), Les Genevrières, La Goutte d'Or (a favorite with foreigners) and Les Charmes.[20]

Excellent red wines, too, are made in Meursault, Puligny, Chassagne and neighboring Monthélie, as well as in Santenay, the southernmost commune of the Côte d'Or. *Premiers Crus*[21] wines from these latter communes are almost always excellent buys, and they are apt to be sturdy and sometimes even long-lived, comparable to those of the vineyards of Gevrey-Chambertin and Morey-St.-Denis. Today these are wines to recommend to the consumer who must keep an eye on the diminishing bulge of the wallet.

Since no wine lover will necessarily wish to drink the *Grands* and *Premiers Crus* exclusively, no one should overlook the Burgundian equals of the regional wines of Bordeaux—in this case known as communal wines. These latter are often of a very high quality when made or endorsed by a good producer. Usually (though not invariably) blends from two or more *Premiers Crus* vineyards, they are simply called Gevrey-Chambertin, Meursault, Pommard, Chassagne-Montrachet and so forth. We have already mentioned those of Nuits-St.-Georges and Beaune as being exceptional. Reputable producers are of course a requisite; thus we once again refer the uninitiated reader to Table F, listing some of the better-known producers, shippers and/or *négociants* of Burgundy. This list, of course, is not exhaustive.

About the only *rosé* of interest made in all Burgundy is called Marsannay, made at Marsannay-la-Côte just south of Dijon, carrying the appellation of either *Bourgogne Clairet* or *Bourgogne Rosé*. Of latter years so-called varietals, both red and white, are also being increasingly exported: wines labeled with grape names such as Pinot Chardonnay, Gamay and so forth. One may be fairly sure that their quality does not match that of the communally labeled wines. No French wine merchant, except in the case of a poor crop he is ashamed of, ever downgrades a wine to a lower classification than necessary. In Burgundy these varietals usually carry the basic *Appellation Contrôlée* of *Bourgogne*. In effect they were created, in a world of rising prices, to com-

---

[20]Many of these vineyards commonly hyphenate their names with Meursault, such as Meursault-Charmes, Meursault-Genevrières, etc.

[21]Some of the lesser wines are sold (legally) as *Côtes-de-Beaune-Villages*.

pete with California varietal wines, the idea being that a Pinot Chardonnay with a foreign label would be more attractive to the consumer than one without. Only experimentation on the part of the consumer can decide what wines, in this varietal class, are of better intrinsic value.

The best recent years for Burgundies were (1958 for Chablis), 1959, 1961, 1962, 1964, 1966, 1967, 1969, 1970, 1971, 1973 and 1976. Occasionally, as we have pointed out, fine wines were made in the intervening years, which wine drinkers will eventually discover after sufficient experimentation. White Burgundies are usually ready for drinking at two or three years of age, whereas most of the *Grands Crus* and *Premiers Crus* reds should be allowed at least a couple of years longer. The traditionally great reds from the northern part of the Côte d'Or have been known to live and improve in the bottle for many years, and it is a crime to drink a well-made Chambertin before it has been allowed eight or ten years to come into its own. Yet, in this very connection, it is unfortunately the case that over all of France—and Burgundy is no exception—the practice of making red wines so that they will mature early and thus "move" faster to the markets of the world is on the increase. Generally speaking, this involves an abandonment of the traditional techniques of making red wine by leaving the stalks, or other tannin-making elements, to ferment a long time with the juice. Tannin adds flavor and long-lasting qualities to the wine, and every good producer knows that short-cut methods reduce the quality of his product. Yet commerce is commerce, and it will be a long time, if ever, before the pendulum swings back. A bottle of well-aged red Burgundy— harsh, tannic and acidic when young, showing a healthy dosage of dregs when aged to softness and charm—is nowadays far more of a rarity than a rule.

TABLE D
Classified Wines of the Côte D'or

Grands Crus
[Entitled to a vineyard *Appellation Contrôlée*]

Côte de Nuits*

(Le) Chambertin	Clos de la Roche
Chambertin-Clos de Bèze	Clos St.-Denis

*All listed wines are red, with the exception of Musigny, whose vineyard also produces a rare, expensive white (Musigny Blanc).

TABLE D Continued
Classified Wines of the Côte D'or

Latricières-Chambertin

Mazys-Chambertin (Mazis)

Mazoyères-Chambertin

Ruchottes-Chambertin

Chapelle-Chambertin

Charmes-Chambertin

Griotte-Chambertin

Clos de Tart

Bonnes-Mares

*(Le) Musigny

Clos de Vougeot

Grands Échézeaux (and Échézeaux)

Romanée-Conti

La Romanée

La Tâche

Richebourg

Romanée-St.-Vivant

Côte de Beaune†

Corton†

Corton-Charlemagne

Charlemagne

(Le) Montrachet

Bâtard-Montrachet

Chevalier-Montrachet

Bienvenues-Bâtard-Montrachet

Criots-Bâtard-Montrachet

Premiers Crus

[Vineyards entitled to the *Appellation Contrôlée* of their own particular commune. Labels need not bear the words *Premier Cru*.]

Côte de Nuits-Red Wines

Commune	*Vineyard*
Fixin	Clos de la Perrière
	Clos du Chapitre
	Les Hervelets
Gevrey-Chambertin	Clos de Ruchottes
	Clos St.-Jacques
	Varoilles
	Fouchère
	Estournelles (or Étournelles)
	Cazatiers
	Combottes
Morey-St.-Denis	Clos des Lambrays
	Calouère
	Les Charnières
Chambolle-Musigny	Les Amoureuses

†All listed wines are white, with the exception of Corton, which may be either red or white (Corton Blanc).

TABLE D Continued
Classified Wines of the Côte D'or

Commune	Vineyard
	Les Baudes
	Les Charmes
Vougeot	Les Petits-Vougeot
	Le Cras
	Clos de la Perrière
Flagey-Échézeaux	Les Beaumonts (Beaux-Monts)
	Champs-Traversin
	Clos St.-Denis
	Les Cruots (or Vignes-Blanches)
	Les Rouges-du-Bas
	Les Poulaillières
	Les Loachausses
	Les Quartiers-de-Nuits
	Les Treux
	En Orveaux
	Les Échézeaux-de-Dessus
Vosne-Romanée	Les Beaumonts (Beaux-Monts)
	Les Gaudichots
	Les Malconsorts (Clos Frantin)
	La Grande Rue
	Les Suchots (Grands Suchots)
	Aux Brûlées
	Les Reignots
	Clos des Réas
	Les Petits-Monts
	Les Chaumes
Nuits-St.-Georges	Les St.-Georges
	Les Boudots
	Les Cailles
	Les Porrets (Porets)
	Les Pruliers
	Les Vaucrains
	Les Cras
	Les (Aux) Murgers
	Les Thorey (Clos de Thorey)
Nuits-St.-Georges-Prémeaux	Clos de la Maréchale
	Les Didiers-St.-Georges
	Clos des Forêts-St.-Georges

TABLE D Continued
Classified Wines of the Côte D'or

Commune	Vineyard
	Les Corvées (Les Corvées-Paget)
	Le Clos St.-Marc
	Clos des Argillières
	Clos Arlot (d'Arlot)
	Les Perdrix (Champs Perdrix)

Côte de Nuits-White Wines

Commune	Vineyard
Fixin	Clos de la Parrière Blanc
Morey-St.-Denis	Mont-Luisants Blanc
Vougeot	Clos Blanc de Vougeot
Nuits-St.-Georges	La Perrière
Nuits-St.-Georges-Prémeaux	Clos Arlot (d'Arlot) Blanc

Côte de Beaune-Red Wines

Commune	Vineyard
Pernand-Vergelesses	Ile-des-Vergelesses
	Les Basses-Vergelesses
Aloxe-Corton	Corton-Bressandes
	Corton-Clos du Roi
	Corton-(Les) Renardes
	Corton-Chaumes
	Corton-Maréchaudes
	Corton-Vigne-au-Saint
	Corton-(Les) Perrières
	Corton-(Les) Grèves
	Corton-Pauland
	Corton-(Les) Meix
	Corton-(Les) Pougets
	Corton-Vergennes
Savigny-lès-Beaune	Les Vergelesses
	Les Marconnets
	Les Jarrons
Beaune	Les Grèves (Grèves de l'Enfant Jésus)
	Les Fèves
	Les Marconnets
	Les Bressandes

TABLE D Continued
Classified Wines of the Côte D'or

Commune	Vineyard
	Le Clos des Mouches
	Le Clos de la Mousse
	Le Cras
	Les Champs-Pimonts
	Les Cent-Vignes
Pommard	Les Épenots (Épenaux) (Grands Épenots)
	Les Rugiens-Bas
	Le Clos Blanc
Volnay	Les Angles
	Les Caillerets
	Les Champans
	Les Fremiets
	Santenots (Volnay-Santenots)
	Les Petures
	Clos des Chênes
	Clos des Ducs
Auxey-Duresses	Les Duresses
	Le Bas-des-Duresses
	Les Bretterins
	Les Écusseaux
	Les Grands-Champs
	Les Reugnes
	Clos du Val
Puligny-Montrachet	Le Cailleret
	Clavoillons
Chassagne-Montrachet	Abbaye de Morgeot
	Le Clos St.-Jean Morgeot
	Morgeot
	Clos de la Boudriotte (La Boudriotte)
	La Romanée
Meursault	Les Cras
Santenay	(Les) Gravières
	Clos-de-Tavanne
	La Comme

TABLE D Continued
Classified Wines of the Côte D'or

Côte de Beaune-White Wines

Commune	Vineyard
Beaune	Clos des Mouches Blancs
Meursault	Clos des Perrières
	(Les) Perrières
	(Les) Genevrières
	(La) Goutte d'Or
	(Les) Charmes
	(Les) Santenots
	(Les) Bouchères
	La Pièce-sous-le-Bois
	Sous-le-Dos-d'Âne
Puligny-Montrachet	Le Cailleret
	Les Combettes
	Hameau de Blagny Blanc
	Le Champ-Canet
	Les Pucelles
	Les Chalumeaux
Chassagne-Montrachet	Les Ruchottes
	Morgeot
	La Maltroie (Château de)

Southern Burgundy and the Beaujolais

Just south of the Côte d'Or, on the Saône River, one comes to the quaint wine town of Chalon. Here begins the region known—for want of a more appropriate term—as Southern Burgundy, embracing three subdivisions: the Côte Chalonnaise, the Mâconnais (thirty-five miles further south) and the Beaujolais. In the sense of the Côte d'Or and Bordeaux, there are no truly great wines made in these areas, but the red wines of Mercurey and Givry of the Côte Chalonnaise and the white Pouilly-Fuissé from the Mâconnais are unquestionably ones of much distinction. Pouilly-Fuissé and its plainer sisters, Pouilly-Loché and Pouilly-Vinzelles—all moderately dry, with a "flintiness" akin to Chablis and the characteristically pungent aroma imparted by the Chardonnay grape—are names that rank extremely high among wine drinkers the world over.

The Côte Chalonnaise covers four officially recognized wine-producing communes: Rully, Givry, Mercurey and Montagny. As in the Côte d'Or, the finest wines are made from the red Pinot noir and the white Chardonnay, though a subtle difference in the soil produces lighter and shorter-lived—and somewhat coarser—wines than those from the Slope of Gold. In view of the prices now asked for the nobility of the Côte d'Or, these are good, solid wines that should not be overlooked or thought of as mere upstarts. In Mercurey, once an important Roman settlement, the vineyards are said to antedate the Romans themselves. Montagny and Rully (also a source of Sparklings) are famous for their exceptionally light-bodied whites. In all four communes certain exceptional vineyards have been awarded a *Premier Cru* status, and are thereby allowed to print the vineyard name on their labels (with or without the words *Premier Cru*, as in the Côte d'Or). Fortunately, many wines of the Côte Chalonnaise are nowadays seen outside of France, especially the reds of Mercurey. These latter may often be wines of considerable distinction.

Pouilly-Fuissé is far and away the finest and best-known white-wine region of Southern Burgundy. Regrettably, because of the great demand for it, more and more of it is being shipped as though it were a blend, simply under the name of Pouilly-Fuissé. In fact, one may have to travel to Paris to find a Pouilly-Fuissé with a traditional vineyard name on its label. As in the Côte Chalonnaise, certain vineyards in the Pouilly-Fuissé region may market their wines under their own names, giving them, in this case, a quasi-*Premier Cru* status. A list of some of the best of these appears in Table E—in almost every case a Pouilly-Fuissé from a bona fide vineyard is vastly superior to one not so labeled. The wines of Pouilly-Loché and Pouilly-Vinzelles, generally made by cooperatives, are never the qualitative equals of Pouilly-Fuissé.

Other whites of the Mâconnais, very similar in type to Pouilly-Fuissé, come from the communes or areas of Viré, Lugny, Clessé, St.-Véran and Chardonnay (the legendary birthplace of the Chardonnay grape). Wines from these five areas have the name Mâcon hyphenated to their own; once again, vineyard names are anything but superfluous.

A *Mâcon-Villages* comes from a larger area yet, and can be good; like-wise, "overflow" wine, simply called Pinot Chardonnay.

In recent years, there has been a rash of white wine from just "south of the border" (the neighboring Beaujolais) labeled Beaujolais Blanc. Also made from the Chardonnay, it is indistinguishable in character from a Mâconnais and a wine to be highly recommended if from a good year and an honest producer.

The reds of Mâcon are usually made from a blend of the Gamay and the Pinot noir; and may be considered in the same qualitative class as a good Beaujolais. *Mâcon Supérieur*, like *Bordeaux Supérieur*, is required by law to contain a small additional amount of alcohol.

Most purists rebel at calling the joyous, thirst-quenching red Beau-jolais—the "toast" of Lyon and the avowed favorite of all France—a Burgundy, and not without good reason. Both grape and soil are totally foreign to the Côte d'Or. About five miles south of the city of Mâcon, bordering the vineyards of Pouilly-Fuissé, the soil changes abruptly to a granite base, and the fermented juice of the otherwise frowned-upon Gamay loses the metallic harshness that it manifests on the Côte d'Or and becomes something entirely delicious and satisfying. A few *rosé* wines of no particular merit are made in the Beaujolais region, for this is predominantly a red-wine region. These reds are probably the fruit-iest and most refreshing in the world—and to be numbered among the few reds which actually taste better at a cool cellar temperature. Most of them are better when young than when aged, and they are not con-sumed in sips—but in gulps. Enormous quantities are imbibed every year in the nearby city of Lyon, most of it at an age so tender that it has never merited the honor of a bottle. Today's fad is to rush the new-est Beaujolais—*Beaujolais Nouveau* or *Beaujolais Primeur*—to Paris, London and New York, hardly before it is out of the cradle. The results are usually disappointing to veteran wine lovers. All red wines need a little age in cask or bottle, even Beaujolais.

Given the amount of Beaujolais that is patently consumed through-out France itself, as well as its omnipresence on the shelves of nearly every wineshop in the world, it goes without saying that there are many more bottles labeled *Beaujolais* than can possibly be produced in a restricted area of central France, even though annual production is estimated at 135,000,000 bottles. Thus it is advisable to heed the nine official geographical superior *Appellations Contrôlées* of the region (see Table E), bearing in mind that an authorized vineyard name on a

TABLE E
Principal Wines of Southern Burgundy

Côte Chalonnaise-Red Wines

Commune (or Appellation Contrôlée)	Recommended Vineyards
Rully	La Fosse
	Marisou
Mercurey	Clos du Roi
	Clos des Fourneaux
	Clos Marcilly
Givry	Clos St.-Pierre
	Clos St.-Paul
	Cellier aux Moines

Beaujolais-Red Wines

Crus de Beaujolais	Vineyard
St.-Amour	Champ Grillé
	Château de St.-Amour
Juliénas	Château des Capitans (Les Capitans)
	Les Mouilles
Fleurie	Clos de la Roilette
	La Madonne
	Le Vivier
Moulin-à-Vent	Les Carquelins
	Le Moulin-à-Vent
	Les Burdelines
Chénas	La Rochelle
	Les Caves
	Les Vérillats
Chiroubles	Le Moulin
	Bel Air
Morgon	Château de Bellevue
Brouilly	Les Bussières
Côte de Brouilly	Le Pavé

Côte Chalonnaise-White Wines

Commune	Vineyard
Rully	Raclos des Jacques
Mercurey	Clos de Petit Clou
Givry	Champs Pourot
Montagny	Vieux Château

TABLE E. Continued
Principal Wines of Southern Burgundy

Mâconnais-White Wines

Commune	Vineyard
Pouilly-Fuissé	Les Chailloux
	Les Bouthières
	Les Prâs
	La Frérie (Frairie)
	Château Fuisŝe
	Château Pouilly
	Les Champs
	Les Perrières
	Les Brûlets
	Les Crays
	Les Chanrue
	Les Chevrières
	Les Vignes-Blanches

[Other *Appellations Contrôlées* for white wines of the Mâconnais include Pouilly-Loché and Pouilly-Vinzelles; Chardonnay, Viré, Lugny, Clessé and St.-Véran.]

Note: Other wines are simply *Mâcon* and *Mâcon Supérieur*. *Grand* or *Premier Cru* or *Tête de Cuvée* on labels of any wines from Pouilly-Fuissé or other parts of the Mâconnais or the Beaujolais are entirely meaningless, and should be viewed with suspicion. *Premier Cru* vineyards are, however, authorized for the Côte Chalonnaise and are indicative of officially recognized quality. The term *Cru de Beaujolais* in Beaujolais refers to one of the nine superior subdivisions. It, alone, is valid.

label—emphatically not meaning a trade name—will almost always mean a better bottle. Of these nine *Appellations*, called *Crus de Beaujolais*, perhaps Moulin-à-Vent, Fleurie and St.-Amour have the highest reputations. Their wines are noted for bouquet and comparative softness, and the better Moulin-à-Vents will actually improve with a few years in the bottle—although most Frenchmen will tell you this is an insane waste of time and storage space. Two other popular *Crus*—more favorites of the French than of foreigners—have the subregional *Appellations Contrôlées* of Brouilly and Côte de Brouilly, wines which are stronger in taste and less delicate than their neighbors. A *Beaujolais Supérieur* is slightly more alcoholic than one simply labeled *Beaujolais*, though not necessarily any better; wines with the appellation of *Beau-jolais-Villages* are communal wines, coming from any one of the thirty-five respected villages of the region. The *ordinaires* of the lot are simply labeled *Beaujolais*.

Vintage years in Beaujolais are often of relatively little significance, although 1971 and 1976 produced wines better than average; those for the balance of the vineyards of Southern Burgundy may, in general, be considered the same as for the Côte d'Or.

Summary

Because of a demand far exceeding the supply, few wines are of poorer quality or more overpriced than the common white Chablis. The two top classifications, *Grand Cru* and *Premier Cru*, are always expensive, but reliable, and often considered the greatest white wines of France. Other wines labeled *Chablis* or *Petit Chablis* should be approached with suspicion. They will nearly always be overpriced for what they are. Any non-French "Chablis" is not even a good imitation. It would do better on the markets of the world with another name.

The Côte d'Or (traditional Burgundy) produces fragrant reds and medium-dry whites that are the qualitative equals of Bordeaux wines. Reds from the northernmost sections (Gevrey-Chambertin, Chambolle-Musigny, etc.) are the finest and require more years (eight to ten) to mature; most of the best whites stem from the southernmost communes of Meursault, Puligny-Montrachet and Chassagne-Montrachet, and may be consumed when three years old or less.

Since most Côte d'Or vineyards are divided among many owners, each making his own wine, the name of a reliable producer on a bottle is of paramount importance (see Table F). And because many communes have hyphenated their names with that of their best vineyard, many a wine drinker is led to mistake an ordinary communal wine or blend for a wine from one of the great vineyards. Example: Gevrey-Chambertin, though it may be of good value, is not from the great Chambertin vineyard, but usually a blend from one or more vineyards of the commune of Gevrey-Chambertin.

The best-known wines of Southern Burgundy are medium-dry white Pouilly-Fuissé and lusty red Beaujolais. Terms on labels of these latter wines, such as *Grand Cru* or *Premier Cru*, have no meaning— but a vineyard name (as well as, in the case of Beaujolais wines, the

TABLE F
Some Recommended Growers and Shippers (*Négociants*) of Burgundy

d'Angerville, J., Marquis
Bavard, Joseph
Belin, J.
Bouchard, Ainé
Bouchard, Père et Fils
Camus, Léon
Cavin, Roger
Clair-Däu
Damoy, Pierre
Domaine Leflaive
Domaine de la Romanée-Conti
Domaine Dujac
Drouhin, Joseph
Engel, René
Faiveley, J.
Fleurot-Larose
Gelin, Pierre
Gouges, Henri
Grivot, J.
Gros, Louis
Jaboulet Ainé
Jaboulet-Vercherre
Jadot, Louis
de Laguiche, Marquis
LaChaize, Domaine de
Lamarche, Henri
Latour, Louis
Lequin-Roussot
L'Héritiers-Guyot
Lupé-Cholet

Maire et Fils
Matrot, Joseph
Maufoux, Prosper
de Mérode, Prince
Moillard, J.
Moillard-Grivot
Mommessin, J.
Monnot, Julien
Moreau, J.
de Moucheron, Comte
Mugneret, R.
Mugnier, F.
Noëllat, Vve.
Pic, Albert
Poirier, Louis
Ponsot, H.
Poupon, P.
Prieur, Jacques
Ramonet, Claude
Ramonet, Pru'hon
Rémy, J. H.
Ropiteau Frères
Ropiteau, Maurice
Ropiteau-Mignon
Rousseau, Armand
Thénard, Baron
Thévenin, Roland
Viénot, Charles
de Vogüé, Comte Georges

appellation of one of the nine superior geographical *Crus de Beaujolais*) should be indicative of the best.

Red Mercurey and white Givry and Montagny are all wines from this region which embody both good quality and good value.

Burgundian varietal wines—named after grapes, such as Pinot Chardonnay—are exported to rival varietal wines of other lands, most specifically California premium wines. If these varietal wines merited a higher classification, few French producers would market them as such.

The Rhône Valley and Provence: The "Classic Growths"

From its headwaters high in the glaciers of the Swiss Alps, beside the perilous Simplon Pass forged by Napoleon as a military and trade route to Italy, the Rhône drops swiftly into the crescent-shaped Lake of Geneva, thence battles with long fingers of the Jura and the Alps before it meanders, in undulating curves, across France. Just above the city of Lyon, it turns abruptly and flows hurriedly toward the Mediterranean. Many of Switzerland's better vineyards border the upper reaches of the Rhône and the shores of the Lake of Geneva—but we are concerned here with those wines which are produced along the Rhône's one-hundred-and-fifty-mile stretch as it rushes from Lyon to the river's delta near Marseille, the Bouches-du-Rhône.

The southernmost stretch of the Rhône Valley is a source of great quantities of wines—a vast majority of them coarse and unappealing, wines that usually shed their individual identities in the carafes of the small bars and *bistros* of France, having been blended with something even less distinguished from Corsica or Tunisia. But upstream, above this vinicultural sea, one comes across four or five isolated atolls of vineyards that have produced superior wines since Roman times, and in some instances probably before. These are known as the "classic growths" of the Rhône. The first of them is to be found about fifteen miles below Lyon, across from the town of Vienne. Here, nestled along the steep slopes of a sheltered, sun-baked arena—a natural hothouse—is a handful of appallingly steep, terraced vineyards called the Côte Rôtie (the Roasted Slope). The Côte Rôtie has two integral parts, known respectively as the Côte Blonde and the Côte Brune, a nomenclature literally based on the differences in color of their respective soils—yet, as one might imagine, the source of inevitable barroom jokes concerning the relative merits of blondes and brunettes. As opposed to that from the Côte Blonde, wine from the Côte Brune is reputed to have superior lasting qualities. Be that as it may, most bottles of Côte Rôtie will be a blend from both. Vineyard names, though authorized, are rare.

The wines of the Côte Rôtie, of a deep red color, are made predominantly from the Syrah grape—a plant traditionally said to be of Persian origin. In France, it is unique to this section of the Rhône Valley. Offensively harsh when young, with sufficient age it develops a rich, velvet, highly perfumed and distinguished wine; but it is so strong in character that modern growers blend it with a small amount of white. Côtes Rôties also have the reputation of living in the bottle for an unusually long time.

Vienne was once a Roman town, but the vineyards are probably older yet, planted by the Greeks after the original plantings near Marseille. Pliny the Younger, seemingly praising the wines of Vienne in the first century A.D., described them as "pitchy"—even now a fair description for improperly aged wines made from the Syrah. Nearly seventeen hundred years later another avid vinophile, Thomas Jefferson, touring the vineyards of France on donkeyback, also admired these wines, and noted in his diary that they possessed "a quality which keeps well, bears transportation and cannot be drunk under four years." The last is an understatement: well-made Côte Rôtie commences to be itself only after eight years.

Just south of the Côte Rôtie are grown the white wines bearing the two *Appellations Contrôlées* of Condrieu and Château Grillet. Here again the vineyards are on abrupt, terraced slopes, and the finely fragrant wines are produced at great expense. The wine of Château Grillet, a minuscule four-acre vineyard with its own *Appellation Contrôlée* (giving it, in effect, a *Grand Cru* status), is nearly impossible to come by except in the best restaurant of Vienne itself, and is considered by many experts to be one of the greatest and most individualistic dry white wines of France, ranking with the Côte d'Or's Montrachets and Corton-Charlemagne and Musigny Blanc. The grape used exclusively for both the wines of Condrieu and Château Grillet is the Viognier, a vine strictly indigenous to this particular little pocket of the Rhône, used nowhere else in France. The wine is unusually delicate, by no means typical of most Rhône whites. Like some of the finer, light Moselles of Germany, its charms are hardly recognizable when con-

sumed away from its home ground. Château Grillet, incidentally, is one
of several French white wines that have a way of becoming seasonally
pétillant—that is, inexplicably undergoing a secondary fermentation in
the bottle which makes them slightly prickly on the tongue, though
only at one season of the year, the spring. We shall have more to say
about this rather spooky, albeit attractive, phenomenon—a subject
which is anathema to the scientific logic of wine chemists, who think
of it only as a result of faulty vinification—when we come to
Champagne.

The next cluster of classic growths is to be found, once again down-
stream, near the busy town of Valence. These are the red and white
wines bearing the *Appellation Contrôlée* of either Hermitage or Croze-
Hermitage, the former being the unmistakable nobility of the two. The
vineyards of Hermitage (sometimes seen on old labels as L'Hermitage,
and not to be confused with a Swiss wine called Ermitage) are spread
over the top of a loaf-shaped hill known locally as the Hill of the Hermit. It owes its name—so the story goes—to a thirteenth-century Cru-
sader who, returning one day from the wars, knelt in exhaustion at a
shrine near the top of the hill, where he received a vision instructing
him to stay and tend the vines, and live in the service of his lord. It is
he, also, who, according to legend, brought the Syrah from Persia, but
the two legends don't exactly jibe.

A well-aged Hermitage, especially a red, is unquestionably the finest
red wine of the Rhône. The area is small, only a few hundred acres of
flinty, stony and shallow soil lying on top of bedrock—manifestly use-
less for growing anything but the wine grape. The roots of the vines
penetrate the cracks and fissures of the rock for their moisture. As in
the Côte Rôtie to the north, the Syrah grape is used for the red wines.
These are usually blends from several vineyards (locally called *mas*)
found in different sections of the hill. Strong wines, dark and with a
deep purple hue, they accumulate an appreciable sediment and improve
in the bottle for several decades. Many decades ago Hermitages were
often used to lend color to and otherwise strengthen lighter wines,
notably those of Burgundy. White Hermitage is dry and unfragrant,
but exceptionally mellow, charmingly honey-colored and possessing
even more prodigious lasting qualities than its red counterpart. Some of
them will live for fifty years.

Surrounding the Hill of the Hermit is the *Appellation Contrôlée* area
of Croze-Hermitage, the source of wines of lesser quality. Also near

Valence and across the river are the communes of St.-Joseph and Cornas, both founts of good red wines, the best made from the Syrah. St.-Péray, another neighboring commune, is noted for its sparkling whites, manufactured by a process which resembles that used for Champagne, which local vintners claim antedates the sparkling-wine industry in Champagne itself. As mentioned elsewhere, by law only sparkling wine from the Cahmpagne area is entitled to the name.

In English-speaking countries undoubtedly the most popular and well-known Rhône red is Châteauneuf-du-Pape, another of the "classic growths." When, in the fourteenth century, the papacy was moved from Rome to the fortress city of Avignon on the Rhône, the first pope to preside in the Church's rebel headquarters was a Frenchman, Clement V, a native of Bordeaux, where a vineyard in Graves bears his name. Although this dissident papal court is known to have been partial to the good wines of Beaune—in fact, the proximity of the Côte d'Or to Avignon is said to have been responsible for the court's tardiness in moving back to Rome—under its fond eye the local wines of Avignon were brought to a degree of perfection they have held ever since. Red Châteauneuf-du-Pape is a wine of great warmth, with much the same richness of flavor and deep purple hue as Hermitage. One of the strongest red wines in France, with a minimum alcoholic content of 12½ per cent (which it often exceeds), it is traditionally made from as many as thirteen varieties of grapes, both red and white. Unfortunately the tendency of many of the growers today is to restrict it to two or three, and predominantly just one, the easy-to-grow Grenache[22]—a part of the lamentable contemporary trend to market wines as soon as possible.

Châteauneuf-du-Pape appears to have been almost entirely unknown throughout France until Napoleonic days, when it was arrestingly brought to the attention of Paris by the antics of one of its growers. This was a venerable noble, the Marquis de la Nerthe, whose vineyard still bears his name and continues to be one of the finest of the region. Famed at the French court as a ladies' man, *bon viveur* and wit, the marquis was once asked how, in his so advanced years, he managed to maintain such astounding health and vigor amid a life of such frivolity, not to say debauchery. Nearly every Frenchman is a born promoter: the Marquis replied, naturally, that his elixir was the wine of his own

[22]Other traditional grapes include the Syrah, the Clairette, the Mourvèdre, the Picpoul and the Terret noir.

vineyard on the Rhône. Châteauneuf-du-Pape was not long in becoming the most popular wine at court, and to this day it is not unusual to hear the old wives' tale that it contains effective aphrodisiacal and medicinal elements.

White Châteauneuf-du-Pape is a pleasantly dry, unfragrant wine—and no serious rival to the honey-colored virile whites of Hermitage, or to the delicate ones of Château Grillet and Condrieu. A far better local white, when one can find it, comes from the nearby commune of Gigondas, which also produces a fair red.

Vineyard names on labels of Châteauneuf-du-Pape are as significant as those of Pouilly-Fuissé, especially in the case of the reds: wines from recognized vineyards are well worth the extra dollars and cents one has to pay. To be at their best, they should be *at least* four or five years old. The vineyards of Châteauneuf-du-Pape were the first of modern-day France to have their own quasi-*Appellation Contrôlée*, a self-imposed regimentation under the influence of the late Baron Le Roy, owner of Châteauneuf's vineyard *par excellence*, Château Fortia. A current by-product of this fifty-year-old movement for excellence and purity is an often seen symbol of the commune's coat of arms, a pope's mitre above two crossed keys, blown into the neck of the bottle. It will at least indicate that the wine is bottled in Châteauneuf-du-Pape itself; and at best it will mean that the grower has conformed to the stringent rules of the town's inner sanctum of growers. The Rhône, unfortunately, has its fair share of growers and bottlers who seek to evade both the laws of the land and the laws of good wine making. The reader must be reminded of that convenient loophole in French law which allows a vintner of one district to appropriate the qualitative terminology of another. Many a Rhône wine can be a "great" or "grand" wine—yet no vineyard along the entire valley is officially authorized to place *Grand Cru, Premier Cru* or *Grand Vin* on its labels. Such is, regrettably, a fairly common practice, and the words *Premier Cru* on a Rhône label (which do have official significance for a wine from the Côte d'Or or Chablis) should constitute grounds for suspicion of the integrity of the bottler and the intrinsic value of the wine.

The non-gentry wines of the Rhône, often highly drinkable, are simply classified as *Côtes-du-Rhône;* other wines, a theoretical notch above the latter in quality, are called *Côtes-du-Rhône-Villages*, an appellation allowed to about fifteen communes in the southern part of the valley.

Two other good regions are the Côtes du Ventoux and the Côtes du Vivarais.

Rosés and the Wines of Provence

Although classified as Rhône wines, the finest *rosé* (pink) wines of France are traditionally associated with Provence, the ancient province which borders the shores of the Mediterranean from the Rhône delta to Italy. The best of them come from the twin communes of Tavel and Lirac, lying in the hills a few miles west of Avignon. Here, away from the river, one finds a bleak and somewhat sinister countryside. The vineyards look baked and parched, and gazing over the landscape one thinks of Keats: "The sedge is withered from the lake, and no birds sing." In winter the two winds that alternately plague this whole Mediterranean area, the nerve-wracking mistral from the north and the stifling desert-born sirocco from the south, course by, unheedful of all in their path. But the wine grape thrives.

Rosé wines are produced by several methods. The first is the obvious simple mixture of red and white wines. In some parts of France this mediocrity is called *vin gris* (gray wine). It rarely results in a more potable drink than a straight white wine tinted with a bit of red cochineal coloring—another method sometimes used to make *rosés*, and inexpensive "pink" Champagnes and sparkling wines. Yet another procedure is the use of red-skinned grapes with white juice, withdrawing the skins from the juice as soon as the desired degree of color is attained. In Tavel and Lirac both red- and white-wine grapes are utilized in the "crush," and all the grapes are withdrawn when the *mélange* has reached the wished-for pinkish tint. The subsequent fermentation is then the same as for white wines, without benefit of skins and stalks.

In this part of the Rhône, the predominant grape for *rosés* is the Grenache, a prolific red grape also used for *rosés* in California and elsewhere, for red wines in Portugal and Spain, and as part of the traditional combination for Châteauneuf-du-Pape. The *rosés* of Tavel and Lirac, considered by most authorities to be the best of their kind in France, are sharp and (for a *rosé*) unusually "winy" in character, with a higher alcoholic content than the average French white wine. The usual color is an orange-pink. They are noted for keeping well in the bottle—though they do not necessarily improve there over the years.

Although it should be pointed out that there is no such thing as a "great" *rosé*, they have their many uses. On hot summer days they can be refreshing, and they hold a distinct overall advantage in that they combine with almost any food. Furthermore, they are usually preferred by novice wine drinkers.

Although Tavel has been for many generations the most widely known *rosé* wine of France, in our opinoin some wines of Lirac—even alcoholically stronger yet—are softer and more delicate tasting. Here are wines made with infinite care, and the vintners of Lirac have an additional, self-imposed standard by which every wine must run the gauntlet of a local tasting committee before it is entitled to the *Appellation Contrôlée*.

Farther south, along the shores of the Mediterranean and in the lovely foothills of the Alpes-Maritimes behind, are the sources of many other good *rosés*, along with scatterings of reds and whites. At Cassis, a quaint fishing village just east of Marseille (the name should not be confused with the black-currant liqueur made in Dijon), dry and refreshing whites and *rosés* are made—wines which, although they do not always travel too successfully, are famous far from the shores of France. The nearby village of Bandol produces an excellent red, as well as a passable *rosé;* a very excellent white and passable *rosés* are made in very small quantity at Bellet on the hillsides above Nice, and in the area of La Palette near the breathtakingly beautiful ancient city of Aix-en-Provence.

The wines of Cassis, Bandol, Bellet and La Palette, and others known as Côtes de Provence, are entitled to their own *Appellations Contrôlées*—but many of the other wines of Provence and the Mediterranean will bear another appellation: *V.D.Q.S.*, standing for *Vins Délimités de Qualité Supérieure. V.D.Q.S.* wines do not have the ranking of the *Appellations Contrôlées* wines, and their vineyards are not always subject to the same strict regulations, the designation having been invented to promote relatively unknown local wines of France. Many of these Mediterranean wines—some good, some not so good—are now appearing on foreign markets, and will be dealt with further in the section entitled "Country Wines."

Certain of the traditional vineyards of Provence have been granted the right to the words *Cru Classé*. The best are listed in Table G.

As in the Beaujolais, vintage years in the Rhône and Provence are actually of minor significance, although it should be mentioned—for the Rhône itself—that the outstanding years of the past twenty years or so have been 1961, 1966, 1969, 1970, 1971, 1976 and 1977.

Summary

The "classic growths" of the Rhône Valley are predominantly red, the principal ones being Côte Rôtie, Hermitage and Châteauneuf-du-Pape. Sturdy and usually dark in color, they require at least four to five years in the bottle, preferably more, before approaching mellowness. White Hermitage, Château Grillet and Condrieu are the outstanding whites.

Vineyard names on labels of all Rhône wines are to be preferred, but not always easy to find. The terms *Grand Cru, Premier Cru,* etc., are not prescribed by law, and wines so labeled can only reflect on the integrity of the vintner, who is probably banking on the ignorance of the public.

The traditionally best *rosé* (pink) wines of France are from the two communes of Tavel and Lirac, near Avignon on the lower Rhône. But many a pleasant, less "winy" *rosé*, along with good whites and reds, are made in Provence, to the south. Many of these do not have *Appellations Contrôlées,* but bear instead the initials *V.D.Q.S.* Some traditional vineyards of Provence are entitled to the term *Cru Classé,* an added guarantee of quality (see Table G).

TABLE G
Principal Wines of the Rhône and Provence

Reds

Appellation Contrôlée	Vineyard
*Côte Rôtie	La Brocarde
	Les Chaveroches
	Grande Plantée
	Tharamount-de-Gron
*Hermitage	L'Ermite
	La Sizeranne

*Côte Rôtie, Hermitage and Condrieu wines are usually blends from different vineyards, and are infrequently labeled with an individual vineyard name. Those so labeled, however, are the unquestionable best.

TABLE G Continued
Principal Wines of the Rhône and Provence

Appellation Contrôlée	*Vineyard*
	La Chapelle
	Burge
	Columbiers
	Le Méal
Cornas	Chambon
	Le Moulin
	Pied la Vigne
Châteauneuf-du-Pape	Château Fortia
	Château de la Nerthe
	Château des Fines-Roches
	Domaine de Mont-Redon
	Château de la Gardine
	Domaine de Nalis (Nalys)
	Domaine de la Solitude
	Clos l'Oratoire des Papes
	Domaine de Beaurenard

Whites

Appellation Contrôlée	*Vineyard*
Château Grillet	Château Grillet
*Condrieu	Chéry
	Basamon
	Côte Chatillon
*Hermitage	Mûrets
	La Chapelle
	Beaumes
St.-Péray	Coteau Gaillard
Châteauneuf-du-Pape	Château Rayas
	Domaine de Mont-Redon
	Domaine de Nalis (Nalys)

LOWER RHÔNE AND PROVENCE

Appellation Contrôlée	*Vineyard*
Tavel	Château d'Aquéria (*rosé*)
	Clos de Vaucroze (*rosé*)
Lirac	Château de Segriès (*rosé*)
Cassis	Marseille
	La Treille

TABLE G Continued
Principal Wines of the Rhône and Provence

Appellation Contrôlée	*Vineyard*
La Palette	Château Simone
Bandol	Domaine A. Tempier
Bellet	Château de Crémant

(Commune)	*Vineyard*
Taradeau	†Château de St.-Martin
	†Château de Selle
Croix Valmer	†Domaine de la Croix
Les Arcs	†Château de Ste.-Roseline
Bormes	†Domaine du Noyer
Cogolin	†Domaine de St.-Maur
Gassin	†Domaine de Minuty
La Garde	†Clos de la Domaine Bastide
La Londe	†Clos Mireille
	†Domaine du Galoupet
Lorgues	†Domaine de Castel Roubine
La Motte	†Domaine de Jos d'Esclans
Pignans	†Domaine de Rimauresq
La Palette	†Domaine de Moulières

†*Crus Classés* of Côtes de Provence.

Wines of the Loire: White Wines

Rising in what is picturesquely called the Massif Central—the great, wild mountains of central France—the Loire flows through a placid countryside in a sweeping six-hundred-mile curve to the Atlantic, its watershed draining some five hundred thousand acres of vines. Even this is probably a low estimate—since in addition to all the regulated vineyards, nearly every peasant has a patch of vines in his own backyard to make wine for his own use. The Loire excels in its white wines, the driest of which are among the driest of all France, the sweetest being as sweet and "luscious" as any of Sauternes or Germany. In between the two extremes there are literally dozens of others, each with its own indisputable special individuality, derived largely from its own particular piece of soil.

Not too far from the headwaters, in the vicinity of the little market town of Pouilly-sur-Loire, are grown two white wines which, in the last few decades, have undergone a spectacular rise in popularity among the wine drinkers of the world. The first of these is Pouilly-Fumé (not to be confused with the white Pouilly-Fuissé of Southern Burgundy), a dry, lightly perfumed white wine possessing what many connoisseurs describe as a "gunflint" flavor. Blanc-Fumé, an alternate name on labels for Pouilly-Fumé, means "white smoke," and the term derives from the particular way a blue, misty dust drifts across the vineyards at harvest time. The grape used here is the Petit Sauvignon, a cousin of one of the three principal white-wine grapes of Bordeaux.[23]

The second white wine from the upper Loire which has gained much favor in past years is that of Sancerre, a commune slightly below and across the river from Pouilly. Like those of the neighboring (but by no means as famous) *Appellations Contrôlées* of Reuilly and Quincy, most Sancerres are bone dry—some of them almost to the point of outright acidity. The French themselves are unusually fond of these ultradry wines, drinking them with shellfish and oysters. In view of the always short supply (and rising cost) of good Chablis, many wine drinkers are turning to these dry whites of the upper Loire.

Yet another popular wine from the vicinity is St.-Porçain, predominantly made as white, though it may also be found as a *rosé*. St.-Porçain is the local wine, or *vin du pays*, of that famous French spa, Vichy, visited periodically by many a French gourmand in order to put his liver right. Years before the magic powers of Vichy water were discovered, however, St.-Porçain was a well-known wine in France. It was a St.-Porçain *oeil-de-perdrix* (the ancient name for a *rosé:* literally, the color of a partridge's eye) which Louis IX served to his guests to celebrate the coming of age of his son. St.-Porçain is dry and refreshing—some people describe it as smelling like freshly peeled apples. One might only add that after a liberal dose of Vichy water, almost any wine would taste like nectar and smell like ambrosia. Two other rare and distinguished *rosés* from this area are Corent and Château Gay, both made near the industrial city of Clermont-Ferrand.

Just below the point where the ambling Loire straightens out and at

[23]It is important to distinguish between two local appellations, the *Appellation Contrôlée* of *Blanc-Fumê-de-Pouilly* or *Pouilly-Fumé*, and that of *Pouilly-sur-Loire*. Wines of the latter are not made from the Sauvignon exclusively, but instead from the Chasselas, a grape also used in Alsace and elsewhere for generally inferior products. Only in Switzerland does the Chasselas make interesting wine.

long last plots its course for the ocean, it passes through what every tourist knows as the Château Country—the playground of the French kings and their courts during the fifteenth and sixteenth centuries. Here, amid the elaborate country seats where the courtiers and their ladies danced away their boredom, sported their falcons and hunted the boar and the stag, one comes upon extensive white-wine vineyards, the wines of which are only just commencing to find their way in any abundance to the outside world. A short distance from the city of Tours, the geographical center of the Château Country, are the vineyards of Vouvray and Montlouis. Wines of the two areas, facing each other across the river, are all but indistinguishable, though the former has the better-known name. A third area, Rochecorbon, is hardly known at all. Neither sweet nor dry, but instead a rather happy combination of the two, made principally from the local white Chenin blanc grape (also the source of one of the better California white varietals bearing that name), these wines differ from most other French whites in that they tolerate considerable aging. They are often stored for several years in deep caves thought to date from prehistoric days, carved into the steep chalk cliffs overhanging the Loire. The rarest (and best) Vouvrays are *pétillant*—slightly fizzy. A Vouvray *pétillant* hardly tastes like wine at all: perhaps the best way to describe one is to liken it to an excellent, gently sparkling cider.

Unfortunately Vouvray *pétillants* do not always travel well, and since they require a higher sugar content in order to pass through the second fermentation in the bottle, they are usually made only in the best years. In other years the wines are either produced as still wines or else turned into sparkling Vouvray (*mousseux*). In France, the best Vouvray *mousseux* is traditionally considered the finest sparkling white wine of the country, next to Champagne, but this is subject to argument. According to the year, Vouvrays may be dry, sometimes almost unpleasantly acid; or semisweet (*moelleux*); or even sweeter yet. Our own ideal is a *moelleux pétillant*, a little sweet and slightly sparkling. A still Vouvray or Montlouis always leaves us a little cold: they seem to require just that added touch imparted by a fizzle or a sparkle. A *pétillant* may sometimes be called a *crémant*.

The most famous as well as the most versatile vinicultural section of the Loire is Anjou—that part lying closest to the mouth of the river. Anjou embraces a myriad of varied wines and *Appellations Contrôlées*, the best known being Saumur, Coteaux de la Loire, Coteaux du Layon, Coteaux de l'Aubance, Savennières, Bonnézeaux, Quarts-de-Chaume, Rosé d'Anjou and Anjou-Rosé-de-Cabernet. Fifty years ago the traditional white vintages of Anjou were sweet—made, like Sauternes, with the aid of the *pourriture noble.* But nowadays wine drinkers rarely ask for sweet wines, and most of the growers have changed to drier versions. The results are not as attractive in a white wine made from the Chenin blanc, and Anjou is fast turning into a land of nondescript *rosés.*

From Saumur, the easternmost section of Anjou, comes a sparkling white wine (Saumur *mousseux*) which is often sweeter than sparkling Vouvray, and by no means of the same quality. The best dry wines, without exception, are from the area of the commune of Savennières, near Anjou's traditional capital of Angers. Its two greatest vineyards, La Coulée de Serrant and La Roche aux Moines, approach such high quality that they are allowed to hyphenate their names to the *Appellation Contrôlée* of Savennières, giving them what would be a *Grand Cru* status (provided such were authorized for the Loire). Coulée de Serrant still graces the tables of the president of France; but it is rarely seen in Chicago. Other superior dry wines of Anjou come from the Château de la Fresnaye (Coteaux du Layon) and the Château de Parnay (Saumur).

For those who continue to like dessert wines in their proper place at the end of a meal—and we are among them—the traditional Anjous *liquoreux* will be found to possess perhaps even more character than Sauternes and Barsacs. Amber in color, with a gentle perfume and a faint flavor of some exotic wild honey, they are among the finest white wines of France. Rabelais, a great connoisseur of wines of the Loire, once said that their aroma spreads itself "like a peacock's tail." Today they are rare; one of the few vineyards still producing them is known as the Quarts-de-Chaume, which, as will be observed in Table H, is also entitled to an *Appellation Contrôlée* of its own. Now divided into four sections, this celebrated vineyard was once owned by an eminent physician so unusually bountiful and democratic that he kept only the wine of one-fourth the vineyard for himself and allowed his laborers to reap the profit of the rest. The doctor's own quarter is now known as the Ancien Domaine du Dr. Bernard, but the wines from it are not as good as those from yet another, the Château de Bellerive. Farther up the little river Layon, a tributary entering from the south, is the commune of Bonnézeaux, again a source of sweet wines of a type which once made Anjou so famous.

Finally, near the mouth of the Loire, are the scattered white-wine vineyards of Muscadet.[24] Much like Pouilly-Fumé and Sancerre, the Muscadets are light-textured and dry, with a unique lemony tang, and are most suitable with seafoods. Made predominantly from the Muscadet grape, which, under the name of Melon, was brought from Burgundy many years ago, the Muscadets have recently undergone a considerable rise in popularity. Originally this transplanted Burgundian grape was tried out in Brittany, one of the few parts of France in which the *Vitis vinifera* has never seemed to flourish (as one writer succinctly put it, "the wines of Brittany are so bad that even the fishermen won't drink them"). People in the wine trade can be as sharp-tongued as any, and the unfortunate vintners of Muscadets are locally subjected to cruel ribbing for their "Breton wines"—even though their vineyards lie predominantly in Anjou. The largest growing area, Sèvre-et-Maine, lies south of the Loire, but the generally better one is in the Coteaux de la Loire, centered on the town of Ancenis, also the source of some good red wine. A lesser white wine made in the Muscadet region comes from a grape known as the Gros Plant—a name frequently seen on labels abroad. Just remember, it is not a Muscadet.

Wines of the Loire: Reds and Rosés

Although the red wines of the Loire live more in the past than in the present, there remains a handful of excellent ones that deserve brief mention, especially as some of them are beginning to reach foreign markets. At Orléans, in the central Loire (the site of Joan of Arc's victory over the British), there is made a pale red wine called Beaugency, as well as another comparable red known as St.-Jean-de-Braye. Centuries ago the red wines of Orléans had the reputation of being the strongest of France, and were great favorites with French connoisseurs, as well as with many traveling Englishmen. It was apparently the wine of Beaugency of which an English courtier noted in his journal during the visit of Charles I: "The wine of this place is so strong that the

[24]Not to be confused with dessert wines from one of the many muscat grapes, variously called Muscat in southern France, Muscatel in California, Moscatel in Portugal, etc.

king's cupbearers are sworn never to give him any of it." Both Beaugency and St.-Jean-de-Braye require quite some age in the bottle before
becoming really potable.

Rabelais's own vineyard, La Dévinière, was at Chinon—but there is
sparse evidence that this talented stumblebum, whose avowed motto
was the single word "Drink," confined himself to the wines of his own
making. Along with the red wine of Chinon, two of his other favorites
came from the nearby vineyards of St.-Nicolas-de-Bourgueil and Bour-
gueil. Wines with these two *Appellations Contrôlées* are still made
today, and are probably the best red wines of the Loire. Although the
predominating grape is the Breton, merely another name for the Cabernet franc of Bordeaux, these Loire reds are considerably coarser and
harder than clarets, and also require long aging. In fact, the wines of
Chinon and its vicinity need at least seven years in the bottle; some
experts specify twice that. In common with Beaujolais, they are better
when drunk cool.

The lower Loire Valley, especially the region of Anjou, produces
thousands of gallons of *rosé* wines, which for most palates tend to be
a little too sweet and cloying, not wearing as well as the *rosés* of Tavel,
Lirac and even Provence. Nor are they as individualistic and delicate
as many of the increasingly popular *rosés* from our West Coast. The
best are marketed under one of the two special *Appellations Contrôlées*
of Rosé-d'Anjou and Anjou-Rosé-de-Cabernet. Like all *rosés*, they
should be consumed when young, for they improve little in the bottle.

The best recent vintage years for the wines of the Loire are 1969,
1970, 1971, 1973 and 1976. Table H gives the principal communes (or
vineyards) accorded authorized *Appellations Contrôlées*, as well as a list
of the best-known vineyards.

TABLE H
Principal Wines of the Loire

Whites

Appellation Contrôlée	*Vineyard*
*Pouilly-Fumé (or Blanc-Fumé-de-Pouilly)	Château du Nozet
	Château de Tracy
	Coteaux des Loges

TABLE H Continued
Principal Wines of the Loire

Appellation Contrôlée	*Vineyard*
	La Loge aux Moines
	Coteau des Girarmes
	Domaine de Riaux
Sancerre	Château de Sancerre
	Clos de la Poussie
	Les Monts Damnés
	Perrières
	Bué (locality)
	Chavignol (locality)
Quincy	Rimonet
Reuilly	Clos des Messieurs
Montlouis	Hameau de la Milletière
Vouvray	Clos le Mont
	Château Moncontour
	Clos de la Taiserie
Saumur	Château de Parnay (Clos Cristal)
Quarts-de-Chaume	Château de Bellerive
	Château de Surronde
	Château de la Guimonière
Coteaux du Layon	Château de la Fresnaye
Coteaux de l'Aubance	Roche de Mûrs
Savennières	La Coulée de Serrant
	La Roche aux Moines
	Clos du Papillon
	Château de Savennières
	Château d'Épiré
	Château de Fesle
Bonnézeaux	La Chapelle
Muscadet	Châteauguy

Reds

Appellation Contrôlée	*Vineyard*
†Vin de l'Orléanais	Beaugency (locality)
	St.-Jean-de-Braye (locality)
Chinon	Rochette-St.-Jean
	Le Closeaux
Bourgueil	Clos de la Salpêtrerie
	Clos des Perrières

TABLE H Continued
Principal Wines of the Loire

Appellation Contrôlée	*Vineyard*
St.-Nicolas-de-Bourgueil	Clos du Fondis
Saumur (Saumur-Champigny)	Château de Parnay
	Clos des Hospices
	Château de Targé

*Not to be confused with the *Appellation Contrôlée* of Pouilly-sur-Loire, wines which are made from the Chasselas grape and are the *ordinaires* of the region.
†*V.D.Q.S.* appellation.

Summary

Of the dry, "flinty" white wines of the upper Loire, the most popular are Pouilly-Fumé and Sancerre (the former is not to be confused with Pouilly-Fuissé from Southern Burgundy). They are excellent with seafoods, good substitutes for the more expensive classic Chablis or Pouilly-Fuissé.

Vouvray, traditionally France's best sparkling wine (*mousseux*), is sweeter than most Champagne, but may often be used as a substitute. Still Vouvray is variable.

The white wines of Anjou are both dry and sweet. The best dry ones come from the commune of Savennières near Angers, the finest sweet dessert wines from the Quarts-de-Chaume and Bonnézeaux vineyards. Anjou *rosés* are pleasant and satisfying, somewhat sweeter than most other French *rosés*.

Muscadet is a white dry wine with a lemony tang, relatively inexpensive and popular, raised on the lower Loire.

Loire reds (Chinon, St.-Nicolas-de-Bourgueil, Beaugency, etc.) are rare but extremely good when sufficiently aged (seven to ten years).

Other French Wines: Alsace

Alsace, the source of what are certainly the most fragrant and flowery white wines in all France, is a tiny district—a verdant little garden spot—tucked away behind the Vosges Mountains in the northeastern corner of the country. Along with its twin province of Lorraine (as the world so well remembers), it was captive German territory for almost fifty years preceding its liberation in 1918—a period which brought the wine industry of Alsace to the brink of disaster. A century ago Alsatian wines were of high quality. But the way to break a Frenchman's spirit is to ruin his wine, and this is exactly what the Germans attempted. Under the German occupation Alsatian viniculture was harnessed to the production of cheap wines for the German market.

In the years since 1918, the Alsatians—cruelly interrupted by the battles of World War II that raged in their vineyards and leveled many of their picturesque villages—have been valiantly putting the pieces back together. Their first act was once again to plant the traditional wine grapes, known in Alsace as "noble grapes," and in view of the dispersion of the old vineyard holdings which had taken place during the occupation, they wisely discarded the tradition that the name of a wine must be married to a particular piece of soil. Thus most Alsatian wines, comparable to the varietal wines of California, go by the name of the grapes from which they derive. Although the best of these are grapes ordinarily associated with Germany, it should be remembered that on Alsatian soil, they simply do not produce white wines which are really comparable to those of the Rhine or the Moselle—and one should not look for such. Alsatian wines are individualistic; if one allows them to stand on their own feet, many of them are very excellent indeed.

There is only the simplest, basic *Appellation Contrôlée* for the wines of Alsace. Previous to 1962 the words were not even required on a label, and the only control laws were locally imposed ones which, in the course of its growing pains, the Alsatian wine industry had laid down for itself. Commune names are not required on a label, but vineyard names, however unofficial, are nowadays increasingly important. The appellation *Vin d'Alsace* or *Alsace* indicates wine from the best or so-called "noble grapes," produced only in certain authorized areas; the highest qualitative appellation is the term *Grand Cru*, indicating a wine which has been chosen for its quality by a local committee working under the Institut des Appellations d'Origine.

There are no Alsatian reds worth mentioning; nor do the *rosés* (*Rosé d'Alsace*), usually made from the Pinot noir, constitute a very distinguished company. One will not need to experiment too long, either, before discerning that there is a vast difference in quality between the wines of one producer and those of another. Among the best shippers to foreign markets are Hugel, Willm, Dopff and Irion, the Domaines Viticoles Schlumberger, Preiss-Henney, and Trimbach.

The following are the principal Alsatian grape names, in general order of excellence;

Riesling. The Riesling grape is the source of all the great German "Rhine wines." In Alsace it produces a medium-dry white wine with a nice bouquet—thought by many to be the finest product of the district.

Gewürztraminer. Wines made from this grape compete in point of sheer strength of fragrance and perfume with almost any other white wine in the world. They also sometimes possess a barely perceptible effervescence, comparable to the *pétillant* white wines of Vouvray and Château Grillet. The German word *gewürz* means spicy, and the Gewürztraminer is simply a "more-so-yet" variety of the commoner but already spice-like Traminer of Germany. In the best years a few producers sometimes make them with the *pourriture noble.* A more exotic, redolent white wine than one of these rare Gewürztraminer *Auslesen* or *Vendanges Tardives* (from sweet, late-picked grapes) can hardly be found.

Sylvaner. A more ordinary grape than any of the above, the Sylvaner produces many of the lesser German wines, including much of the popular Liebfraumilch. In contrast, an Alsatian Sylvaner may be acid and hard—at best, light and pleasant.

Muscat. In Alsace this grape brings forth a dry white wine with a strong, enticing aroma that is never quite justified by the taste which follows. Nor is any typical "muscat" flavor in evidence.

Pinot gris or *Tokay.* Some will tell you this is the grape of the celebrated Hungarian dessert wine, the "liqueur of wines." Actually, any relationship is impossible and is certainly not corroborated by Alsatian Tokay, which is simply dry, "flinty" and refreshing.

The *ordinaires* or most common wines of Alsace, formerly called Zwickers, were usually made from the Chasselas grape, a grape we have already referred to in connection with the inferior wine from the region of Pouilly-sur-Loire. The Chasselas is in the process of being exterminated from all good Alsatian vineyards. Better than these are wines called Edelzwickers, which, by local law, must be a blend of two or more "noble grapes." Edelzwickers are not frequently seen outside of France, but are to be recommended when found with the label of a good producer.

Even the best and most carefully made Alsatian wines do not improve in the bottle, and the majority of them should be drunk young. Like the wines of Germany, they come in thin, tall bottles, here called *flûtes d'Alsace*. These wines, unusually light in color, are consumed in their native land from prettily decorated goblets, designed to enhance their gaiety. The best recent years in Alsace are 1975, 1976 and 1977.

Table I lists the leading vineyards or "brand names" of the best producers.

Wines of Other Districts and "Country Wines"

Other traditional French wines from far-flung districts sometimes seen on foreign markets are those of the Jura, Monbazillac and Jurançon. The Jura is a small mountainous area northeast of the Côte d'Or. Chiefly noted for its amber-colored white wines, dry and rather heavy, and for its *rosés*, which are quite similar to (and compare favorably with) those of Anjou, the Jura also produces two vinous curiosities. One of these, formerly made in other parts of France (notably in Hermitage on the Rhône and in Alsace), is called *vin de paille* (straw wine). In effect, straw wine is raisin wine. The grapes are put out to dry in the sun on straw mats (hence the name) until they have reached a completely withered condition and have attained an exceptionally high sugar content. The fermentation may require as much as a year; the wine, needless to say, is sweet and thick, and correspondingly strong.

The second curiosity of the Jura is made in the commune of Château-Châlon, and called *vin jaune* (yellow wine). This Sherry-like, dark-colored liquid derives from being allowed to remain, after its initial fermentation, in barrels open to the air for a period of six years or more. Bit by bit a crusty yeast forms on the surface of the wine, producing a progressive oxygenation which results in a yellow color and a somewhat bitter taste—though, to many connoisseurs, not an unpleasant one. *Vin jaune* is in effect a very mild, unfortified Sherry—and in view of the history of the Jura, not illogically so. For a brief period of time, as a result of one of those territorial jugglings that were always taking place through the intermarriages of Europe's nobility—the Jura was under Spanish control. No doubt this is the root of the close relationship between the wine of Château-Châlon and Sherry.

Château-Châlon has its own *Appellation Contrôlée*, and its yellow wines are bottled in individualistic square bottles, *clavelins*. The other two best-known wines from the Jura (white and *rosé*) go by the appellations of Arbois and Étoile. Vintage years for the district are roughly the same as for the Côte d'Or.

Monbazillac, the sweet white wine made in the Dordogne Valley upstream from St.-Émilion and Pomerol, is sometimes disparagingly referred to in France as "poor man's Sauternes." This accusation is not entirely fair. Made with the *pourriture noble*, and with the same grapes as those of Sauternes (though in different proportions), the wines of the *Appellation Contrôlée* of Monbazillac are softer and more mellow than the *liquoreux* of Bordeaux, though they lack the characteristic "rusty" taste of many Sauternes and Barsacs. An appreciation of them need not be so often a matter of an acquired taste. They are endowed with sweetness and sunlight. Children, among others, dote on them. Vintage years for Monbazillac correspond to those of Bordeaux.

The heady, orange-colored wines of Jurançon spring from an isolated district in the foothills of the Pyrénées, near the fashionable, fox-hunting town of Pau. Whether it was actually Jurançon (instead of the strong brandy from nearby Armagnac) which was so hastily brushed across the lips of the minutes-old Prince of Navarre—later to become Henry IV of France—is still a matter of considerable dispute among the respective publicizers of the two. In any event, Jurançon was to become one of the king's favorite wines, and its fame was spread far and wide by this native of the Béarn, himself born at Pau. Jurançon is made predominantly from two native grapes of the Pyrénées, the Marsencs (Gros and Petit). It has much fragrance and a peculiar musky tang, rather similar to what is often referred to as the "foxy" taste of New York State and other eastern United States wines. Persons who are accustomed to these wines will find Jurançon an interesting comparison at least; to others it may almost be unrecognizable as a wine of France.

Jurançon, traditionally a *liquoreux* wine made with the *pourriture noble*, now more often dry, possesses a reputation for an exceptionally long life in the bottle. It, too, may be slightly *pétillant*. Only in good years is the *pourriture noble* encouraged, giving the wine an extra sweetness. Almost all French wines have their folklore, and just as Châteauneuf-du-Pape (thanks to its romping old marquis) is widely thought to be an aphrodisiac, Jurançon is considered a valid treatment for marital discord, an accepted means of bringing estranged lovers together again. This, in itself, bodes well for its continued life on earth.

Vintage years for Jurançon in general correspond with those of Bordeaux.

In latter years, in one part the result of the rising prices of the traditional French wines, in another part the increasing demand for wine of all types (and especially those with foreign appellations), many importers with the aid of the French government have promoted what they call the "Country Wines of France." Certainly the term is a misnomer, since many of these wines—Mâconnais, Muscadets, Alsatians—are not "country wines" at all, but simply good and recognized wines from well-known districts which hadn't yet become known or sold well abroad. Many of them have been covered, in their proper places, in the foregoing pages. Thus we find it difficult to agree absolutely and entirely with the generalization of one critic, who dismisses them all as "sows' ears with silk labels." Yet the reader must be cautioned against the romance of these "country wines." It should be evident that if many of them were as good as advertised, they would long since have become better known in their own land, which has always imported large quantities of wines to quench its thirst.

Among the dry whites (and even reds) appearing on shelves are wines from the general region of Entre-Deux-Mers, the pie wedge of land between the Médoc and St.-Émilion. These bear various appellations such as Premières Côtes de Bordeaux, Loupiac and Cadillac. In general they turn out to be weak and watery-tasting, and cannot even be compared to an ordinary Graves. Far more interesting are the whites from the diagonally opposite corner of France, the ancient province of Savoie, bordering Switzerland. Two of the best, also with *Appellations Contrôlées* of their own, come from Crépy and Syssel. The whites of Crépy—a small region on the south shore of the Lake of Geneva—are crisp and very dry indeed. Those of Syssel, a town on the upper Rhône between the Alps and the Jura, are often of exceptional value. The best known is called Roussette de Syssel, a soft, fragrant white made from a white Rhône grape locally called the Altesse. Certain sparkling wines from this area compare favorably with other French sparklings, even Champagnes.

Next to the sprawling wine country above the Bouches-du-Rhône near Marseille (a source of "blending wines") comes the vast region of Languedoc, which can best be defined as a large triangle extending from the Rhône across to Carcassonne and down to the Spanish border.

Most of the mentionable wines of Languedoc (Coteaux du Languedoc) are classified as *V.D.Q.S.*, though one, Fitou, containing sources of coarse reds, has earned a dubious *Appellation Contrôlée* of its own. Another area, Corbières, has not, but at least the appellation in Corbières is awarded only to a wine that has run the gamut of a local tasting committee. The best red of the region is probably St.-Georges-d'Orques, made near Montpellier—many years ago the salvation of a group of British, exiled in Languedoc by Napoleon. Red wines of the area are made from Rhône grapes; the whites are usually from the Muscat, tend to be very sweet and are usually fortified. Of these, Muscat de Frontignan is perhaps the best known. On the western boundary of Languedoc is a small white-wine district making a fair sparkling, known as Blanquette-de-Limoux.

These days one will also run across three other reds, from the southwest—Gaillac, Cahors and Bergerac. Cahors was once a rival, a hundred years or so ago, of Bordeaux itself, but quality has suffered. Gaillac's traditional best is a sweetish white—not marketable today. It is doubtful if the consumer will find any of these as rewarding as many of the lesser Côtes-du-Rhônes and Côtes-du-Rhône-Villages already mentioned, which are in general softer on the palate and equally easy on the pocketbook.

None of the above—especially the wines of Languedoc—would merit mention in these pages, had it not been for the commercial "country wine" promotion responsible for bringing them to our shores.

Summary

Alsatian wines, nearly all white, are noted for their fragrances, and except for those rare ones made from late-picked grapes, they are all moderately dry. Like California varietals, they are usually named after the grape from which they are made, but vineyard and brand names are becoming increasingly important. Alsace did not have *Appellations Contrôlées* regulations until 1962; previous to that year the term did not appear on labels. Often of excellent quality, they do not rank with the best German wines, even though most are made with the same grapes. Alsatian wines should be drunk young.

The vineyards of the Jura Mountains produce good whites and even better *rosés*, the principal appellations being Arbois and Étoile. Jurançon, made near the Pyrénées, is orange-colored and heady; white Monbazillac, the most famous dessert wine of the Dordogne, resembles Sauternes, though milder in taste. The best years for the Jura are roughly the same as for the Côte d'Or; those for Jurançon and Monbazillac parallel those of Bordeaux.

Among the so-called "country wines," good whites come from Crépy in the foothills of the Alps and Syssel on the upper Rhône. Wines of southern districts, such as Languedoc, Gaillac, Cahors and Bergerac, usually red, must be exceptional to be worth any price.

TABLE I
Other Wines of France

PRINCIPAL ALSATIAN WINES

Commune	Wine for Which Commune Is Most Noted
Bambach	Riesling
Ribeauvillé	Pinot Gris (Tokay)
	Riesling
Bergheim	Gewürztraminer
Hunawihr	Riesling
	Pinot Gris (Tokay)
Riquewihr	Riesling
	Muscat
	Gewürztraminer
Mittelwihr	Gewürztraminer
Equisheim	Riesling
Soultzmatt	Sylvaner
	Riesling
Guebwiller	Gewürztraminer

LEADING ALSATIAN VINEYARD (OR BRAND) NAMES FROM VARIOUS GROWERS

Clos des Amandiers	Kitterlé
Clos des Capucins	Au Moulin
Clos des Sorcières	Brand
Clos des Maquisards	Schonnenberg
Clos de Zahnacker	Osterberg
Clos Ste.-Hune	Mandelkreug
Gansbrönnel	Käfferkopf
Muhlforst	Socières
Sporen	

T A B L E I Continued
Other Wines of France

WINES OF THE JURA, SAVOIE, THE DORDOGNE, THE PYRÉNÉES, ETC.

Jura

Appellation Contrôlée	*Vineyard (or Wine)*
Château-Châlon	Château-Châlon (yellow)
Étoile	(*rosé*, white)
Arbois	(*rosé*, white)

Savoie

Appellation Contrôlée	*Vineyard (or Wine)*
Crépy	(white)
Syssel	Rousette de Savoie (or Syssel)
	(white)

Dordogne

Appellation Contrôlée	*Vineyard (or Wine)*
Monbazillac	Château de Monbazillac (white)
Bergerac	Château de Monplaisir (red, white)

Pyrénées

Appellation Contrôlée	*Vineyard (or wine)*
Jurançon	Pourtau (white)
	Perpigna (white)

Others

Appellation Contrôlée	*Vineyard (or Wine)*
Coteaux des Languedoc (*V.D.Q.S.*)	St.-Georges-d'Orques (red)
	Muscat de Frontignan (white, sweet)
Corbières (*V.D.Q.S.*)	(red)
Gaillac	(red, white)
Fitou	(red)
Cahors	(red)
Blanquette-de-Limoux	(white)

CHAPTER 3

Wines of Germany

North Country Vineyards

The 50th parallel, which in Europe is the approximate northernmost limit for the wine grape, slips between Land's End and the Scilly Isles, skirts the top of France, bisects the little Duchy of Luxembourg and passes through the center of the greatest wine districts of Germany. In fact, the northern part of these districts are the sole exception to this vinicultural rule: only the insignificant red-wine vineyards of the Ahr, the famous Rheingau and the little river called the Moselle (Mosel), twisting and turning every which way between its precipitous banks, push north of the parallel.

In comparison with France, Germany produces a mere trickle of wine—less than one-seventh. All the fine wines of Germany are white, and the finest of these are indelibly associated with the Riesling grape, which is undoubtedly indigenous and has been cultivated for wine in Germany for a thousand years or more. The Riesling is the "noble" grape of the North Country. Although it is by no means unique to Germany, nowhere else does it truly excel. In California, for example, it produces a somewhat less distinguished (though good and fragrant) dry wine—although the very sweet versions compare favorably with

those of Germany. In Bordeaux, especially parts of Graves, it is sometimes used for surreptitious blending; in Alsace, the Rhineland's neighbor, it vies for high favor with the Gewürztraminer. Yet nowhere in
the world but in the Moselle and the Rhine regions will one find a
Riesling as subtle, fragrant or as delicate. A fine German wine made
from the Riesling is a true aristocrat.

The Riesling is a lover of sun — and of poor, preferably stony soil.
If proof were ever needed of the maxim that adversity is the ally of the
wine grape, it is here. There is a saying on the Moselle that "where a
plow can go, no vine should grow," and certainly there are few places
in the world where wine is made under more torturous and impractical
conditions. Many of the great wines of Germany come from vineyards
that have been terraced along the steep cliffs, amid outcroppings of rock
where nothing else could possibly grow. The stone-laden terraces
themselves are oftentimes reached not by paths or roads, but by flights
of steps. When such earth as nature has begrudged them is washed
away, it must be carried back up the cliffs in baskets or pails, by hand
or with pulleys.

Nor is it just the terrain that taxes many German winegrowers. For
although in favorable years the aristocratic Riesling rewards him for
his pains several times over — and in the best years enables him to make
his justifiably celebrated sweet, fragrant wines — it fails him cruelly in
other years. In fact, the climate in parts of Germany is so capricious
that one is in luck to have as many as three truly satisfactory years in
a single decade. A passable German wine needs a hundred days of sun
to shine on the grapes; for a great wine, one hundred and twenty. In
off years, in order to bring about a sufficient fermentation, the grapes
in the vat must perforce be sugared, which never enhances the quality
of wine — and even then the product may be so poor that it must be
sold for the manufacture of *Sekt* (German Champagne), in the process
of which it is sweetened once again. Or perhaps the crop in a mediocre
year will go into *Tafelwein* (*ordinaire*) — or Liebfraumilch, Germany's
most widely exported wine, the origin and nature of which may be of
some concern to the reader, who might best receive clarification at the
start.

One often hears the criticism that the classification and labeling of
German wines are overmeticulous, yet compared to the system of grading and labeling carried on in most other countries of the world, this
can be a blessing. Once one gets the hang of it, it is possible to know

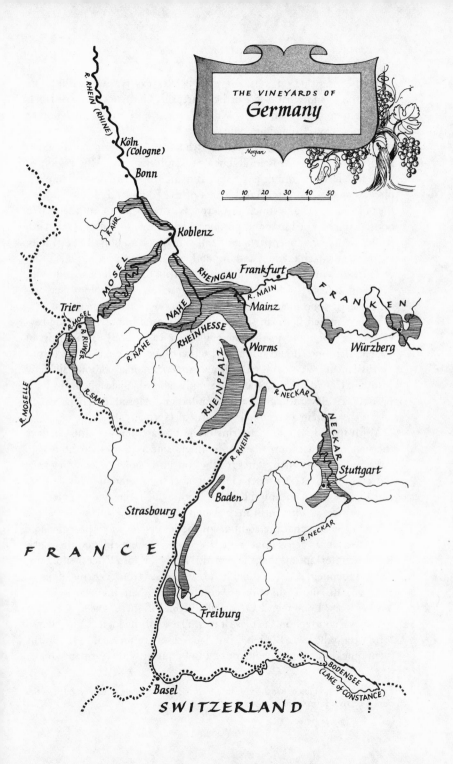

THE VINEYARDS OF
Germany

Morgan

0 10 20 30 40 50

R. RHEIN (RHINE)

Köln
(Cologne)

Bonn

R. AHR

Koblenz

MOSEL

RHEINGAU

Frankfurt

R. MAIN

Trier

R. MOSEL

R. RUWER

NAHE

Mainz

FRANKEN

R. NAHE

RHEINHESSE

Worms

Würzberg

R. MOSELLE

R. SAAR

RHEINPFALZ

R. NECKAR

NECKAR

R. RHEIN

Stuttgart

Baden

Strasbourg

R. NECKAR

F R A N C E

Freiburg

BODENSEE
(LAKE OF CONSTANCE)

Basel

SWITZERLAND

from the language on most German bottles exactly where the wine came from—and what it is. Furthermore, this German system of labeling is nationwide—something which does not hold true for most other European wine-producing countries.

The two principal exceptions to the logic of German labels are Liebfraumilch and Moselblümchen, its equivalent from the region of the Moselle. The former is a regional name for what is often simply a blend of wines from several districts of the Rhineland. Although neither of them is drunk much in Germany, this is not to say that when bottled and shipped by good producers (the firms of Sichel, Deinhard, Rudolf Müller, Langenbach and Valkenberg are among the best) they cannot be drinkable wines and of good value. But it must be added that the aura of wines named Liebfraumilch (Milk of the Holy Virgin) and Moselblümchen (Little Flower of the Moselle)—terminology that artfully catches the imagination of the unknowing consumer—has frequently tempted German shippers and domestic importers to add several dollars or more to the fair value of a case. The real point is, of course, that one should not expect either wine to be any more distinguished in its way than a Bordeaux *Supérieur* or a communal blend from the Côte d'Or, or something simply labeled Châteauneuf-du-Pape without a vineyard name. Liebfraumilch and Moselblümchens are, in effect, the principal "regional" exports of Germany.

With these two regional terms cleared away, one may then believe the statement that most German vintners sincerely do their utmost to assess and identify their wines for the consumer's benefit, and do a very thorough job of it. A proper German label for a wine of quality invariably bears the name of the place from which the wine comes—in adjectival form. This form may at first be confusing, but if one keeps in mind the fact that the addition of the letters "er" to a proper name renders it an adjective, one will have little trouble. Hence the name Rüdesheim(er) means that the wine is "from" or "of" Rüdesheim. Similarly, Hochheimer from Hochheim, Wormser from Worms. This is, after all, no more difficult to comprehend than the terms "New Yorker" or "Londoner." Occasionally one of these adjectival forms becomes a contraction, such as Binger instead of the logical Bingener— "from the village of Bingen." But such cases are unusual.[1] One learns them quickly enough, even from a brief contact with German wines.

---

[1] One will also notice that the year in which the wine is made is usually given in this same adjectival form, such as *1959er*.

Of great importance on a German label, as a guide to quality, is the name of the particular vineyard. If one knows the language, many of these names evoke colorful pictures. Schloßberg means the vineyard on the hill with the castle; Sonnenberg, a vineyard on the sunny hill; Glöck, the vineyard of the clock; Schwarze Katz, the black cat's vineyard. In some exceptional cases (such as Schloß Johannisberg or Steinberg, two vineyards of universal renown), the name of the town is omitted from the label—but this, again, is applicable only to a sparse handful of the best, comparable to the French system of allowing a separate *Appellation Contrôlée* for Montrachet or Château Grillet.

Under a new German "liberalizing" wine law promulgated in 1971 (which, in this writer's opinion, was not really a contributory aid to any consumer wishing to find the best or the best value) the wines are nowadays divided into three categories:

1. *Tafelwein,* the *ordinaire* of the country, which need not concern us here;
2. *Qualitätswein,*[2] which must contain 8½ per cent alcohol and *may* be labeled regionally (*Anbaugebiet*); also by the district (*Bereich*); also as from one of the newly created collective vineyards (*Großlagen*) as well as the individual vineyard (*Einzellage*)—all this provided 75 per cent of the wine made is in the smallest-named area;
3. *Qualitätswein mit Prädikat.* This, the highest category, specifies wine made only from an approved grape, with a minimum of 10 per cent alcohol.[3]

Both categories of *Qualitätswein* must be tested, approved and given a number by an official committee, and the number must appear on the label. The 75-percent provision also applies to the year, as well as to the predominant grape if its name is printed on the label.

Prior to 1971, a German vintner (who always prints his name and address on the label) informed the consumer of his quality wines exactly what degree of sweetness the wine had, whether it had been estate-bottled and—in the case of the very finest wines—what cask it had come from. The commonest terms for casks were *Fuder, Stück* and *Faß*—thus *Fuder* 129 meant the one-hundred-and-twenty-ninth cask put down that particular year. Inasmuch as many German wines,

[2]Sometimes printed as *Qualitätswein b. A.*

[3]A list of traditional vineyards and their respective districts and collective vineyards is given in Table J.

especially the sweeter ones, vary in subtle ways from cask to cask, this courtesy allowed the wine drinker the opportunity of duplicating a bottle which he may think especially fine—or of avoiding a repetition of one he doesn't like.

Degrees of sweetness (under the new law, and covering the top category of *Qualitätswein mit Prädikat* only) are, first and driest, *Kabinett*[4] wines, which must be made from fully mature grapes without sugar added in the vinification process to raise the alcoholic content; *Spätlese*, from late-picked, even more mature grapes; *Auslese*, from specially selected sweet grapes; *Beerenauslese* and, finally, *Trockenbeerenauslese*. As one would assume for a country with so short a growing season, the most prized wines of Germany are the sweetest, made in the all too infrequent years in which the *pourriture noble* (the German term is *Edelfäule*) has had time to settle. Thus a *Spätlese* will be richer and sweeter than a *Cabinett;* an *Auslese* is an even sweeter one. A *Beerenauslese* (picked-off berries) or a *Trockenbeerenauslese* (raisined picked-off berries) will be very sweet indeed, the grapes having been plucked one by one as they turned, or sometimes become so ripe and lush that they are about to fall to the ground.[5] Logically these sweet wines are the most expensive of all German wines. In their native land, they are often taken between meals, very much as we drink coffee and tea. At the other end of the scale, two other terms now in use, but not officially required, are *Trocken* and *Halbtrocken*—dry and slightly sweet, respectively.

Many German producers also go so far in their honesty as to print the name of the grape on the label. In place of the Riesling, which, like all the superior wine grapes of the world, is a stubborn producer and comparatively slow to ripen, many of the lesser German vineyards use the Silvaner, or one known as the Müller-Thurgau, a cross of the two. In certain parts of Germany, good wines are also made with the Gewürztraminer, a grape we have already met in nearby Alsace. Other grape names seen on bottles will be Rülander (Pinot gris); Kerner; Morio-Muscat and Scheurebe. If two grape names appear, the dominant grape must be the first mentioned.

[4]The term originally specified wine which was put aside for the owner's exclusive use or for entertaining important personages.

[5]In certain unusual years, late frost in the early growing season—the enemy of the wine grape—enhances the quality of these very sweet wines. The product is called *Eiswein* (ice wine). Owing to the actual freezing of the grapes, the result is an even higher concentration of sugar than belatedly picked grapes would ordinarily produce.

The best German wines—like the French—are always estate-bottled. The *Aus dem eigenen Lesegut* (from our own harvest) is the new term, although *Keller-Abfüllung* (cellar-bottled) and *Schloßabzug* (bottled at the castle or manor) will be seen on bottles for some years yet. But inasmuch as most German vineyards (*Lagen*) are divided and subdivided among many owners, comparable to the situation on the Côte d'Or, the name of a reliable bottler or shipper on a label is always of importance, as the wine drinker will soon enough discover by experience. Another auspicious signpost of quality may be found in wines from vineyards owned or managed by the German state—of which there are a great many. Labels of state-produced wines bear the term *Staatsweingüter*—indicating wines made with traditional Teutonic thoroughness, usually of good quality.

As with so many French wines, it is of primary importance to remember that a bottle without a year can only mean a poor year, or a blend of two years or more, and the wine should definitely be suspect—just as a bottle that does not carry an individual vineyard, or collective vineyard name will almost certainly be inferior. As we have said, abject slavery to a vintage chart is arch foolishness—yet it is perhaps less so in the case of German wines than of those of other countries. Good wines here are rarely made in poor years.

The best recent vintage years have been 1971, 1975, 1976 and 1979. It is well to remember that dry German wines are ready to drink within a couple of years and, with the exception of the various sweet *Spätlesen*, *Beerenauslesen*, etc., none of them profit by remaining very long in the bottle.

The Southern Regions of the Rhine

Just beyond the point where the Rhine is finally swallowed up by Germany, north of the Alsatian city of Strasbourg, one comes to the first (and largest-producing) of the half-dozen famous German wine regions. This is the Rheinpfalz, or Palatinate—so named by the Romans, the first known cultivators of the wine grape in Germany, for one of Rome's seven hills. Unlike most of the up-and-down vineyard land in Germany, the Palatinate—a high plateau on the west bank of the Rhine which the Germans call the "Pfalz"—is a garden spot, a continuation of the terrain and way of life of neighboring Alsace. It is filled with orchards and truck gardens and vines, grotesque, timbered houses in villages with twisting, narrow streets. The sun shines longer and brighter in the Palatinate than in other parts of the Rhineland, and the predominant grapes here, the Silvaner and the Müller-Thurgau, flourish as nowhere else.

The best vineyards of the Palatinate, however, restrict themselves to the Riesling, and the finest wines of all come from a small concentration of upland villages known locally as the Weinstraße (wine street). Quarries abound in this part of the Palatinate, and the ground of many of the vineyards is covered with their rubble, holding the sun's heat throughout the cool nights. The wines, which have for years been uncommonly popular in England, are milder and less acid than those from any other part of the Rhineland, and they mature faster. *Auslesen* and other sweet wines from the Palatinate are apt to be honey-sweet.

Although the Palatinate is Germany's largest wine-producing region, embracing some fifty thousand acres in vines, the vineyards of the Weinstraße total only about four thousand. The balance of the region is low-lying, and devoted almost solely to Sylvaner and lesser grapes for the production of *Tafelwein*—the *ordinaire* that the Rhinelanders drink themselves from pitchers and carafes. *Tafelweins* are relatively low in alcohol, harsh and undistinguished. They are rarely exported.[6] Wines of the Weinstraße most often seen abroad are those of Ruppertsberg, Deidesheim, Forst and Wachenheim, though there are other villages, such as Bad Dürckheim, Ungstein and Königsbach, that are nearly as famous. The traditionally best vineyards of the Rheinpfalz are listed at the end of this chapter.

Conterminous to the Palatinate, also on the west bank of the river, is a region producing more widely known wines, the Rheinheßen (Heßia or "Heße"). The vineyards of the Rheinheßen, their vines neatly tailored on high wires, hug the riverbank all the way from Worms to Mainz. Again, in contrast to the northern regions of the Rhineland, the land rolls gently up from the river, and there is little need for terracing except for a small section upriver from Nierstein—the source of the best of the Rheinheßen. Although the wines, the best-known of which are perhaps the Niersteiners, are moderately dry, soft, fruity and pliant, they are generally more deficient in character and finesse than those of the Rheinpfalz and the other great regions of Germany, and are more readily acceptable to uninitiated palates. Some of them are raised on the red sandstone soil so typical of the region, as

---

[6]The principal exception is Moselblümchen from the Moselle.

reflected by the names of many of the traditional vineyards: Rothen-berg (red hill), Scharlachberg (scarlet hill), Goldberg (golden hill). Unfortunately, many of the colorful names have been eliminated by the collective nomenclature of the new German wine law.

In addition to being the home of such familiar wine names as Nier-steiner, Oppenheimer and Bodenheimer, the region is also the original fount of the omnipresent Liebfraumilch. In fact, the finest *Lage* of Worms, a twenty-five-acre tract that surrounds the Liebfrauenkirche (Church of Our Lady), is probably the source of the term. In great years wines from the Liebfrauenkirche,[7] traditionally one of the best vineyards of the Rheinheßen, can be as filled with multiple exotic tastes and subtleties as any. Anyone who has tasted it at its best will perhaps not wonder why the name might have been plundered and dragged into the mud. Of the fifty-thousand-odd acres of vineyards in the Rheinheßen, it has been estimated that all but about 10 per cent of their production emerges, one way or another, as Liebfraumilch—made in large part from the Silvaner and the Müller-Thurgau.

Although the mass of vineyards of the Rheinheßen ends abruptly where the river turns sharply westward at Mainz, technically the region includes two other famous wine towns facing the celebrated Rheingau region further down the river. These are Ingelheim, which produces mediocre red wines, and Bingen, at the junction of the Rhine and the Nahe. Bingen is the source of some superb white Rhine wines, described by connoisseurs as "robust and racy." The town also once manufactured most of the corkscrews of Germany, known colloquially as "Bingen pencils." The apocryphal story behind this bit of wit has to do with a presiding bishop of Bingen who, having called a meeting of his priests and finding himself without a pencil with which to make the necessary notes, asked if anybody perchance had brought one. The clerics obediently probed the depths of their habits—but no one could produce anything but a corkscrew. The adjectival form of Bingen on labels, as we have mentioned before, is Binger.

In order not to travel too far ahead of ourselves in this vinous journey down the Rhine, we must digress for a moment and cross the river to inspect two minor, though still significant, wine regions. These com-

---

[7]Wine from this vineyard is now called Liebfrauenstift-Kirchenstück under the new law.

prise the vineyards along the steeply sloped valley of the Neckar—the home of "student wines" to those who knew the university city of Heidelberg—and those of Franconia, on the river Main. The wines of the Neckar are made under climatic conditions so severe that each winter the vines are often taken off their wires, laid on the ground and covered with straw to protect them against the frosts. Neckar wines shine only in the very best years—but when at their zenith they are entirely comparable, in delicacy and fragrance, to Moselles. The finest of them are made from the Riesling and Müller-Thurgau grapes. The Neckar is also the traditional home of a German *rosé*, less popular now than formerly, called Schillerwein. The word (which is not related to the poet Schiller) means "glistening play of colors"—certainly a pretty word picture for a *rosé* and hardly less promotionally imaginative than the terms Liebfraumilch and Moselblümchen.

Franconia's wines (colloquially known as Steinwein or Frankenwein) hold a unique reputation, based in part on the squat flagons in which they have been traditionally bottled for generations. Unchanged in style or shape since the eighteenth century, this particular bottle is known as *Bocksbeutel* (or *Boxbeutel*), an entirely realistic word having to do with one-half of a part of a male goat's anatomy. The name Steinwein is often construed to mean that these bottles were once made of stone; but the truth is that it derives from Würzburg's oldest (and Germany's largest) vineyard, Stein, which lies close to the middle of this charming, ancient German city. Steinweins are generally from the Silvaner grape, or the cross, the Müller-Thurgau, and are rather different from the general run of German wines. Very dry, with an unsuspected alcoholic potency, they live a long time and often remind one of the white wines of northern France, such as those of Chablis. Some of them are exported. Not so long ago they were relatively inexpensive—in terms of most German wines, a major asset in itself—but unfortunately this is no longer the case.

The Rheingau

It will come as a surprise to many that out of Germany's comparatively minuscule total of two hundred thousand acres planted to wine grapes (compared with France's more than three million), only about twenty thousand produce superior wines. Certainly the greatest concentration of these is to be found in Germany's small (seven-thousand-acre) region, the Rheingau—an impressive series of vineyards following the Rhine for about fifteen miles along its north bank, from its confluence with the Main to just below its confluence with the Nahe at Bingen. Throughout this stretch the river's course turns almost due westward. The vineyards, filled with coarse pieces of quartz and fragments of slate, literally stew in the sun, protected from the north winds by the forested Taunus Mountains behind.

It is said that the Emperor Charlemagne (whom we remember as the owner of vineyards in the Côte d'Or), while occupying the great palace he had built in Ingelheim, across the Rhine from the Rheingau, one day noticed a spot on the opposite bluffs where the snow melted sooner than elsewhere, and commanded the planting of the vines that now constitute the famous vineyards of Schloß Johannisberg. Charlemagne may have been the first member of Europe's nobility to note the virtues of the Rheingau, but he was certainly not the last. Among others, in later years, was Queen Victoria, whose fondness for German wines took the form of hypochondria. Visiting the Rheingau in the middle of the last century, so contagious was her enthusiasm that she managed to have a vineyard, Viktoriaberg (by no means the best), named after her. Among others, one of the Queen's coined phrases was "Frankenwein is *Krankenwein*"—sick wine; and it was the dour Queen herself who was responsible for the platitude of the last century: "Good hoc keeps off the doc." She was referring, of course, to the wines of the village of Hochheim, the first that one meets in the Rheingau. To the wines of this particular village the British term "Hock," throughout the British Isles a generic name for all German wine, owes its derivation.

Hochheim borders the Main and lies on relatively low ground—but as the river rounds the bend and starts on its westward course the hills appear, and we are in the land of the gods. Here are the greatest vineyards of the Rheingau, if not of all Germany: Schloß Johannisberg and the nearby Steinberg at Hattenheim—with Schloß Vollrads at Winkel and the Marcobrunn at Erbach ranking as close seconds.

Steinberg, the Clos de Vougeot of German vineyards, surrounded by a mile and a half of walls built by Cistercian monks in the twelfth century, is now owned by the German state. Schloß Johannisberg was founded as a Benedictine monastery in the same century, and has been owned for one hundred and fifty years by one of the oldest of all noble Germanic families, the Metternichs.[8] The present *Schloβ* (castle), an imposing building overlooking its sloping vineyards and the Rhine, was used by the Germans as an observation post during World War II, and was consequently heavily bombed by the R.A.F. Happily, it has now been restored. Although their character in the last decade seems to have fallen off, here are wines that have earned the praises of wine drinkers for centuries. Full of power and character, the dry ones are slightly piquant, the sweeter ones unbelievably fragrant. At both the Schloβ and Steinberg, one finds the very epitome of German care and attention to detail in the art of wine making. To guard against contamination and infection of the vines, visitors have been known to be asked to shed their shoes before entering the vineyards; and the cellars—the first in Germany to install glass-lined steel tanks to replace wooden casks—are perhaps even more sanitary and free from contamination than a modern hospital.

The wines of Schloβ Johannisberg, made in various grades (six in most years, more yet in the best years), are labeled in their own way. The lowest grade bears a red seal (*Rotlack*). Next in quality comes the white seal (Weisslack), followed by a rose or pink seal (*Roselack*)— this being at least a semi-sweet *Auslese* wine. The sweeter and most expensive wines bear orange, white, blue or gold seals, in an ascending order of excellence. But let us not whet the reader's thirst too hastily: he must be warned that a *Trockenbeerenauslese* from a great year may cost him half a fortune. A fine Steinberger may cost even more. Thus it is significant to know that although the wines of these particular vineyards are among the indisputable best, there are other vineyards in the villages of Johannisberg and Hattenheim[9] that are nearly as excellent; the traditional best are listed at the end of this chapter.

Another outstanding Rheingau wine comes form the village of Rüdesheim, almost the westernmost of the region, where the multitudinous terraced vineyards are scattered over the face of the steepest of

---

[8]A family of vinophiles for generations. It was, in fact, Prince Metternich who—in the course of negotiations for the hand of Marie-Louise of Austria—first brought to the attention of the lowly born Emperor Napoleon the existence of the rare Sherry-like *vin jaune* of the Jura, Château-Châlon.

[9]Wines are labeled adjectively Johannisberger and Hattenheimer after the villages, with labels supplemented by individual or collective vineyard names.

bluffs. It is important to remember that Rüdesheim vineyards append-ing the word *Berg*—indicating that they are situated on the most pre-cipitous part of the bluff—have the reputation of being the finest. (Examples: Berg Rottland, Berg Lay, etc.) Other villages with deservedly international fame are Winkel (with Schloß Vollrads, the largest privately owned vineyard intact on the Rhine), Hallgarten, Erbach (the principal vineyard is Marcobrunn) and Rauenthal.

Although the average alcoholic content of German wines is appre-ciably lower than that of French wines (most Rhine wines rarely attain more than 10 per cent, and Moselles tend to be lower yet), the wines of the Rheingau are exceptions. They are not only comparatively strong in alcohol but also less sweet or sugary in the respective cate-gories for wine made from late-picked grapes—*Auslese, Beerenauslese* and *Trockenbeerenauslese.* Aptly described by experts as "brisk and silky," they are certainly the most touted of all German wines, and if for this reason only, it should not be forgotten that there are extreme variances in quality among poor, good and excellent years—that a famous Rheingau of an inferior year can be as unappealing and undrinkable as any, and not worth any price. These wines are natural pitfalls for the "wine snob." The reader should also not allow himself to become unduly concerned, especially in connection with these wines of the Rheingau, over the relative sameness of them. Although there is a considerable difference between the rather earthy wines of Hochheim at one end of the Rheingau and the far more elegant ones of Rüdesheim near the region's western end, the subtle variations of taste between one village and the next tax even the powers and palates of the experts. German wines are versatile, to be sure, but there are subtleties of differences that are not always easily spotted by uninitiated palates. Thus the experimenting wine drinker should not despair if he cannot at first tell the difference between a Moselle and a Rheingau, or a Rheinpfalz and a Rheinheßen, much less a Schloß Johannisberg and a fine Steinberg.

The Moselle

Rising high in the Vosges Mountains of northern France, passing through one of the most fought-over territories on earth, the Moselle River is joined in Germany by two tiny streams, the Saar and the

Ruwer, before commencing its snakelike route to the Rhine. In fact, so circuitous is the course of this extraordinarily beautiful little river that over a distance of forty miles, as the crow flies, it triples its length and—in its predominantly northeasterly path—runs eight times due north, seven times due south and once nearly due west.

All the best Mosel-Saar-Ruwer vineyards face south; thus some of them are on the left bank, others on the right, and most of them so precipitously placed as to induce violent vertigo. In the upper reaches of the region the finest wines come from the Scharzhofberg and Scharzberg vineyards of the Saar, and the villages of Maximin Grün-haus and Eitelsbach on the Ruwer. Made exclusively from the Riesling, reaching their zenith of perfection only once or twice in a decade, they are the most gracious and fragrant, fruity and above all crisp, of all German wines. They are also the palest of all German wines; and Moselles from the Saar and Ruwer watersheds, especially, are apt to be slightly *pétillant* (or *spritzig*), a quality which rarely detracts from the charm of any light white wine.

The seven principal villages on the Moselle proper (known as the Mittel-Mosel) are Piesport, Wehlen, Zeltingen, Graach, Bernkastel, Erden and Ürzig. Concentrated in a small area at a place where the little river suffers its most active peristalsis, these villages are responsi-ble for the majority of Moselles encountered in foreign countries. Of the seven, the wines of Piesport and Wehlen are traditionally consid-ered the finest—equaled perhaps only by those of a few outstanding vineyards of Graach, one of the best of which is appropriately called Himmelreich (Kingdom of Heaven). Also at Graach is the superb vineyard of Josephshöf, owned for more than a century by the old wine-making family of Kesselstatts. Few German wines of a great year can be as luscious or pervasively fragrant as a Josephshöfer *Beerenauslese*.

Ranking close, certainly in terms of international reputation, to Schloß Johannisberg and Steinberg, is the Moselle with the colorful name of Bernkasteler Doktor—from the principal vineyard of Bern-kastel. Perhaps because of its picturesque and easy-to-remember name—comparable to the Côte d'Or's Volnay and Pommard—Bern-kasteler Doktor became one of the first Moselles to attain popularity in England and America. Some experts find a distinctive "smoky" flavor in it. In our opinion, the wine does not necessarily merit the high prices that it so often brings. If one must sample "the Doktor," however, the two best from this tiny vineyard are from the famous Thanisch family, and J. Lauerburg, a small but very excellent producer.

Scattered Vineyards

Other good German white wines are produced in the region of Nahe, whieh adjoins the Rhine to the south, and in the area of Baden in the foothills of the Black Forest, across the swift-flowing river fi om Alsace. The best of the Baden (Badische) wines, made near the city of Freiburg, derive from Silvaner, Müller-Thurgau, Pinot blanc (rare) or Pinot gris (here the Ruländer) grapes. Curiously enough, although neither the Chasselas nor the Pinot gris ever seems to constitute the source of distinguished wines elsewhere, they bloom in this particular part of Germany. The best vineyards of Baden surround the villages of Ihringen (Winklerberg), Achkarren (Schloßberg, Traubengarten), Durbach (Schloßberg), Endingen (Steingrube) and Oberrotweil (Henkenberg)—names of prophesiable value to drinkers of German wines in future years. Wines from the neighboring region of Württemberg are of less worth, but the rarely seen wines known as *Seeweins*, grown along the placid shores of the Lake of Constance, the principal source of the Rhine, are delicious in their own habitat. Regrettably they are not made in sufficient quantity to warrant export.

The red wines of Germany, made in larger quantities than one might think, are almost all exclusively lowland wines. They are virtually never exported. The best of them, made far down the Rhine in the Ahr Valley, near Bonn, usually derive from the German version of the Burgundian Pinot noir, here called the *Spätburgunder* (late Burgundian). Soft but also too austere for a red wine, they lack character and require no further mention, except as a reminder to visitors of Germany that they often constitute a momentary (and most welcome) respite from what may be a plethora of whites. Comparable reds are also made at the lower extremity of the Rheingau, at the state-owned vineyards of Aßmaushausen.

With the exception of Steinwein and Frankenwein, German still wines come in tall, slim bottles known as *Flaschen*. For purposes of quick identification, it is well to know that the wines of the Moselle (and *Sekt*) are shipped in green bottles, other German wines in brown bottles.

Summary

All the best German wines are white, with the sweeter ones classified (and priced) according to the degree of sweetness: the driest is *Kabinett* from normally ripe grapes; *Spätlese* (from late-picked grapes); *Auslese* (picked even later); *Beerenauslese* (a definitely sweet wine); *Trockenbeerenauslese* (the sweetest). *Tafelwein* is the lowest grade, followed by *Qualitätswein b. A.* and *Qualitätswein mit Prädikat*, the highest.

Liebfraumilch, Moselblümchen and Frankenwein are "regionals"; the first two tend to be overpriced for what they really are.

The finest German wines come from the regions of the Rheingau (on the Rhine) and the Moselle (Mosel). The former have more body and character; the latter are the more delicate and aromatic. Other regions are the Rheinpfalz, the Rheinheßen, the Neckar and Franconia (Frankenwein or Steinwein is shipped in flagon-like bottles).

Most dry German wines are ready to drink after a year or two, and need no further aging. The sweeter ones improve in the bottle. Recent great years are 1971, 1975, 1976 and 1979.

TABLE J
Principal Traditional Vineyards of Germany

MOSEL-SAAR-RUWER

District (*Bereich*): *Bernkastel*

Village	Collective Vineyard (*Grosslage*)	Vineyard*
TRITTENHEIM	Michelsberg	Trittenheimer Apotheke
		Trittenheimer Altärchen
		Trittenheimer Falkenberg
		Trittenheimer Laurentiusberg
		Trittenheimer Clemensberg
		Trittenheimer Sonnenberg
NEUMAGEN	Michelsberg	Neumagener Laudamusberg

*Note: Some of these traditional vineyards, specifically those of less than 12 acres, were banned by the law of 1971 from using their own names on labels. However, there are many bottles—especially ones containing sweet wines—still extant. Manifestly these represent, in most instances, a finer quality than wines now pooled and bottled under a collective vineyard label.

TABLE J Continued
Principal Traditional Vineyards of Germany

Village	(Grosslage)	Vineyard*
		Neumagener Engelgrube
		Neumagener Rosengärtchen
DHRON	Michelsberg	Dhronhofberger
PIESPORT	Michelsberg	Piesporter Goldtröpfchen
		Piesporter Lay
		Piesporter Schubertslay
		Piesporter Falkenberg
		Piesporter Güntherslay
		Piesporter Taubengarten
		Piesporter Treppchen
WINTRICH	Kurfürstlay	Wintricher Geyerslay
		Wintricher Grosser Herrgott
		Wintricher Rosenberg
		Wintricher Ohligsberg
		Wintricher Neuberg
		Wintricher Sonnseite
BRAUNEBERG	Kurfürstlay	Brauneberger Falkenberg
		Brauneberger Juffer
BERNKASTEL	Badstube	Bernkasteler Doktor (und Graben)
		Bernkasteler Lay
		Bernkasteler Schloßberg
		Bernkasteler Doktor (und Bratenhöfchen)
		Bernkasteler Schwanen
		Bernkasteler Pfalzgraben
		Bernkasteler Rosenberg
GRAACH	Münslay	†Josephshöfer
		Graacher Abtsberg
		Graacher Heiligenhaus
		Graacher Himmelreich
		Graacher Domprobst
WEHLEN	Münslay	Wehlener Sonnenuhr
		Wehlener Klosterlay
		Wehlener Rosenberg
		Wehlener Nonnenberg
		Wehlener Lay

†Designates that vineyard labels its wine only with vineyard name.

TABLE J Continued
Principal Traditional Vineyards of Germany

Village	(Grosslage)	Vineyard*
ZELTINGEN	Münslay	Zeltinger Schloßberg
		Zeltinger Himmelreich
		Zeltinger Rotlay
		Zeltinger Sonnenuhr
		Zeltinger Stephanslay
		Zeltinger Kirchenpfad
ERDEN	Schwazlay	Erdener Treppchen
		Erdener Prälat
		Erdener Bußlay
ÜRZIG	Schwarzlay	Ürziger Kranklay
		Ürziger Lay
		Ürziger Würzgarten
		Ürziger Urglück
KINHEIM	Nacktarsh	Kinheimer Hubertuslay
		Kinheimer Rosenberg
CRÖV (OR KRÖV)	Nacktarsh	Cröver Niederberg
		Cröver Petersberg
		Cröver Heislay
TRABEN-TRARBACH	Schwarzlay	Trarbacher Schloßberg
		Trarbacher Königsberg
		Trarbacher Huhnersberg
		Trarbacher Ungsberg

District (Bereich): Schwarz Katz

Village	(Grosslage)	Vineyard*
ZELL		Zeller Burglay
		Zeller Dommhen
		Zeller Nußberg
		Zeller Schwarze Katz

District (Bereich): Saar-Ruwer

Village	Collective Vineyard (Grosslage)	Vineyard*
ENKIRCH	Scharzberg	Enkircher Steffensberg
		Enkircher Herrenberg
		Enkircher Montenubel
		Enkircher Battereiberg

TABLE J Continued
Principal Traditional Vineyards of Germany

Village	(Grosslage)	Vineyard*
WILTINGEN	Scharzberg	†Scharzhofberg
		Wiltinger Rosenberg
		Wiltinger Braune Kupp
		Wiltinger Gottesfüß
OBEREMMEL	Scharzberg	Oberemmeler Hütte
		Oberemmeler Karlsberg
		Oberemmeler Altenberg
AYL	Scharzberg	Ayler Kupp
		Ayler Herrenberg
OCKFEN	Scharzberg	Ockfener Herrenberg
		Ockfener Bockstein
SERRIG	Scharzberg	Schloß Saarstein
		Serriger Heiligenborn
		Schloß Saarfels
MAXIMIN GRÜNHAUS	Römerlay	Maximin Grünhäuser Herrenberg
EITELSBACH	Römerlay	Eitelsbacher Karthäuserhofberger Kronenberg
		Eitelsbacher Karthäuserhofberger Sang
KASEL (OR CASEL)	Römerlay	Kaseler Niesgen
WALDRACH	Römerlay	Schloß Marienlay
MERTESDORF	Römerlay	Brutusberger Lorenzberg
		Brutusberger Treppchen

RHEINGAU

District (Bereich): Johannisberg

Village	Collective Vineyard (Grosslage)	Vineyard*
RÜDESHEIM	Burgweg	Rüdesheimer Berg Bronnen
		Rüdesheimer Berg Lay
		Rüdesheimer Berg Burgweg
		Rüdesheimer Berg Roseneck
		Rüdesheimer Berg Muhlstein
		Rüdesheimer Berg Schloßberg

TABLE J Continued
Principal Traditional Vineyards of Germany

Village	(Grosslage)	Vineyard*
		Rüdesheimer Bischofsberg
		Rüdesheimer Berg Rottland
		Rüdesheimer Berg Hellpfad
GEISENHEIM	Burgweg	Geisenheimer Rothenberg
		Geisenheimer Decker
		Geisenheimer Katzenloch
		Geisenheimer Klaüserweg
		Geisenheimer Lickerstein
		Geisenheimer Kosackenberg
		Greisenheimer Mäuerchen
		Geisenheimer Mönchspfad
JOHANNISBERG	Erntebringer	†Schloß Johannisberg
		Johannisberger Hölle
		Johannisberger Mittelhölle
		Johannisberger Goldatzel
		Johannisberger Hansenberg
		Johannisberger Klaus
		Johannisberger Sterzelpfad
		Johannisberger Kerzenstück
		Johannisberger Nonnhölle
WINKEL	Honigberg	†Schloß Vollrads
		Winkeler Jesuitengarten
		Winkeler Dachsberg
		Winkeler Hasensprung
		Winkeler Kläuserweg
HALLGARTEN	Mehrhölzchen	Hallgartener Deutelsberg
		Hallgartener Jungfer
		Hallgartener Hendelberg
		Hallgartener Würzgarten
		Hallgartener Schönhell
		Hallgartener Rosengarten
ÖSTRICH	Gottesthal	Östricher Lenchen
		Östricher Eiserberg
		Östricher Klostergarten
		Östricher Hölle
		Östricher Magdalenengarten
		Östricher Doosberg

TABLE J Continued
Principal Traditional Vineyards of Germany

Village	(Grosslage)	Vineyard*
		Östricher Deez
		Östricher Pfaffenberg
		Östricher Klosterberg
HATTENHEIM	Deutelsberg	†Steinberg
		Hattenheimer Wißelbrunnen
		Hattenheimer Nußbrunnen
		Hattenheimer Mannberg
		Hattenheimer Engelmannsberg
		Hattenheimer Haßel
		Hattenheimer Wilborn
		Hattenheimer Rothenberg
		Hattenheimer Pfaffenberg
		Hattenheimer Hinterhausen
		Hattenheimer Bergweg
ERBACH	Mehrhölzchen	†Marcobrunn
		Erbacher Steinmorgen
		Erbacher Brühl
		Erbacher Hinterkirch
		Erbacher Herrenberg
		Erbacher Siegelsberg
		Erbacher Hohenrain
		Erbacher Honigberg
		Erbacher Rheinhell
KIEDRICH	Heiligenstock	Kiedricher Waßerrose
		Kiedricher Turmberg
		Kiedricher Heiligenstock
		Kiedricher Gräfenberg
		Kiedricher Sandgrube
RAUENTHAL	Steinmacher	Rauenthader Baiken
		Rauenthaler Rothenberg
		Rauenthaler Herberg
		Rauenthaler Wieshell
		Rauenthaler Gehrn
		Rauenthaler Wulfen
		Rauenthaler Pfaffenberg
ELTVILLE	Steinmacher	Eltviller Sonnenberg
		Eltviller Kalbspflicht

TABLE J Continued
Principal Traditional Vineyards of Germany

Village	*(Grosslage)*	*Vineyard**
		Eltviller Langenstück
		Eltviller Klumbehen
		Eltviller Taubenberg
		Eltviller Monchhannach
WALLUF	Steinmacher	Wallufer Walkenberg
		Wallufer Unterberg
		Wallufer Mittelberg

District (*Bereich*): *Hochheim*

Village	*(Grosslage)*	*Vineyard**
HOCHHEIM	Daubhaus	Hochheimer Kachenstück
		Hochheimer Rauchloch
		Hochheimer Raaber
		Hochheimer Stielweg
		Hochheimer Sommerheil
		Hochheimer Domdechaney
		Hochheimer Stein
		Hochheimer Hölle
		Hochheimer Daubhaus

RHEINHEβEN

District (*Bereich*): *Nierstein*

Village	*Collective Vineyard* *(Grosslage)*	*Vineyard**
BODENHEIM	Sankt Alban	Bodenheimer Kahlenberg
		Bodenheimer Rettberg
		Bodenheimer Braunloch
		Bodenheimer Ebersberg
		Bodenheimer Hoch
		Bodenheimer Silberberg
NACKENHEIM	Sankt Alban	Nackenheimer Rothenberg
		Nackenheimer Stiel
		Nackenheimer Rheinhahl
		Nackenheimer Fenchelberg
		Nackenheimer Engelsberg
NIERSTEIN	Auflangen	Niersteiner Glück
	Rehbach	Niersteiner Flächenhahl
	Gutes Domtal	Niersteiner Hipping

TABLE J   Continued
Principal Traditional Vineyards of Germany

Village	(Grosslage)	Vineyard*
OPPENHEIM	Güldenmorgan	Oppenheimer Goldberg
		Oppenheimer Kröttenbrunnen
		Oppenheimer Sackträger
		Oppenheimer Kreuz
		Oppenheimer Herrenberg
DIENHEIM	Güldenmorgan	Dienheimer Goldberg
		Dienheimer Tafelstein
		Dienheimer Kröttenbrunnen

District (Bereich): Wonnegau

Village	(Grosslage)	Vineyard*
WORMS	Liebfrauenmorgan	Wormser Liebfrauenstift

District (Bereich): Bingen

Village	(Grosslage)	Vineyard*
BINGEN	Sankt Rochuskapelle	Binger-Büdesheimer Scharlachberg
		Binger Eiselberg
		Binger Rochusberg
		Binger Ohligberg
		Binger Schloßberg
		Binger Schwätzerchen
		Binger-Kempter Rheinberg
		Binger Rosengarten

RHEINPFALZ

District (Bereich): Mittlehardt-Deutshe-Weinstrasse

Village	(Grosslage)	Vineyard*
KALLSTADT	Saumagen	Kallstadter Krenz
		Kallstadter Nill
		Kallstadter Kobnert
		Kallstadter Steinacker
UNGSTEIN	Honigsachel	Ungsteiner Michelsberg
		Ungsteiner Spielberg
		Ungsteiner Herrenberg
BAD DÜRCKHEIM	Feuerberg	Dürckheimer Speilberg

TABLE J. Continued
Principal Traditional Vineyards of Germany

Village	(Grosslage)	Vineyard*
		Dürckheimer Hochneß
		Dürckheimer Schenkonböhl
		Dürckheimer Michelsberg
		Dürckheimer Fuchsmantel
WACHENHEIM	Mariengarten	Wachenheimer Gerümpel
		Wachenheimer Bächel
		Wachenheimer Goldbächel
		Wachenheimer Bohlig
		Wachenheimer Bechbächel
		Wachenheimer Wolfsdarm
FORST	Mariengarten	Forster Jesuitengarten
		Forster Ziegler
		Forster Freundstück
		Forster Langenacker
		Forster Kirchenstück
		Forster Kranich
		Forster Ungeheuer
		Forster Langenmorgen
DEIDESHEIM	Hofstück	Deidesheimer Grainhübel
	Mariengarten	Deidesheimer Hochenmorgen
		Deidesheimer Dopp
		Deidesheimer Geheu
		Deidesheimer Leinhöhle
		Deidesheimer Kränzler
		Deidesheimer Grain
		Deidesheimer Kieselberg
		Deidesheimer Rennpfad
		Deidesheimer Kalkofen
		Deidesheimer Langenmorgen
RUPPERTSBERG	Hofstück	Ruppertsberger Nußbien
		Ruppertsberger Hoheberg
		Ruppertsberger Mandelacker
		Ruppertsberger Reiterpfad
		Ruppertsberger Gaisböhl
		Ruppertsberger Hofstück
		Ruppertsberger Kieselberg

TABLE J Continued
Principal Traditional Vineyards of Germany

NAHE

District (Bereich): Kreuznach

Village	Collective Vineyard (Grosslage)	Vineyard*
BAD KREUZNACH	Kronenberg	Kreuznacher Kröttenpfuhl
		Kreuznacher Kahlenberg
		Kreuznacher Narrenkappe
		Kreuznacher Hinkelstein
		Kreuznacher Forst
NIEDERHAUS	Sonnenborn	Niederhäuser Hermannsberg
		Niederhäuser Hermannshöhle

District (Bereich): Schloss Böckelheim

NORHEIM	Burgweg	Norheimer Kirschheck
		Norheimer Götzenfels
		Norheimer Kafels
		Norheimer Dellchen
SCHLOβ BÖCKELHEIM	Burgweg	†Schloβ Böckelheim
		Schloβ Böckelheimer Kupfergrube
		Schloβ Böckelheimer Kupferberg
		Schloβ Böckelheimer Königsfels
		Schloβ Böckelheimer Königsberg

FRANKEN

District (Bereich): Maindreieck

Village	Collective Vineyard (Grosslage)	Vineyard*
WÜRZBURG	(None)	Würzburger Stein
		Würzburger Steinmantel

TABLE J Continued
Principal Traditional Vineyards of Germany

Village	(Grosslage)	Vineyard*
		Würzburger Jesuitenstein
		Würzburger Innere Leiste
		Würzburger Felsenleiste
ESCHERNDORF	Kirchberg	Escherndorfer Lump
		Escherndorfer Kirchberg
		Escherndorfer Eulengrube
RANDERSACKER	Ewig Leben	Randersacker Pfülben
		Randersacker Hohberg
		Randersacker Teufelskeller
		Randersacker Spielberg

CHAPTER 4

Italian Wines

Wines of the Alps and the Plains

Although only a handful of Italian wines may ever be compared in quality with the best of France and Germany, this little nation, half the size of France, produces more wine than any country on earth. Italy holds several other vinous world's records, too. The first is for the exportation of table wine: in 1979 Italy passed the mark and became the largest importer of wine to the U.S. The second is for the production of Vermouth, in which she far outstrips her closest rival, France. The third is national per capita consumption: the average Italian drinks even more wine than the average Frenchman, at an annual rate approaching forty gallons.

Italy makes eight times as much red wine as white, and, as is so amply illustrated by Germany, white-wine grapes flourish best closest to the northern limit of the wine belt. Thus one might think of Italy as the converse of Germany, whose red wines, it will be recalled, are hardly worthy of mention. It has been estimated that Italy has more than two thousand different wines—not to mention seven hundred different grapes. If this chapter were expanded in proportion to the number of Italian wines now exported to the U.S., it would exceed all reasonable bounds. The well-known, traditional Italian wines, with a few notable red exceptions, are inexpensive and highly drinkable, meriting identification and descriptions—but assessments can usually only be given in pastel shades. Most of them need no laying away or aging; they should be drunk and enjoyed within a few years of their birth. This in fact is the viewpoint of a great majority of Italians themselves. In Italy, wine is simply *vino*—the going beverage. Even in the better restaurants of Italy the waiter asks if one wants red or white, then vanishes to fetch it. A wine list must sometimes be extracted just short of using force; and when perchance one spies a pearl, it will usually have been stored, cork up, on a hot shelf over the bar.

One often hopes that it will not be too long in the future of the civilized world before someone comes up with a universal system for the naming and classifying of wines. Meanwhile, the wine drinker can only resort to familiarizing himself with the principles, such as they may be, behind each individual country's systems—and let experience (and many a mistake) teach him the finer points. The basic problem with Italian wines is simply the fact that their names, as found on labels, are divided between grape names and place names; the most confusing aspect being that certain varieties of grapes are grown in many different parts of the country, while others are confined to small regions or even individual vineyards. Thus a wine called Barbera (from the grape of the same name) may be produced on the plains of Piedmont or among the Veronese hills, rendering it in effect a regional wine; whereas white Soave, for example, is made only around Soave, a little hill town between Verona and Venice.

The average Italian wine maker is not as conscientious, or as artful, or as caring as his French or German equivalent. In 1963 the Italian government embarked on a gargantuan effort to regulate and classify Italy's wines and demarcate the better vineyard areas: much progress has been made, but even now the job is far from finished. There are just too many scattered wines and vineyards, traditional names and grapes, to be conquered in a day. To date, however, most of the better-known areas—such as Barbaresco, Barolo, Soave, Chianti, etc.—have been brought into line. Their wines may be labeled *Denominazione di Origine Controllata* (*DOC* for short); the superior title, awarded only to given wines from top regions, is *Denominazione Controllata e Garantita* (*DOCG*).

Perhaps the best rule of thumb for the novice to remember is that the five principal Italian wines named after grapes (all red) are Barbera, Nebbiolo, Dolcetto, Freisa and Grignolino—and assume that any other name on a label, with or without the grape name, is a place name, until one learns otherwise. Since the superior wines of the world always derive from the most suitable soils, it goes without saying that those Italian wines which are named geographically are the best. There is one infamous exception: Chianti. Chianti is a specific place name—a small delimited region. But several million gallons of it produced each year still don't exactly come from there.

Wine, as we have said, is the blood of Italians, and just as many an Italian in the United States buys California or New York grapes and makes his own wine in his cellar, the grape is grown in every backyard from the boot top to the toe of the Italian peninsula, and on the islands of Sardinia and Sicily. Yet there are, in effect, only seven major vineyard areas responsible for superior Italian table wines—all of them surprisingly small. From north to south, these are the mountainous Tyrol in the north, once part of Austria; the plains of Lombardy and Piedmont, the latter largely known abroad as the source of Asti Spumante, the best-known Italian sparkling wine; Verona in the province of Veneto (Venice); Chianti, south of Florence; the region of Orvieto in Umbria; and finally the slopes of volcanic Mount Vesuvius below Naples.

As would be expected, the vineyards of the Tyrolean Alps, sky-high in the valleys and steep approaches of the Brenner Pass to Austria, are predominantly filled with Austrian and German wine grapes, and their best wines are the aromatic whites that derive from the Traminers and the Riesling. One of the more famous Rieslings (which often come in tall, green Rhine-wine-type bottles) is from Terlano; that made from the Traminer is often called *Traminer aromatico*. Also grown in the Tyrol are several excellent reds, Guncina, Santa Giustina and another with the somewhat incongruous name—for an Italian wine, at any rate—of Kuchelberger (no doubt a relic of the Austrian days). These Tyrolean Alps are also the source of a lively *rosé* called Lagrein Rosato, deliciously fruity and fragrant, probably the best Italian *rosé*. Lagrein is the name of a minor grape—not one of the predominant five. Although none is truly outstanding, the white and *rosé* wines of the Tyrol are fresh, fragrant and pleasant. Long popular with the Swiss and the Austrians, the day may not be far off when they will be exported elsewhere in more quantity. Three red wines of the Tyrol are

THE VINEYARDS OF
Italy, Sicily and Corsica

0   50   100   150
MILES

SWITZERLAND • Innsbruck
Brenner Pass
AUSTRIA

FRANCE

Milan
LAKE GARDA
Verona
Trieste
Venice
Turin
Asti
R. PO
Genoa
Nice

YUGOSLAVIA

ADRIATIC SEA

Florence
R. ARNO
Siena

I T A L Y

Orvieto
R. TIBER
Rome

CORSICA
(French)

SARDINIA
(ital.)

Naples
Capri

TYRRHENIAN
SEA

Palermo • Messina
Marsala
SICILY
Catania

TUNISIA

also to be recommended: Lago di Caldaro, Santa Maddalena and Valtellina.

The vineyards of Piedmont, that part of Italy closest to France, are split in two by the river Po, Italy's longest river. Near the headwaters, in the rolling country south of industrial Turin—whose grime and soot are forgiven once one knows it as the Mecca for such gastronomic treasures as the celebrated lavender (or white) truffle and those thin, crispy Italian breadsticks called *grissini*—is a tremendous stretch of vineyards, said to produce three times more wine than all the vineyards of New York State and California put together. Most of this is of inferior quality: white, sweetish Moscatello, used either as a basis for herb-laden Vermouth or for the manufacture of Italy's best-known "Champagne," Asti Spumante, a sparkling white wine with an unmistakable Muscat flavor. But Piedmont is also noted for some excellent regionals (those named for the grape). Perhaps the best white is the green-gold Cortese, made from the grape of the same name, a dry (*secco*) pale wine that is best when sold under the label of Gavi. The reds include Freisa, fragrant and fruity, and Barbera, sturdy and coarse, which, like many another Italian common red wine, is apt to be *frizzante* (*pétillant*). The Italians themselves think of this as adding to the charm of a red wine. When made for export, however, they are usually still wines.

Piedmont is also responsible for superior geographically named wines, all red—perhaps the only Italian wines to which the adjective "great" may be justly applied at all. These are, respectively, Gattinara, Carema, Barbaresco and Barolo—all named for the villages in which they are grown. Made from the indigenous Nebbiolo grape, here are wines that are full-bodied, individualistically fragrant and slow to mature, reminiscent in bouquet and taste of good Burgundies. Barolo is often called the "Prince of Piedmont." Sometimes startlingly alcoholic, it is universally acknowledged as the best of the lot. If one is fortunate enough to come across an old bottle (or has the patience to wait for a young one to mature), he will not be disappointed. Another Piedmont red, fast disappearing and probably more of a curiosity than anything else, is the rare, sweet Dolcetto, one of the few unfortified red dessert wines in the world. Wine snobs—and many another—will find it both incongruous and distasteful. Ordinary Dolcetto from Piedmont is dry. Sweet Dolcetto does not resemble, and should not be confused with, a far better known sweetish type, a specialty of Veneto, known as Recioto, made with partially raisined grapes principally as Valpolicella or Soave (see Table K). Dry Recioto—when the sugar has been completely fermented out—is called Amarone.

Here, too, is the source of Nebbiolo Spumante, a ruby-colored, sweetish (*abboccato*) equivalent of Sparkling Burgundy, at its best when made by a process similar to the *méthode champenoise* of the Champagne district in France. But most wine drinkers will agree, we think, that the most commendable sparkling wines of Piedmont are the white Astis.

In the United States an increasingly popular Italian dry white wine is Soave, which owes its name to an intriguing little walled town just east of the city of Verona, on the road to Venice. Soave might well be called the Italian Chablis. Exceptionally light in color, it is dry and mild (*soave*, coincidentally, also means suave or mild). As with Chablis, the vines are grown on chalky soil, giving the wine a comparable "flinty" quality. Soave is shipped in tall, slender bottles similar to those of Alsace and Germany, and it is an excellent companion to almost any dish demanding a light white wine, especially fish. One may be certain that it will offend few palates. And as with all traditional Italian wines—Bardolino, Valpolicella, Chianti, etc.—the addition of the term *Classico* on a label means a better product.

Three excellent reds of Veneto are the twins Valpolicella and Valpantena, fragrant and soft and subtle, and Bardolino, a coarser and sturdier wine than the others, often called the Beaujolais of Italy. Valpolicella was a great favorite of Julius Caesar; today a bottle of Valpolicella *Classico*, well aged, is considered to be one of Italy's "near greats." But Bardolino has a more modern glamour in that it is raised in what are among the most spectacular vineyards in the world, above the fabulously beautiful Lake Garda. Overlooking this jewel of all Italian inland seas, its crystal-blue waters mirroring the peaks of the surrounding mountains, the tiny village of Bardolino is one from which many a traveler has found it all but impossible to leave. On the opposite shore is Chiaretto, the source of an excellent *rosé* of the same name. *Rosé* wines of the surrounding region are often sold under the name of Chiarello. They are all good—but poor travelers.

Two rare white wines, and one less distinguished red now making big inroads abroad, are natives of this region. One is white Verdiso, dry and delicate; the other, better known, is the sweeter, redolent Prosecco, also white and usually found as a sparkling wine, though better when made as a still one. The Prosecco grape, known as the Glera, was well known in the days of the Romans, when it was religiously thought to possess the power to prolong life. The third wine, made to the south near Bologna, thus not properly a product of Veneto, is the semi-sparkling (*frizzante*), sugary red Lambrusco. The current wave of Lambrusco's popularity in the U.S.—as the successor to Spanish Sangria, Cold Duck and Portuguese *rosés*—baffles most serious wine lovers. Perhaps the testimony of a leading Italian gourmet—himself by no means a Lambrusco fan—may shed some small light on the phenomenon. After describing the heavy regional cuisine of Modena-Romagna (Lambrusco's birthplace), he adds that Lambrusco is one wine that "cuts through, like a knife" all oils and fats, sausages and dense sauces. So why not Lambrusco with reheated pizza and cheeseburgers?

Wines from the Hill Towns

Ordinary red Chianti, once the most exported table wine on earth, has no doubt had a larger part in alienating novice wine drinkers than all the other wines from all countries of the world taken together. Shipped the world over in those squat, round bottles known as *fiaschi*, picturesquely wrapped in straw jackets and enticingly decorated with red, white and green strands reflecting the Italian tricolor, 90 per cent of it was haphazardly made, improperly aged and inadequately corked. After a shipment has sat for a month or two on the sunny docks of Livorno or Genoa, and an individual bottle has rested cork up for the better part of a year on some merchant's shelf, it is no wine to buy to enhance Sunday dinner—except possibly when you've invited your mother-in-law. The end result, more often than not, is a sour, bitter liquid with an overpowering, unpleasant "burnt" taste. With well-made Chianti—a comparatively scarce wine—this same "burnt" flavor is one of its more attractive elements.

In one sense ordinary red Chianti may be likened to Liebfraumilch and Moselblümchen—it may be almost anything. Made in the province of Tuscany around Florence, it can be among the cheapest of all red wines, and its production is enormous. Much of it is simply a base of any common Tuscan wine, doctored and flavored with heavily boiled-down grape juice concentrate—contributing the "burnt" flavor.

But there is such a thing as fine Chianti, coming from the traditional zone, now given the *DOC* of *Chianti Classico*, that embraces parts (and only parts) of villages strung along the Via Chiantigiana, the ancient winding hill road running south from Florence to Siena and thence to Rome. Not too long ago the entire Chianti region was as much a caldron of graft and fraudulence as Burgundy in the 1920's and 1930's; then in recent years, under the guidance of the Barone Ricasoli—whose Brolio Chianti is among the best on the market—the best growers organized themselves into a group called the *Consorzio per la Difesa del Vino Tipico del Chianti* (the Society for the Protection of Genuine Chianti Wines). Their mark or symbol (*Marco Gallo*) on bottles is a black cockerel. Bottles bearing the *Marco Gallo* are what the consumer should still look for. The very finest, often labeled *Chianti Classico Riserva* to indicate superior wine from these best vineyards, are not shipped in the straw-jacketed *fiaschi*, but in ordinary bottles resembling those of Bordeaux. Another mark of distinction is the term *Imbottigliato alla tenuta* or *al Castello*, meaning estate- or castle-bottled, expensive wines that demand an age of from ten to fifteen years; in the hands of a good producer they often get at least part of it before being shipped.

Certain other Chiantis, not made in the "classic" zone, often use the mark or symbol of a cherub on labels. This is by no means the qualitative equal of that of the black cockerel, but the reader may at least know that a *fiascha* decorated by a cherub is better than one unadorned.

A well-made, aged Chianti, very much like a traditional Châteauneuf-du-Pape, has body and substance—for Chiantis are among the rare Italian wines made from a blend of several grapes. In the case of the reds, two native ones are used: the Sangiovese, the Canaiolo nero, and the white Trebbiano and Malvasia—to which are sometimes added the juices of either the Cabernet or the Malbec, both of which, as the reader will remember, are ingredients of red Bordeaux. A rare, expensive cousin of Chianti, Brunello di Montalcino, a wine of great power and requiring much age, is made in the hills of Siena, largely the product of proud hill-town family.

White Chianti—*Toscana Bianco* (Tuscany White)— is a dry and rather dull wine principally from the Trebbiano grape, though it may contain a certain amount of Burgundian Chardonnay, or of Roussanne, one of the ingredients of white Hermitage. The best white of Tuscany traditionally comes from the village of Pomino, but it is no exception to the general rule that the finest dry white wines are made in northern climes.

Another white of central Italy, from the vineyards of Montefiascone on Lake Bolsena, goes by the intriguing name of Est! Est!! Est!!! The words, which bear the ring of some Madison Avenue promotion more than the name of an ancient wine, are actually the Latin for "It is! It is!! It is!!!" The rather incredible myth behind them involves a bibulous German bishop, whose practice when traveling was to send his comparably bibulous valet ahead to assess the wines at the various inns en route. For taverns offering outstanding wines, the valet had instructions to chalk on the inn's outside wall the word *Est*—thus conveying to the master who followed that the wine *Est bonum* (is good). In this instance the servant exceeded himself in recording his enthusiasm for the Moscatello wine of the Umbrian village of Montefiascone. The bishop naturally stopped for the night—but the tale ends gloomily. He never resumed his journey, and drank himself to death. Anyone who doubts the legend may visit the bishop's nearby tomb.

Est! Est!! Est!!! is made in two versions, one a dry wine, the other a dessert wine. The latter is one of the few Italian white dessert wines that are produced as such. Except for the potent white Cinque-Terre[1] from Liguria near Genoa, perhaps its only serious rival comes from the region of Orvieto (also in central Italy), the source of two other white wines, one also dry, the other sweet. Like ordinary Chianti, Orvieto is sold in flask-like bottles, known as *pulcianelli*. Dry Orvieto,[2] exported in some quantity, has a peculiar, leathery taste, not unlike an inexpensive white Graves. We hazard the guess that the reader will prefer the sweet version, which he should find excellent with fruits and desserts. Other whites from this region are Frascati from Rome, Verdicchio dei Castelli di Jesi, and Velletri. All of them are strong in alcohol, markedly golden in color, and tend to be dry. Verdicchio, made close to the Adriatic coast near the port of Ancona and shipped in green amphora-shaped bottles, has a slightly spicy, individualistic quality, faintly reminiscent of an Alsatian Gewürztraminer. After Soave, Verdicchio is probably the most popular traditional Italian wine found abroad.

---

[1] Also to be found as a red and as a rare *rosé*, the latter being especially delicious.

[2] Like the Portuguese wines of Vinho Verde, most Orvieto grapes are grown under what are usually considered impossible vinicultural conditions—what the Italians call *coltura promiscua* (promiscuous farming). The vines are not grown in conventional vineyards, but as part of small-farm crops, being allowed to climb trees or trellises, or to seek out their livelihood amid garden crops.

Except for Marsala and Moscato, the fortified wines of Sicily (the Italian counterparts of Sherry and Port), the only remaining Italian wines of importance are Lacryma Christi (Tears of Christ) and Capri. True Lacryma Christi is raised on the slopes of Mount Vesuvius; it is principally a dry white wine with a treacherously high alcoholic content. But the reader should be warned that it may also be found as a sweetish sparkling wine, one of Italy's sparkling "generics"—and not made on or near the slopes of Vesuvius.

There is also a sparse amount of red and *rosé* Vesuvian Lacryma Christi, but neither is as good as the white. The white wines from Capri are dry and refreshing, though hardly notable. Most of them have never seen the Isle of the Blue Grotto—but are made on the mainland around the Bay of Naples.

The rage today for Italian wines has even surprised the Italians, and many rabbits (mostly white) have been hastily pulled out of hats, resulting in the creation of many new brand names involving fantasy or romantic bits of history. More often than not the origin of the wines behind these labels is unclear, and it is safe to say that all of them are distinctly inferior products, stemming from vineyard areas never before heard of except locally. They have no place in these pages. But among those not in this category—wines from non-classical but still recognized vineyard areas—we should mention Corvo from Sicily, the white soft and velvety, the red—with sufficient age—a distinguished product; red Sangiovese dei Colli Pesaresi from the same region as Verdicchio, and Venegazzù from the easternmost corner of Veneto, made with the same ingredients as red Bordeaux and considered by some to be one of Italy's best; plus a spate of clean, honest wines from the comparatively untrammeled region of Friuli-Venezia Guilia, bordering Yugoslavia. The best of these latter are red Merlot and Cabernet, and white Pinot Bianco and Pinot Grigio (Pinot Gris). Most Friuli-Venezia labels carry the term Collio—which means hill or slopes. Two famous hill districts are Collio Orientali and Collio Goriziano.

One need pay little attention to vintage years in Italy, even those from the northernmost region, the cool Italian Tyrol of the Alpine valleys. Years are increasingly appearing on labels—and of course should a year be mentioned for an Italian red (especially a *Classico* or a *Riserva*), the consumer may be reasonably sure that it is one which the producer hopes he (the consumer) will have the patience to age. In all likelihood this temporary abstention will be amply rewarding.

Summary

Although Italy produces a handful of good white wines, four-fifths of her output is in reds. Confusingly, some Italian wines are named after grapes and may come from almost any part of the country (and thus vary greatly in quality); others are named for places, and these are the best. A good rule of thumb: remember that the following five Italian wines (all red) are named after grapes—Barbera, Nebbiolo, Dolcetto, Freisa and Grignolino—and assume that all others are place names until you learn otherwise.

The exception is Chianti—the name of a small geographic area which is even nowadays prostituted. The best Chiantis, labeled *Classico*, should also bear a seal with a black cockerel. They are usually shipped in standard (Bordeaux-type) bottles—not the familiar flagon covered with basketwork. A superior Italian *Classico* or *Riserva* needs age: ten years is a good minimum.

In 1963, after centuries of confusion leading to mass misnomers and frauds, Italy initiated its first official wine laws, which are now in effect with *most* of the best-known vineyard areas. The rank of quality is defined by the words *Denominazione di Origine Controllata* (*DOC*); of super quality by *Denominazione Controllata e Garantita* (*DOCG*).

Barbaresco, Barolo, Valpolicella and Valpantena are four other excellent Italian reds, now exported in quantity. Two good dry whites are Soave and Verdicchio dei Castelli di Jesi; the best *rosés* are Lagrein Rosato and Chiaretto (Chiarello).

Vintage years for Italian wines are not important, except that a year on a bottle of a superior *Classico* or *Riserva* red usually means that the producer hopes the wine drinker will have the patience to allow it sufficient age. Usually these years will be 1961, 1964, 1971, 1975 and 1977.

TABLE K
Principal Italian Wines

Reds

Wine	Region
Barbaresco	Piedmont
*Barbera	Piedmont (principally)
Bardolino	Veneto
Barolo	Piedmont
Brunello di Montalcino	Tuscany
*Cabernet	Northern regions
Caldero	Italian Tyrol
Carema	Piedmont
Chianti	Tuscany
Cinque-Terre	Genoa (Liguria)
Corvo	Sicily
*†Dolcetto	Piedmont (principally)
*Freisa	Piedmont (principally)
Gattinara	Piedmont
Ghemme	Piedmont
*Grignolino	Piedmont (principally)
Lambrusco	Bologna (principally)
*Merlot	Northern regions
Montepulciano (Nobile di)	Tuscany
Santa Maddalena[1]	Italian Tyrol
Valpantena	Veneto
Valpolicella	Veneto
Valtellina	Italian Tyrol

Whites

Wine	Region
Capri	Campania
Chianti	Tuscany
Chiaretto (Chiarello)	Veneto
††Cinque-Terre	Genoa (Liguria)
*Cortese	Piedmont

[1]Known in Switzerland and Austria, where it is inexpensive and popular, as St. Magdalener.
*Grape name.
†Made both as a dry and as a sweet.
††Sweet.

TABLE K Continued
Principal Italian Wines

Wine	Region
Corvo	Sicily
†Est! Est!! Est!!!	Umbria
Frascati	Rome
*Gewürztraminer	Northern regions
Lacryma Christi	Campania
*Lagrein Rosato	Veneto
†Orvieto	Umbria
*††Prosecco	Veneto
Soave	Veneto
Terlano	Italian Tyrol
*Traminer	Northern regions
*Verdicchio dei Castelli di Jesi	Adriatic
Verdiso	Veneto

Sparklings (*Spumantis*)

Wine	Region
Asti (white)	Piedmont
Lacryma Christi (white)	(Generic)
*Nebbiolo (red)	Piedmont

CHAPTER 5

The Wines of Portugal and Spain

Consumos, Pastos and Reservas

The wines of the Iberian Peninsula—those of Spain and her little neighbor, Portugal—once served to slacken the thirst of Rome. Cicero alludes to the lush vineyards of Lusitania (the Roman name for Portugal); and wines were being shipped from the Roman port of Tarragona, on Spain's Mediterranean coast, long before the legendary conversion of the Iberians by St. Paul. In fact, the Iberian vineyards of that day appear to have been even more widespread and bountiful than those of southern France.

Yet perhaps the most intriguing thing about wine making in Portugal and Spain in our time is that modernity has only recently begun to catch up. In Portugal the grapes travel from vine to vat over roads engineered and paved by the Romans centuries ago, in primitive basketwork ox carts with solid wooden wheels and creaking axles, of a design unchanged since Roman times. In both countries the grapes are often still trod by human feet; every part and appendage of the grape that nature intended for wine—animal, vegetable and mineral—may be

[136]

found in the fermenting vats. Only at the largest and most progressive vineyards does one come across newfangled contraptions used today throughout most of the wine-making world. Shortcut methods of stripping the grapes from their stems and stalks, to produce a lighter and faster-maturing wine, or using a centrifuge to clarify it, are looked on with suspicion. The end result, as is to be expected, is wine which, when young, is coarse and usually distasteful—overburdened with tannin and acids—yet when adequately aged often proves to be of unusual quality.

The wine drinker is to be cautioned, even so, that he will not find Iberian wines very similar to French or German wines. There is no Spanish Château Lafite-Rothschild, nor a Portuguese Schloß Johannisberg. Iberian soils and climates differ vastly from those of France and Germany; most Iberian wine grapes are indigenous, unrelated to those found elsewhere. The wines have a different taste; one needs to get used to them. Yet once their harshness and robust youth, especially with the reds, have been placated by time, one will hardly fail to spot a unique richness and depth of flavor which can only be the result of sound (and commendably old-fashioned) vinicultural practices. The best Iberian wines are still made as wines were made in France a hundred and fifty years ago.

Both Portugal and Spain rely heavily on wine as an integral part of their national diets—and, for the most part, very bad wine it is. The *ordinaires*—those known as *vinhos de consumo* in Portugal and *vinos de pasto* in Spain—are unbelievably raw concoctions. They are always consumed very young—and with the exception of the so-called *vinhos verdes* (young wines) of Portugal—happily never come our way. Red *consumos* and *pastos* pucker the mouth and cloy the throat; the whites may smell disarmingly enchanting—like fresh apples or peaches, perhaps—but when swallowed give rise to disappointment. Unless one has never known anything better, they simply cannot be said to be potable.

In both countries the finer wines almost invariably go by the classification of *Reserva*—a term used to indicate the proudest product of a producer from a vintage year he considers superior. Before it is released for sale a white Portuguese or Spanish *Reserva* will usually be at least five years old; a red, ten. This will have involved two or three years in the barrel, followed by approximately the same period in the bottle for the whites—and a minimum of five years in the barrel for the reds. In the Rioja region of northern Spain, the universally

THE VINEYARDS OF
Portugal
and Spain

0   50   100   150
MILES

Bay of Biscay

FRANCE

GALICA

R. MIÑO

Haro

RIOJA

R. EBRO

VINHO
VERDE

DOURO
(PORT)

R. DOURO

R. DUERO

Valladolid

Barcelona

Oporto

Tarragona

DÃO

Madrid
Toledo

R. TAJO (TAGUS)

COLARES

VALDEPEÑAS

BUCELAS
Lisbon

R. GUADIANA

SETÚBAL

PORTUGAL

SPAIN

ALGARVE

R. GUADALQUIVIR

SHERRY

MÁLAGA

Jerez
Cádiz

Málaga

MEDITERRANEAN SEA

ATLANTIC

OCEAN

MOROCCO

ATLANTIC

SPAIN

PORTUGAL

Lisbon

Madrid

OCEAN

Madeira
Is.(Port)

600 Miles

MOROCCO

acknowledged source of the finest wines of that country, some of the top producers still age their *Reserva* red wines "in the wood" for ten years, followed by ten or more in the bottle! For good Iberian wines this is none too much—and by local standards, of course, *Reservas* are expensive wines. Yet when one learns that a glass of *consumo* or *pasto* at a Portuguese or Spanish bar costs only the equivalent of a few pennies, it follows that even the price of a *Reserva* abroad cannot be high. In view of the spiraling prices of wines from other European countries, it is not surprising that we see more Iberian wines. Of late years, also, many Iberians have been concentrating on making wines for foreign tastes, producing them so they are ready to drink far sooner.

Reservas are vintage wines—but with a difference. Whereas the advent of a bountiful year, such as 1959 in France or Germany, sent every vintner scurrying—virtually before his grapes were crushed—to market his wine in a bottle bearing the magic year, a *Reserva* of Portugal or Spain is rarely designated as such until it has been at least two years in the barrel. At that time its intrinsic quality is assessed and, if it passes the test, it is chosen for a *Reserva* status and a long life. Otherwise it is bottled forthwith and released. The word for vintage on Portuguese labels is *Colheita;* on Spanish ones, *Cosecha.* The important point for the wine drinker to bear in mind is that the presence of either of these two words with a year does not necessarily indicate that a wine has been given sufficient age in the producer's cellar to become truly fine. We shall cover this aspect more fully when dealing with the wines of the two countries separately.

Portuguese Wines

Portugal, in many ways, may be numbered among the more fortunate countries of Europe. A land of happy and incredibly hospitable people, it is endowed (thanks to the Romans) with well-engineered roads, an enviably diversified agriculture, the best sardines and the finest cork. Portugal ranks third, after France and Italy, in wine consumption per capita, but its wine industry is only beginning to come into its own. As recently as fifty years ago, with the exception of the fortified dessert wines of Port and Madeira, only three Portuguese wines were known at all to the outside world—the balance, however good, being restricted to internal consumption. These were the sweetish white Moscatel of Setúbal, a dry white wine known as Bucelas and the strong and oftentimes unappealingly harsh (when young) red

Colares. During the past decades, however, the Portuguese government has made appreciable efforts to develop its wine industry, with emphasis on exports. Although much remains to be done before any vast number of Portuguese table wines (except *rosés*) become well known to foreign palates, under the supervision of the Junta Nacional do Vinho (National Wine Board) great strides have been made in isolating the most suitable grapes and in educating the vintners.

The Junta Nacional initiated state-owned cooperative cellars to serve the small vintners, and even conducted schools for wine waiters—a vital innovation in a country where perhaps only at the ultra-cosmopolitan Ritz Hotel in Lisbon did one even find wineglasses of suitable size and proportion, or waiters who did not persist in filling them to the very brim. In almost any Iberian restaurant a red wine on its way to your table may have been shaken like a Daiquiri; it may well have arrived in one's glass well chilled—whereas its white sister would perhaps have been the temperature of warm broth.

A white wine in Portuguese is a *vinho branco;* a red is a *vinho tinto* (incidentally, the same word, *tinto,* is used for red in Spain). A *rosé* is a *rosé* or a *maduro,* sometimes a *clarete;* and all table wines go by the term *vinhos de mesa. Doce* is the usual term for sweet wine; *adamado* (literally: "for dames") the colloquial one, though frequently seen on a label. In addition to the two regions producing Port and Madeira, the Junta Nacional officially recognized six other regions for the production of *vinhos de mesa,* for each of which it has established rules and vinicultural specifications comparable to the *Appellations Contrôlées* of France. Wines from each of these regions are authorized to bear the insignia of their respective *União Vinicola Regional* (Vinicultural Union)—abbreviated on sticker labels as *U.V.R.* Whereas the presence of an official sticker is a guarantee of genuineness, it should not be automatically construed, as will be seen in Table L, that there are not other good Portuguese wines from unregulated sections of the country.

Proceeding from north to south, the officially recognized regions and their wines are as follows:

Vinho Verde (or *Minho*). The northwestern section of Portugal, extending from the Douro River (the home of Port) northward to the Spanish border. In addition to being one of the more beautiful and verdant parts of the country, the Vinho Verde region has certain picturesque vinicultural practices. Comparable to the Orvieto section of Italy, the vines are allowed to climb high on trees along the fence rows (a practice which gives rise to many accidents, especially after bibulous noon hours, during harvesting), or strung on trellises surrounding each field, which is planted with other crops, such as corn and potatoes. The Vinho Verde is a country of small landowners, and each square of land is so planned that if one crop fails or falters, the profits from another will bring the family through the winter. And since the vines grow along with crops of fruits, grains and vegetables, they often receive a copious fertilization—the exact opposite of the usual treatment of the wine grape in other parts of the world.

Vinho Verde (the wine), which may be red, white or *rosé*, is not, as one might expect, "green" wine—but young wine. Intended to be drunk young, it is customarily bottled very early in the spring following its birth, when it is undergoing a second, or so-called malolactic, fermentation. This renders it mildly sparkling (*pétillant*) and is responsible for a great part of its charm. Unfortunately, when exported to the United States—because of the high tax levied on anything of a sparkling nature—it must be a comparatively still wine. White Vinho Verde, slightly acid and relatively low in alcohol, is especially pleasant as an accompaniment to those many fish and seafood dishes for which the Portuguese are so renowned. The *rosé* is usually less acid. Red Vinho Verde, a very popular *vinho de consumo* among the northern Portuguese, is something else again. Smelling enticingly like a concentrate of fresh raspberries, its particular degree of rawness strips the very lining from the mouth and throat. The Vinho Verdes are all made from indigenous grapes, the predominant red one being the Vinão (with varying dosages of many another unfamiliar: the Barraçal, the Espadeiro, the Azal Tinto, the Cainhos and the Brancelho). White Vinho Verde comes principally from the Azal Branco and the Dourado.

Dão. The fertile, rolling countryside along the river Dão in central Portugal, surrounding the quaint town of Viseu, is the largest and most important area of Portugal producing *vinhos de mesa*. Well-aged reds from the Dão—labels should at least bear the word *Velho* (old), *Garrafeira* (selected) or, better yet, *Reserva*—are all wines of much character, with strong bouquets reminiscent of red Burgundies. The similarity is not coincidental. Although in years gone by Dão wines were made from half a dozen or more indigenous grapes, Dão vintners have been concentrating on a grape known as the Pinta Pinheira, recently identified as the Pinot Aigret, once used for the celebrated still red wines of Champagne and extreme northern Burgundy. Although promising efforts are being made by many of the Dão producers to create younger wines that are more palatable and attractive, traditional Dão reds usually require an aging of ten years. The best *Reservas* are often found at twice this age. The white wines of the Dão are perhaps the most universally appealing whites of Portugal. Made principally from the Arinto grape (a cousin of the Riesling), sometimes with the addition of a little juice of the Sémillon (of Bordeaux), they possess body and smoothness, and are reminiscent both in taste and character of a white Hermitage or any other sound white wine of the central Rhône.

Bucelas. White Bucelas, once known in England as "Lisbon Hock," and before that, in Shakespeare's day, as Charneco (Charneca is a village in the Bucelas region), is one of the three traditional *vinhos de mesa* of Portugal to have been exported in any quantity. Also made from the Arinto or Riesling, in the hands of good producers it is a clean, very dry wine, reminiscent of a superior Graves. At those periods in history when French wines were either barred from England or subject to a prohibitive tariff, Bucelas from Portugal always took a sharp rise in popularity. It eventually fell from grace, however, when Portuguese vintners gave in to the temptation of fortifying it with brandy, comparable to Port and Madeira. Nowadays, under the guidance of an enlightened officialdom, Bucelas is again coming into its own. Its vineyards, spread across a lovely up-and-down countryside fifty miles north of Lisbon, are among the more beautiful in all Portugal.

Colares. Red Colares is another of the classic wines of Portugal. Traditionally known as "Ocean Wine" because of the proximity of its vineyards to the sea, it is produced from the Ramisco grape—distinctly a native of Portugal—under conditions that are certainly among the most extraordinary in the world. North of Lisbon's fashionable seaside resort of Estoril (Coast of the Sun), the road zigzags along a jagged, mountainous coastline, covered with heather and dotted with round stone windmills. High on a bleak promontory in the distance is the lighthouse of Cabo de Roca—the westernmost point of Continental Europe. Suddenly the road descends steeply to a level countryside where magnificent beaches line the coast, and where for several miles inland a receding ocean has left a land of pure sand. The only crops at Colares are pines and vines. As one trudges through the groves of turpentine pines, one never expects to come across a clearing filled with grapevines, nor—unless one stumbles on a vineyard which is being newly planted—would one ever guess that the roots of these particular vines often penetrate thirty feet of sand to obtain moisture from a basic clay subsoil. In fact, planting the vines at Colares is no simple affair: to dig a narrow trench in thirty feet of sand requires shoring up the sides, and as the excavation proceeds, the diggers cover their heads with ludicrous wicker baskets that may allow them to breathe for a time in the event of a cave-in. When the roots are finally embedded in the moist clay, the trenches are filled up gradually, year by year, as the shoots of the vines lengthen. Frequently the original ground level is not obtained for four or five years.

The sandy vineyards (*areias*) of Colares are additionally unique in that they have never been beset by the *phylloxera*, the curse which at one time devastated nearly all the vineyards of Europe. The sands of Colares are too fine and deep for the tiny aphids to burrow through and reach the roots. In consequence, Colares is one of the few wines extant which is still made from grapes not grafted to American wild-grape root stock. Strong in taste and exceptionally high in alcohol, it probably requires more age in the barrel and bottle than any other Portuguese red; but when adequately matured it does possess a softness and a flower-like bouquet comparable to that of a good St.-Émilion. White Colares, made from the Arinto grape, lacks distinction.

Carcavelos and *Moscatel de Setúbal*. Known in Portugal as *vinhos generosos*, meaning table wines fortified with alcohol, even though they are not subjected to the same aging and special blending processes of Port or Madeira. Carcavelos, from a small (and fast-disappearing) group of vineyards in the western suburbs of Lisbon, is a sweetish red with an alcoholic content approaching 20 per cent. Almond-tasting and definitely demanding an acquired taste, it is drunk as an *apéritif* and is exported chiefly to Scandinavia. Though the Junta Nacional designated the Carcavelos region as an authorized *União Vinícola*, the government does not appear to be encouraging its production.

Moscatel de Setúbal is produced both as a red and as a white wine—the latter being, loosely speaking, the Sauternes of Portugal. Made, as its name implies, from a variety of the same Muscat grape responsible for many other fortified wines (including France's Roussillon and Muscat de Frontignan), the best of it is labeled under the names of

Palmela and Azeitão—two villages in which it is most successfully produced. The vineyards lie on the peninsula south of Lisbon, in a warm pocket behind the Arrabida Mountains just west of the fishing town of Setúbal. Moscatels are heavily fortified, and have a characteristic grapy flavor by no means appealing to everyone. Because of the lagging world demand for sweet dessert wines, its producers try to develop an attractive dry wine that will be below 15 per cent in alcohol. The results have not been outstanding; much of it has gone to Germany for *Sekt*.

The Setúbal region is also the best-known source of another Portuguese red, Periquita, made from the grape of the same name. Like the Ramisco, the Periquita flourishes in sandy soil, and until comparatively recently the Periquita vineyards of Setúbal were free of the *phylloxera*. Periquita in its youth has an enticing aroma—but the reader is cautioned to beware of tasting it until it has attained a seasoned age, when it should resemble a light but very good Médoc.

Portuguese *rosés*, nowadays as ubiquitous as the stars, are in a class by themselves: they need neither to be *Reservas* nor *Garrafeiras*—and some of them are among the best and most potable *rosés* in existence. *Rosés* are made all over Portugal with almost equal success. Certainly one of the most popular goes by the brand name of Mateus, which comes in an attractive brown *Bocksbeutel* and is made in a massive, ultra-modern plant near Oporto. A blend of strictly local grapes—the Alvarelhão, the Bastardo, the Touriga and the Souzão—Mateus is found abroad both as a still and as a carbonated wine. In our opinion, the former is far preferable. Its strongest competitor, sold abroad as Lancers, comes from the Setúbal region, and tends to be a harsher wine—attributable, no doubt, to the presence of the virulent Periquita in the mixture. Two other *rosés*, even more recommendable to the serious wine lover, are Lagosta (the lobster) from the Vinho Verde region and Moura Basto. Portuguese *rosés* are always ready to drink when bottled, and their labels rarely carry a vintage year.

Unlike the wines of France or Germany, even the best of Portugal are almost never associated with a vineyard (*quinta*), but instead carry a regional or brand name. For this reason we have included in our listings of Portuguese wines (Table L) the names of some of the larger and more reliable wine houses (*adegas*), the quality of whose wines may in general be counted on.

TABLE L
Wines of Portugal

Reds (*Tintos*)

Bussaco (Buçaco)	So-called "claret" from central Portugal. Two of the best: Quinta de San Miguel and the Caves do Mosteiro.
*Carcavelos	A sweet, fortified red wine, best as an *apéritif*.
Cartaxo	The best is produced by the Adega Cunhas.
*Colares	Portugal's traditionally finest red. Three of the best producers are the Visconde de Salreu, Jorge da Silva and the firm of Tavares e Rodrigues.
*Dão	Two outstanding names: Grão Vasco and San Pedro.
Douro	One good red is called Imperial Evel—a lively, tart wine, resembling a California Zinfandel.
Grantom and Lagoa (Algarve)	Few good wines are made in Algarve, the southernmost province of Portugal, but the light reds of Grantom and Lagoa are exceptions.
Mealhada	A fragrant red from a district north of Lisbon, requiring much age. Among its best producers is the firm of Carvalho, Ribeiro e Ferreira.
Pinhel	A light and pleasant red made in central Portugal to the south of the Douro region.
Serradayres	Traditional brand name for an excellent red table wine, the best of which is made in the province of Estremadura.

Whites (*Blancos*)

*Bucelas	Made from the Arinto or Riesling grape. A dry wine reminiscent of a white Graves. The best producer is J. Camillo Alves.
Bussaco (Buçaco)	White Bussacos resemble the whites of the central Loire. They are clean and slightly sweet, with delicious, mild aromas. Those from

*Indicates an officially recognized region, table wines from which are entitled to bear the authorized *U.V.R.* sticker.

TABLE L Continued
Wines of Portugal

	the Caves do Mosteiro are to be highly recommended.
Douro	Granjo, slightly sweet but with excellent body, resembles French Monbazillac. Other recommendable whites are Planalto, Compo Grande, Grão Vasco Branco and Ermida.
Lagoa	A dry white with a lovely yellow tinge, from Algarve on the southern coast, where very little good wine is produced. Low in alcohol.
*Moscatel de Setúbal	The best is bottled as Palmela and Azeitão. Fortified with grape alcohol to attain a content of 18 per cent, often called the Sauternes of Portugal. The principal producer is José Maria da Fonseca; this firm also produces a dry Moscatel ("Branco Seco").
Obidos	A walled town north of Lisbon whose whites are peculiarly light and refreshing, with a nice aroma. One of the best comes from the Quinta Gaieras.
Santarém	A town north of Lisbon on the Tagus River. The whites of Santarém are fruity and dry, with a pleasing aftertaste. The best (and rarest) comes from the Quinta Abidis.
*Vinho Verde	"Young wine" from northern Portugal. Acidic and light, it can be most refreshing. The rarest of all from the Vinho Verde region is Moncão—light and mellow, with a delicate bouquet of wild flowers.

Rosés

Among the most popular Portuguese *rosés* now exported are Mateus (Douro), Lancers (Setúbal) and Lagosta (Vinho Verde).

Recommended Wine houses

The following is a partial list of reliable Portuguese wine houses:
Carvalho, Ribeiro e Ferreira
Caves Aliança
José Maria da Fonseca

TABLE L Continued
Wines of Portugal

Real Compania Vinicola do Norte de Portugal
Sociedade Agricola de Quinta da Aveleda
Sociedade Agricola e Comercial dos Vinhos Messias
Sociedade Agricola Moura Basto
Sociedade Comercial dos Vinhos de Mesa de Portugal (Sogrape)
Sociedade dos Vinhos Borges e Irmão
Tavares e Rodrigues
Vinicola do Vale do Dão

Spanish Wines

There is probably no better bargain in the world than a fine old vintage of Spain—and oftentimes nothing harder to find, even in Spain itself. The truly good wines of Spain are produced in lamentably small quantities, and almost entirely for domestic consumption. Furthermore, traditional Spanish wine making *in general* can only be described by the word "casual"—a fault which has been the basis for the often-heard criticism of them: their variability. Not only from year to year, but even between one bottle and another of the *same* year from the *same* vineyard and with identical labels, Spanish wines have varied enormously. Regrettably, Spanish government agencies responsible for guiding the industry reflect this very same casualness. Nominal regulations and standards exist for the vineyards of most of Spain's forty-nine provinces—and many Spanish wines are entitled to an official label of quality, *Denominación de Origen*—yet an official sticker on a bottle of Spanish wine remains all but meaningless. In fact, it may frankly be said that the only reliable mark of quality on any bottle of Spanish wine is that of the unofficial organization of vintners of the Rioja region (*Garantía de Origen*), the indisputable source of Spain's best wines. However, this is not to say that many individual producers are making far better wines today than formerly, especially for export purposes.

Leaving the wines of the Rioja aside for the moment, most other Spanish table wines may be divided into two classes: the regional wines (*vinos del país* or *vinos de la tierra*) and those from a particular set of vineyards associated with a specific town. Far and away the most pop-

ular and widespread of the regionals, often called the Beaujolais of
Spain, is Valdepeñas (Valley of Stones). Valdepeñas may be either red
or white, though the red is far better, and more frequently exported. It
is produced in tremendous quantity on the arid high tablelands of New
Castile, south of Toledo in the central part of the country. High in
tannin, often more than a little vinegary, it is almost always drunk in
its native land when less than a year old. Because of its power (not
necessarily alcoholic), the Spaniards call it *peléon*—a word which
means fighter. The fact that a *chato* or small glass of it costs the equivalent of a few pennies in a Madrid bar has no bearing on the fierceness
of the fighter: even in small quantities *peléon* can be a most invigorating
drink.

The second most popular regional wine of Spain is probably Ribero
(or Ribeiro), from the lovely province of Galicia, north of the Portuguese border. Galician vineyards are in effect merely a continuation of
the vinicultural pattern of Portugal's Vinho Verde region to the south.
Galicia is also a country of small landowners, where each individual
plot of corn or oats has its quota of grapevines climbing the trees or
strung on neat trellises along the walls or hedgerows, and its tomblike
little corncrib raised high on granite posts and surmounted with a cross.
Like the wines of the Vinho Verde, Ribero is usually *pétillant* and
rather acidic—nonetheless, it is much coveted by the Spaniards. The
best of it is white. Curiously, the most popular drink among the Gali-
cians themselves is the excellent sparkling cider that abounds in this
particular corner of Spain.

On the opposite corner of Spain is Catalonia, the source of many
more refined and localized wines. Among others are those called Prior-
atos, or Tarragona wines, from the Mediterranean city of the same
name—strong wines that were once fortified with brandy and, as such,
known to our forefathers as "Tarragona Port." Now many Tarragona
wines go to France to be made into *apéritifs*, as does much of the white
(and very pleasant) wine of Alicante, the Mediterranean city of Spain
where "the sky is always the bluest." Catalan wines can be red, white
or *rosé*. Some of the best and most exportable still wines are made in
considerable quantity near Villafranca del Panadès by a firm called
Torres, many of the more successful ones made from French and German grapes; and sparklings by Cordorniú, from the same area, have also
won international recognition. Others, acceptable to foreign palates, are
the reds, white and *rosés* or Perelada, made north of Barcelona along

the forbidding but extraordinarily beautiful Costa Brava. Another is Alella, a rather heavy and sweet white, also made near Barcelona. Alella comes in slim, tall bottles, comparable to those of Germany; the best known is the white Mafiel, though there is also a red Alella of lesser quality.

One comes upon a few other gems scattered elsewhere across Spain. There is the exceptionally delicate white Rueda, from Valladolid, northwest of Madrid. Considered by many to be the finest white wine of Spain, and certainly in a class with the whites of the Rioja, Rueda is hard to find away from its home ground, and it is rumored that much of it is surreptitiously wasted for blending with inferior whites. Yet another fragrant white wine comes from Yepes, a small town east of Toledo in central Spain. Two reds in the same class are worthy of mention. Although one often hears that no wine but Sherry is made in the region of Jerez de la Frontera, the fact is that this area is the source of two of the pleasantest red wines of Spain. One of them, known as Carlo, is a fragrant wine from Sanlúcar de Barrameda, a seaside town on the southern coast just above the gleaming, whitewashed port of Cádiz; and from the village of Rota, a few miles down the coast, comes a light red wine, much savored by Spaniards, known as Tintillo.

Wines of the Rioja

The best proof of the comparative excellence of Riojan wines is that on the wine lists of nearly every good hotel and restaurant in Spain they appear almost to the exclusion of all others—the exceptions being an occasional Alella or a Rueda, or perhaps a better-than-average Valdepeñas.

The Rioja is the Côte d'Or of Spain—and of about the same size and proportions. Its center is the little wine town of Haro, which lies on the Ebro River in the northeastern part of the country, just south of the foothills of the Pyrénées. The climate of the Rioja is more rigorous, and the summers shorter, than on the southern tablelands where the mass of Spanish wine is produced, and the resultant wines more resemble those of northern countries, such as Germany and France. In fact, the Ebro at Haro could be taken for a mountain river of France itself. Lush fields and groves of poplars line its gravelly banks, and the swift-flowing, opaquely green mountain water abounds with fish. To the north is the high protective plateau of the Sierra de Cantabria, over the top of which a fifty-mile-long, low-lying cloud is apt to appear and slide dramatically down into the valley—like a great white blanket not tucked in—only to disappear as it meets the tepid air below.

Unlike most other vineyard areas of the world, the Riojan country-side, dotted with little landlocked lakes and walled hill towns that bespeak the days of a more prosperous Spain—a Spain with colonies and a world trade—is one of diversified agriculture. The vines are inter-spersed with crops of wheat, olives and fruits; the soil is unusually fer-tile for vineyard land—bright red clay, filled with small stones. One phenomenon of the region is that until the beginning of our century it was free of the *phylloxera*—and thus for more than thirty years an important source of wine for other European nations at a time when their own vineyards were giving forth only a comparative trickle. This undoubtedly is the origin of the labeling practice of so many Riojan wines with quasi-French names—"Spanish Claret," "Spanish Chablis," "Spanish Burgundy" and so on—terms which are now being gradually discarded, or forbidden as misleading by other countries.

Needless to say, no white Rioja ever really tasted like a Chablis or a Rhine wine, and a well-aged Rioja red—a *Reserva*—can be only remotely compared to a good Burgundy or a Bordeaux.[1] The old wives' tale so often heard, that the Rioja was colonized in the 1880s by Bor-deaux vintners who introduced French grapes and taught the Riojans how to make wine in the French manner, is hotly denied by the Riojans themselves, who are justly proud of their own wine-making traditions. The truth of the matter appears to be that a Riojan delegation, visiting France some thirty years before the *phylloxera* was ever heard of, did bring back a certain number of French vines to be tried out on the banks of the Ebro. Of these, only two seem to have survived, and then only in a minor capacity—Bordeaux's red Cabernet Sauvignon and the Grenache, itself by no means strictly French. As with the Portuguese wines, the grapes used in Spain are indigenous varieties whose connec-tion with the accepted ones of France, Germany and Italy have never been thoroughly traced. Along with the Grenache or Garnacha, Riojan wines are made chiefly from the native Tempranillo (the *tinto* for the

[1] Some Riojan producers do still make a distinction between what they conceive of as a Bordeaux type (claret or *Cepa Burdeos*) and a Burgundy type (*Cepa Borgoña*). Neither actually involves the use of French grapes—the only difference being that the Burgundy type is made as a lighter and less dry wine.

reds, the *blanco* for the whites), with several other natives called Graciano, Mazuelo and Viura.

However little the French had a hand in it, the fact remains that the best wines of the Rioja are still fermented and aged very much as those of Bordeaux and Burgundy were many decades ago—without any shortcut methods. This accounts for their extreme rawness when young—as well as the fact that a properly aged *Reserva*, once its copious dosages of tannins and acids have been sufficiently "married" in the bottle, may be a very good wine indeed. The best Riojan whites, provided they have not been kept in casks too long, have a softness and body one rarely finds elsewhere; the reds possess an almost overpowering bouquet, a richness of color and a finesse that renders them among the finest.

The Rioja region is traditionally (though not officially) divided into three parts, the best of which is known as the Rioja Alta (upper), adjoining Haro. Rioja Alta wines are lighter in alcohol than others of the region and are acknowledged to possess the greatest "breeding"; those of the Rioja Baja (lower), the part surrounding the industrial town of Alfaro to the southeast, are of less repute. The other section (the Rioja Alavesa, on the north bank of the river) is in general the source of what the Spaniards deem "wines for ready drinking." Paradoxically, the two very best *bodegas* or wine houses, those of the Marqués de Riscal and the Marqués de Murrieta, are to be found in or near this "middle ground." The largest and best *bodegas* of the Rioja are entitled to affix a locally authorized sticker of origin, assuring an added rank of quality.

In recent years many of the leading *bodegas* of the Rioja—along with some in Catalonia—have been attempting to tailor their wines for better acceptance abroad; that is, making the reds thinner and ready to drink sooner, and modifying the Iberian tradition of keeping both reds and whites overly long in wooden casks, thus preserving their natural freshness. This movement has been a boon to the foreign consumer who is forced to pay unrealistic prices for French and German wines. In this same connection, though, the reader should be warned against a recent trend among certain other Spanish producers, that of shipping their cheapest wines under false varietal or grape names, such as Pinot Chardonnay or Pinot Noir. The trend—comparable to the French "Country Wines" effort—is obviously aimed at competing with California premium wines, capitalizing on the public's ignorance and the glamour of a foreign label. Recently the United States, for one, has been successful in banning some of these Spanish "varietal" labels, but not necessarily the wines themselves.

A vintage year in Spain is known as a *cosecha*—and Spanish labels often bear the adjectival variation *cosechado*, meaning "of the vintage" of such-and-such a year. On the label of a good producer the term *Escogida* (specially chosen) may have significance; but the reader should be warned that the two most common terms used for "old"— *Pasado* and *Viejo*—mean little. The best producers give the *cosecha*, or else the terms *5° Año, 6° Año*, etc., to indicate how long the wine was kept in barrel and bottle before release. As with Portuguese wines, good or bad vintage years do not exist in the sense that they do for France and Germany. A year for a *Reserva* is purely a matter of a decision on the part of a particular vintner that a wine is deserving of further age—and this decision is not made until the wine has been in the barrel for several years. For example, 1932 may be a *Reserva* year for one producer, whereas 1934 might be for his neighbor. The wine drinker may be certain, however, that in the case of the best Riojan producers, the word *Reserva* with a year on the label is an intended mark of quality.

Riojan wines are not labeled with vineyard or geographical names, but instead have a trade or house name bestowed upon them by their producers, whose establishments throughout Spain are called *bodegas*— the equivalent of *caves* in France and *adegas* in Portugal. Table M lists a number of the best Riojan producers.

TABLE M
Principal Spanish Wines

REGIONAL WINES
Reds (*Tintos*)

Wine	*Locality*
Alella	Catalonia
Carlo	Cádiz
Perelada	Mediterranean
Priorato (Tarragona)	Catalonia

TABLE M Continued
Principal Spanish Wines

Ribero (or Ribeiro)	Galicia
Rota Tintillo	Cádiz
Valdepeñas (El Morenito)	Central Spain
Villafranca del Panadès	Catalonia

Whites (*Blancos*)

Alella (Mafiel)	Catalonia
Alicante	Mediterranean
Perelada (*rosé* also recommended)	Mediterranean
Ribero (or Ribeiro)	Galicia
Rueda	North-Central Spain
Yepes	Central Spain
Valdepeñas (El Morenito)	Central Spain
Villafranca del Panadès	Catalonia

TRADITIONAL WINE HOUSES (*BODEGAS*) AND WINES OF THE RIOJA*

Reds (*Tintos*)

Compañía Vinícola del Norte de España	*Cune* Imperial Reserve Viña Real *Reserva Oro* "Royal Claret"
Franco Españolas	
La Rioja Alta	Viña Ardanza *Reservas* "904" and "890"
López de Heredia	Viña Tondonia *Reserva* Viña Bosconia *Reserva*
Marqués de Murrieta	Castillo Ygay Ygay
Marqués de Riscal	Traditionally one of the finest producers of the Rioja. The *Reservas* and the older wines are to be especially recommended.
Palacios, Ignacio	*Reserva* Especial
Paternina, Frederico	All *Reservas*

*Trade or house names are given in the right-hand column.

TABLE M Continued
Principal Spanish Wines

Vega Sicilia
Valbuena

Not strictly Riojan wines, the reds of Vega Sicilia and of Valbuena are among the best in Spain. The vineyards of Vega Sicilia have been taken over as a government experimental station, but excellent old wines are still in circulation.

Whites (*Blancos*)

Compañía Vinícola del Norte de España	*Cune*
	Monopole *Reserva*
La Rioja Alta	*Reserva* Blanco Extra
López de Heredia	Viña Tondonia
	Viña Zaconia
Marqués de Murrieta	Castillo Ygay

Rosés (*Rosados*)

Rosé wines from López de Heredia, the Marqués de Murrieta and the Bodegas Bilbainas are especially recommended. Riojan *rosés*, locally called *ojo de gallo* (cock's eye), are strong in taste and color and may be likened to those of the lower Rhône in France. Bottles rarely carry a vintage year (*cosecha*).

Summary

Portuguese and most Spanish wines are made from native grapes (and thus taste different from other European wines), as well as by old-fashioned methods that require more aging than most other wines. A well-made, five-year-old white is usually, by Iberian standards, just ready to drink—a red needs much more time yet. For our palates, a five-year-old Iberian white has too much of the taste of oak, and many producers of both countries are beginning to catch on.

The best are "vintage wines" called (in both countries) *Reservas*. Other terms meaning "very old" or "selected," generally indicative of quality, are *Garrafeira* (Port.) and *Escogida* (Sp.). Common terms meaning "old" (*Velho*, Port.; *Pasado, Viejo*, Sp.) cannot be relied on.

The Portuguese excel in *rosé* wines and their white Vinhos Verdes. The best traditional Portuguese wines are white Bucelas and red

Colares, rarely exported. Dão reds are excellent when ten years old or more—especially if the word *Reserva* is present on the label.

Spain's most popular red—its "Beaujolais"—is vinegary, young Valdepeñas. Better, lighter and more readily drinkable wines also come from Catalonia. But the indisputably best wines of Spain are from the small northern Rioja region. Inexpensive Riojas (usually intended for export) are labeled with quasi-French names: "Spanish Claret," "Spanish Chablis," etc. For the best Riojas, all bearing the trade names of the traditionally finest wine houses or *bodegas*, see Table M.

Vintage years for both countries are inconsequential. A vintage year of a *Reserva* is meaningful: first as an indication of the wine's true age, second as an indication of its producer's pride in this particular wine.

CHAPTER 6

Wines of Other European Countries

Switzerland

In proportion to her size, the little country of Switzerland consumes a great deal of wine, most of which is imported. She is one of Spain's very best customers, as well as Italy's, and each year the produce of many of France's top vineyards are cornered by the Swiss. Beaujolais is a great favorite—and, strange as it may seem, a bottle of Romanée-Conti or Chambertin is a far more common sight in the window of a Swiss wineshop than in a French one.

Very few Swiss wines reach other countries. The great majority of them are white, the best made from either a Riesling-Sylvaner combination (in Switzerland imitatively called the Johannisberg) or the Chasselas grape, in some parts of Switzerland called the Fendant. If the lowly Chasselas, which we have already met in Alsace and at Pouilly-sur-Loire, can be said to excel anywhere, it does so on the high, terraced vineyards of Switzerland, the loftiest in the world.

Swiss wines, like the pure mountain air in which they are grown, are known for their freshness and zest, and for their "clean" tastes. Swiss wines were favorites of the Romans, who probably brought the red

Pinot noir and Gamay from Burgundy, the white Riesling, Sylvaner and Chasselas from Germany, and perhaps the red Merlot from south-western France. Nowadays they are produced on the Rhine in the north and the Rhône in the south, on the lakes of Neuchâtel and Léman (Geneva), and in Italian-speaking Switzerland around the semi-tropical lakes of Maggiore and Lugano.

Traditionally, Swiss wines are consumed young—reds, whites and *rosés* alike.

Over the years the wines of Neuchâtel, Switzerland's largest lake, east of the Jura Mountains (the Swiss do not consider the Lake of Geneva a Swiss lake, since it also possesses French shores!), have come to be the best known abroad. Neuchâtel's vineyards are chalky and rich in minerals; its white wines, made from the Chasselas, are dry, piquant and oftentimes a bit prickly on the tongue, and are the classic accompaniment for cheese *fondue*. Because of this faint fizziness they are locally called "Star Wines," and often poured into the glass from a considerable height above the table to bring out the effect of their pretty bubbles.

The vineyards of Neuchâtel are also the source of Switzerland's best red, Pinot noir, from the grape of Burgundy. Swiss Pinot noir is a light-colored, fragrant red wine that, with sufficient age, sometimes matches a good Burgundy. From Neuchâtel, too, comes one of Switzerland's best *rosés*, also from the Pinot noir and often called Oeil-de-Perdrix— the ancient wine term meaning the pink of a partridge's eye. Some Neuchâtel is labeled Cortaillod, after the best village for *rosés*.

Few parts of the globe are more romantic than the Swiss shores of the Lake of Geneva, overlooking the distant towering French Alps. Known as the Vaud, it consists of three vinous subdistricts: Chablais, upstream from where the Rhône enters the lake; Lavaux, bordering the lake east of Lausanne; and La Côte, the stretch between Lausanne and Geneva. Nearly all Vaud wines are white and go by the generic name of Dorin, though many of them use the name of the commune or village, an added sign of quality. In the section called Chablais, the more famous villages are Aigle, Yvorne, Ollon and Bex. Better wines yet come from Dézaley, Épesses, Cully, and St. Saphorin, in Lavaux. Two famous Swiss whites, Clos des Moines and Clos des Abbayes, are vineyards owned by the city of Lausanne, producing superior wines which the Swiss ordinarily reserve for official functions. La Côte's Mont-sur-Rolle, Bougy, Féchy and Vinzel are thinner and less outstanding. Fragrant reds are also produced from a blend of Pinot noir and Gamay grapes. Labeled "Salvagnin," they are apt to be wines which bespeak a comparative quality, since the appellation must be bestowed by an official tasting committee.

At the easternmost tip of the Lake of Geneva, north of the city, is the canton of Mandemant. The fruity and oftentimes subtly sparkling whites of this area are labeled "Perlan," but there are also rare "specialty" wines made from the German Riesling and Sylvaner grapes, as well as the Aligoté, the Chardonnay and the Gamay.

Switzerland's best vineyards, however, are to be found in the canton of Valais, near the mouth of the Simplon Tunnel, on the headwaters of the Rhône above the Lake of Geneva. Here the terraced vineyards climb to a height of three thousand feet, while high Alps shield them from winds and storms. The Valais is the most arid section of Switzerland, and water for the vines is often carried by mountainside canals from the glaciers far above. The rich bottomland of the Valais is famous for its fruits, especially the pears used to make Switzerland's famed pear brandy.

The Valais produces two excellent white wines, one *rosé* and one red. The latter is known as Dôle, blended from the Pinot noir and the Gamay. Soft and satisfying, neither sweet nor entirely dry, Dôle tastes like a cross between a Beaujolais and something from the Côte d'Or. The other red wine of the Valais is Goron, also a blend of the two same grapes—the difference being that the juices of the Gamay predominate in the latter, whereas with Dôle it is the other way around.

The two leading white wines of the Valais are Johannisberg and Fendant. Comparable to Dôle, Johannisberg is also a blend, in this case of the Riesling and the Sylvaner of the Rhine. It is fragrant and delicate with a virile tang and a marked touch of nobility. Fendant du Valais is more prevalent—a smooth, medium-dry white made from the Chasselas.

A fragrant, dry Rosé de Gamay also comes from the Valais, along with a number of scarce and not too interesting white "specialty" wines, among others: Malvoisie, Ermitage (from a grape of the lower Rhône), Arvine, Amigne and Humagne. Except for Ermitage, their grapes are indigenous, and the wines—even though the Swiss tout them—are nothing spectacular.

A small quantity of reds from the Pinot noir (here called the Klevner), available only to tourists, are made in scattered vineyards to the north and east, but the Italian-speaking section of Switzerland, around the resort lakes of Maggiore (Locarno) and Lugano, is the source of good red wines which are increasingly exported. From vineyards basking on the semi-tropical foothills of the Alps, the Swiss produce a soft red Merlot, one of the principal grapes of Bordeaux. A Merlot from Ticino should be labeled with the term Viti, guaranteeing its quality and authenticity. A lesser red from the area is called Nostrano—quaintly meaning "our wine."

Freshness and vigor constitute the charm of all Swiss wines and—as may be said of the wines of almost any land—they are at their best when served with native dishes. They should be consumed when young, and vintage years are of little consequence. Swiss wines offer few inexpensive "finds": it pays to buy the more costly ones.

Among the best producers are: Château d'Auvernier, Ville de Neuchâtel and Chatenay (Neuchâtel); Gilliard and Vins des Chevaliers (Valais); Badoux, Fonjallaz, Comtesse and Deladoey-Desfayes (Vaud—Lake of Geneva).

Hungary and Yugoslavia

Among the few wines to emerge from behind the Iron Curtain are those of Hungary—a country which, prior to the *phylloxera* period, ranked fourth among the wine-producing nations of Europe. Though few may have tasted it, nearly everyone has heard of Tokay (Tokaji), the legendary sweet wine of Hungary, which at its best is more like a golden liqueur than a wine. But the honey-sweet Tokay is by no means the only Hungarian wine of excellence. The Hungarians have known how to make a good wine for a thousand years, and their government—whatever else one may think of it—seems not to have impeded them. Many of the traditional cellars are still there, as is father-to-son wine making.

The finest wines of Hungary come from the tiny wine district of Somló in western Hungary and from Lake Balaton, a large lake southwest of Budapest which the landlocked Hungarians call "Our Hungarian Sea." The wines of the Balaton region are all white, and the best are either from the Riesling grape (Italian type) or the Hungarian Furmint, this latter also being the grape responsible for Tokay. Olasz Rizling, the most common (note the Hungarian spelling of Riesling), is a full-bodied white wine with a lovely flowery fragrance. Badacsonyi Kéknyelü, the most expensive (and tongue-twisting), is a delicate sweetish wine with a marked aroma, once traditionally drunk in its own land from bowls large enough to accommodate the nose comfortably.[1] Another popular Balaton wine is Furmint of Balaton, a pleasant and light white from a grape which—according to one distinguished Hungarian expert anyway—is supposed to have had its origin in the hills of northern Italy. The three best areas on Balaton's shores are Csopak, Balatonfüred and Badacsony, and the finer wines will have these names coupled to that of the grapes, such as Furmint, Szürkebarát (Grayfriar) and Kéknyelü. The adjectival Balatoni covers wines for the whole area.

The tiny Somló region, locally known as Somló Hill, is an extinct volcano that rises like an island in a sea of wheat plains in the western part of the province of Vesztera in central Hungary. Somló Hill might be called the Clos de Vougeot of Hungary. Its wines were known for their excellence long before Tokay was ever heard of, and owe their long and distinguished existence to Stephen I, the first king of Hungary, who sagely perpetuated the vineyards in the thirteenth century by founding a nunnery among the best of them. As with the Clos de Vougeot, passing troops are habitually halted and brought to attention to salute Somló Hill.

The white wines of Somló are pungent and an unusually brilliant green. Their traditional medicinal and curative qualities are almost too numerous to mention. Reputedly they aid the digestion, clear the kidneys, combat anemia—as well as being an "appetizer which causes neither headache nor dyspepsia." A traditional custom of the Hapsburg family was to take a glass of Somló before their nuptials to insure the procreation of male offspring.

Tokay, Hungary's most renowned wine, is made near the northeastern village of the same name, on the river Tisa. There are two forms of Tokay, sweet and dry. The latter is usually called Szamarodni, and is the more prevalently exported. It can be a good wine, but never a distinguished one. Sweet Tokay—Eszencia or Aszú—is basically made from selected (aszú) grapes that have been attacked by *botrytis* and all but dried on the vine. The unpressed juice or seepage from these, very sweet and syrupy, is then added to the wine of ordinary ripe grapes in varying proportions, depending upon how sweet the producer wishes the wine to be. The terminology for this proportion is known as *puttony*[2] (actually the name for the collecting tubs used locally in the vine-

---

[1] When exported, Kéknyelü is not a dessert wine, but a dry and refreshing one.
[2] Often seen alternate terms are *puttonos* and *puttonys*.

yards). The greater the number of *puttonys* indicated on the label, the sweeter the wine. Five puttonys, for example, is very sweet indeed.

Tokay Aszú is dark golden in color, and highly perfumed. The legendary wonders of this rarest of all wines became so exaggerated throughout the civilized world that at one time it was actually rumored to contain gold. The legend was further expanded when an Italian humanist, after visiting Hungary, asserted that the hills of Tokay contained veins of gold ore, and that golden shoots were to be found on some of the vine stocks. This report in turn prompted the immediate visit of the most notorious Swiss alchemist of his time, a man named Parcellus. Parcellus conducted prolonged experiments with wine, grapes and soils—only to come up with the rather lame diagnosis that the soil of Tokay was unusually blessed with minerals, and that Hungarian sunshine, "like a thread of gold, passes through stock and roots into the rock." Hungarian Tokay, incidentally, should not be confused with either the Tokay of Alsace, a dry wine which bears little resemblance even to Szamarodni, or Tokay of California.

Although the majority of Hungary's good wines are white, two good reds, Egri Bikavér (Bull's Blood) and Nemeskadar, nowadays both found on foreign wine shelves, are good bargains. The former, certainly one of the world's most realistically named wines, is made from a combination of Pinot noir and red Bordeaux grapes. It has a peculiar clove-like fragrance, and when given sufficient age, it may be a wine of considerable character.

An even better, though rare, red comes from the small district of Villány near the Yugoslavian border. It is called Villányi Burgundi, and is made from the noble Pinot noir brought directly a hundred or so years ago from the Côte d'Or.

All Hungarian exports of wines are handled by a government monopoly, Monimpex—a bureaucratic entity which could, if it wished, channel far better wines of its nation to those on the outside of the Iron Curtain, as well as afford some pronounceable translations for their labels. To our regret, Hungary does not export its best.

The wines of Yugoslavia have been known to Europe since the Middle Ages, carried thence by traders journeying from the Middle East. In recent years they have been seen increasingly on foreign markets; in fact, Yugoslavia is the world's tenth-largest producer of wine. They are not of the same quality as those of Hungary (meaning those one never sees outside Hungary), nor have they been improved by the imposition of Marshal Tito's wine cooperatives. They are, however, relatively inexpensive. The best of them come from Slovenia, that part of Yugoslavia adjacent to Italy and Austria; the best two towns are Maribor and Ljutomer, names often seen on labels.

Most Yugoslavian wines are named after their grapes, such as Traminer, Sylvaner, Italian Riesling and a local grape known as the Šipon (Chipon), related to Hungary's Furmint. Šipon produces a dry and fairly palatable white that the wine drinker, in this day of high prices, may find useful for daily drinking. A certain quantity of German (Rjanski) Riesling is used in the better vineyards, with comparably good results.

Yugoslavian reds are in general inferior to the whites, and the labels usually bear French grape names, such as Merlot, Cabernet and Pinot. The country also produces a sweetish Port-like red called Prošek, and a popular, pleasing *rosé*, Ružica. Many unusual country wines, some of them privately made and hoarded, may be found along the islands and shores of the Dalmatian coast, but these are for tourists only. Yugoslavia's large cooperatives are nowadays cultivating the Pinot noir and Gamay, with an eye to mass export. Already, Germany affords a large market for Yugoslavian "Burgundy."

Austria

The Austrians are a traditionally gay and lighthearted people, with a sparkling humor and the watchword of *Gemütlichkeit*. Vienna in its heyday was the capital of "Wine, Women and Song"—and as many a visitor knows, the atmosphere of an Austrian *Weinstube* (wine café) is anything but heavy-footed. Wine aptly fits the national mood.

As would be logical from the foregoing, not too many years ago only the best Austrian wines ever saw a bottle. But now Austria is seeking to export her wine, and we may see many of them in the months and years to come. Austrian wines may be likened to German wines—except that they do not reach such towering heights. Although the common ones, or *ordinaires*, of the country are generally made from the German Veltliner, the finest spring from other German grapes: the Riesling, the Sylvaner and the Traminer. Some of the best Austrian vineyards are to be found in the suburbs of Vienna, of which Grinzing (the wine is called Grinzinger) is probably the most famous. Others are Neustift, Nussdorf and Kahlenberg.

Thirty miles or so up the picturesque Danube is the wine region of Wachau, which produces well-known whites called Dürnsteiner, Loubner, Kremser and the somewhat less distinguished wine named after the region itself, Wachauer.

It is from south of Vienna, however, in what is known as the "wine quarter" of Burgenland, where Austria's best-known and most frequently exported wine is produced. This is called Gumpoldskirchener—a spicy and charmingly scented white, whose red counterpart is rather disappointing in its coarseness. Certainly a better and milder red, also from the Burgenland, is Vöslauer.

Austrian labels bear not only the town name, but that of the grape as well—and, comparable to German wines, a good year brings forth a *Spätlese* or an *Auslese*, or even a *Trockenbeerenauslese*. It is well to bear in mind that these probably will not be as luscious as their German namesakes, but one may be assured they will be easier on the pocketbook. Vintage years for Austria are generally the same as for Germany.

Romania

Known as Thrace in Greek times, Romania traces its wine making back to several thousand years before the Christian era. In Roman days Romanian wines were the favorites of the emperors; years later, in the fifteenth century, they were an important source for Russia and Hungary. In recent years Romanian wines have spread to Europe, as well as to North America.

Proceeding clockwise from the north, Romania is rimmed by Russia, the Black Sea, Bulgaria, Yugoslavia, Hungary and then Russia again. The country is split in two—from north to south—by the Carpathian Mountains, whose southern ranges fan out westward towards Yugoslavia. Two of its best vineyard areas are to be found in the Carpathian foothills: one, Dealu Mare to the southeast in the direction of Bucharest, known for its spicy reds; the other, an area called Târnave in the northwest corner of the country—a land once known as Transylvania. Târnave is famous for its whites. A third district of much renown is Murfatlar, near the Black Sea.

Romanian vineyards are subject to strict regimentation—the laws governing appellations, pruning and all aspects of production being quite comparable to the *Appellations Contrôlées* of France. The vines include innumerable exotic, indigenous varieties, as well as familiar

European plants such as the Cabernet sauvignon, the Merlot, the Pinot noir, the Traminer and the Muscat. Several of these latter (notably Cabernet sauvignon and Pinot noir) are exported to North America, varietally labeled. Dry, spicy and remarkably inexpensive, they are shipped under the brand name of *Premiat*.

Unfortunately for those of us on this side of the Iron Curtain, the Romanians have not thus far seen fit to export any wines made in the traditional style of the country. These descendants of the Thracians have a distinct sweet tooth—and the wines they are fondest of, and make best, are sweet, red and white alike. Probably the most famed of all is a white from Transylvania called Cotnari, familiarly known as the "Flower of Moldavi"—so named because its pervasive fragrance makes one feel as though transported to some lush flower garden. Made from botrytised, raisined grapes, it is said to rival Sauternes and Tokay in its sweet richness. Other comparable sweet wines, generally varietally named, derive from variants of two strictly indigenous grapes, the Feteasca and the Grasca. Among the wines made sweet from eastern European grapes are the Muscat, with a redolent peach bouquet and a honeyed taste—and sweet Cabernet Sauvignons and Pinot Chardonnays.

Greece

The wines of Greece were once considered the best of the world. Times have changed—or, properly speaking, the world's tastes changed as the northern wine-growing sections of Europe were developed. Nonetheless, Greece exports a good deal of wine today, inferior wines which go principally to France for blends to make *ordinaires* and to Germany for the equivalent.

Greek wines divide into three general classes: sweet, dessert wines containing a fairly high percentage of alcohol, of which the one called Maphrodaphne is the most commonly seen abroad; ordinary table wines, red and white and *rosé*, perhaps the best being a delicate white called Pallini; and doctored wines, those which derive from the early periods of Grecian wine making, when neither bottles nor corks existed, and wine was stored in decorative crocks called *amphorae*, which were sealed with skins to keep out the air. Even though wine in that ancient day was drunk young and almost always watered, the *amphora* system was anything but successful in terms of preserving or aging the wine. Thus the wine—to combat the vinegar-making yeast and many another airborne enemy—was doctored with spices such as cloves, peppercorns, various aromatics and (chiefly) sandarac, a resin used today principally as an ingredient in the manufacture of varnishes. Yet it should not necessarily come as a surprise for the reader to learn that in modern Greece resinated wine is still preferred—in fact, nearly half the wine made in Greece is still resinated. Wine is so often a matter of habit and usage. Just as many a farm child brought up on whole milk rebelled at the taste of pasteurized milk; or as the native of northern Portugal, accustomed all his life to the cloying red Vinho Verde, spurns anything else—so the Greek prefers his Retzina that tastes like pine needles. Some commentators proclaim that resin is needed to combat the tastes of certain Greek foods. Other authorities say that after several bottles of Retzina, one overlooks the pine needles and begins to taste wine. The latter never seem to mention whether the several bottles should be consumed all in the same sitting or in easy dosages.

Summary

Not much Swiss wine is exported, but among the best to be found abroad will be whites called Johannisberg, Fendant, Neuchâtel, Aigle and Dézaley, all appropriate to cheese dishes and Swiss food in general. Pinot Noir and Dôle are the best reds.

The best-known Hungarian wine abroad is the very sweet Tokay Aszú, but it is a rarity. A dry version (Szamarodni) is also exported. Two good exported Hungarian reds are Egri Bikavér (Bull's Blood) and Villányi Burgundi. The former needs much aging.

Yugoslavian wines, usually named after French or German grapes (the chief exception is Šipon, a dry white), are not always very well made—but their low price renders them worth a try.

The best Austrian wines are white, all made from German grapes, such as the Riesling, the Sylvaner and the Traminer. They are similar to German wines, and less expensive—but one should not look for any "greats." One of the most popular is Gumpoldskirchener.

In Greece, wine of the Retzina type—instilled with resin—is still considered a delicacy. Three other more potable wines (to the European-trained palate) are sweet Maphrodaphne (often seen in the United States), the delicate white Pallini, and Santa Helena.

The Romanians' favorite wines are sweet, but several dry reds and whites of exceptionally good value are exported to North America, notably Cabernet Sauvignon and Pinot Noir under the *Premiat* label.

TABLE N
Principal Recommended Wines of Switzerland, Hungary, Yugoslavia, Austria, Romania and Greece

SWITZERLAND

White	Red
Fendant (Valais)	Dôle (Valais)
Johannisberg (Valais)	Goron (Valais)
Neuchâtel (Neuchâtel)	Cortaillod (*rosé*) (Neuchâtel)
Dorin (Vaud)	Oeil-de-Perdrix (*rosé*)
St. Saphorin (Vaud)	Pinot Noir (Neuchâtel)
Villette (Vaud)	Salvagnin (Vaud)
Yvorne (Vaud)	
Cully (Vaud)	
Dézaley (Vaud)	
Épesses (Vaud)	
Aigle (Vaud)	
Ollon (Vaud)	
Bex (Vaud)	

HUNGARY

White	Red
Tokay (Tokaji) Aszú (sweet)	Egri Bikavér
Tokay (Tokaji) Furmint (dry)	Villányi Burgundi
Olasz Rizling (dry)	Nemeskadar
Badacsonyi Kéknyelü (sweet)	
Somlói Furmint (dry)	
Szamarodni (dry)	

YUGOSLAVIA

White	Red
Šipon (Chipon) (de Maribor)	Prošek (sweet)
Silvaner (Château de Maribor)	Ružica (*rosé*)
Traminer	Cabernet (Château de Dobrovo)
Rjanski Riesling	Merlot (de Breda)

TABLE N Continued
Principal Recommended Wines of Switzerland, Hungary, Yugoslavia, Austria, Romania and Greece

AUSTRIA

White	Red
Grinzinger	Vöslauer
Neustift	
Nussdorf	
Kahlenberger	
Dürnsteiner	
Gumpoldskirchener	
Loubner	
Kremser	
Wachauer	

ROMANIA

White	Red
Dry Riesling	Cabernet Sauvignon
	Pinot Noir

GREECE

White	
Retzina (Retsina) (resinated)	Maphrodaphne (sweet)
Pallini (dry; semi-sweet)	Kokkinlini (*rosé;* resinated)
Hymettus (dry)	Pendeli
Muscat of Samos (sweet)	Demestica
Santa Helena (dry)	Nemeae

CHAPTER 7

Wines of the New World

California

Few Americans—even Californians—know that the state of California produces four times more table wine than is imported into the United States from all other countries of the world. This is in addition to millions of gallons of California Port, Sherry and other "fortified" wines. California itself, furthermore, not only drinks almost half of what it produces, but also consumes nearly a quarter of all United States imports. This is simply part of the truth that people of wine-growing areas of the world like and drink wine. The average adult American drinks around thirty gallons of milk a year (less milk than a Frenchman or an Italian drinks wine), about one and a half gallons of spirits and close to two gallons of wine. California has an average wine consumption per capita of more than four gallons.

Although all the principal grapes used for wine in California—unlike those of the Eastern states—are the *Vitis vinifera*, and thus are of European origin, California wines cannot truthfully be said to taste exactly like European wines. There are certain strong resemblances, and some California producers have succeeded in making something that is considerably more than just reminiscent of its European counterpart. But beyond this point, we can only be deceiving ourselves if we attempt to draw similarities. More important yet, we would be doing a considerable disservice to all concerned. California Cabernet Sauvignon, made from the principal red Bordeaux grape, does—in the hands of the best producers—taste and smell much like a Médoc or a red Graves; but a California Cabernet Sauvignon also tastes and smells like itself. In a California Pinot Noir (from the Burgundy grape) one often finds the intriguing bouquet of a red from the Côte d'Or—a Volnay, perhaps—yet for any devotee of the wines of the Golden Slope, the anticipated ensuing tastes are just not quite there. Twenty years ago anyone who went along with the sanguine promoters of white California Chardonnay and claimed an exact identity with white Burgundy should have had both his head and his palate examined, even though Chardonnay was the most creditable white wine made in California at the time. But progress has changed all that. One sometimes wonders if California wine makers realize just how lucky they are. The best traditions of wine making in the Old World involve a man making wine—give and take a good or bad year—as well as his grandfather did. In the New World, the sky's the limit. In the Old World, furthermore, all the best places for wine grapes have been found and worked for generations; there are no more good ones. On our West Coast, new *microclimates* in surprising, never-before-thought-of areas are turning up all the time; and modern technology enables skillful blending of grapes from distant areas to make even better wines. In fact, the truly exciting aspect of California wines is that one rarely visits a California vineyard without tasting *one* wine, anyway, which is better—more distinguished and distinguishable for its own individual character—than it was the year before. Sensible Alsatians, for instance, long since abandoned the idea of promoting their wines as "Vins du Rhin" or attempting to produce something to rival a Schloβ Johannisberg—and most Californians are shedding the old idea that emulation or exact duplication of European types is the ultimate goal.

In comparison to the confusing systems of names and classifications of most European wines, the terms on California labels may be unfolded with a disarming simplicity. California table wines divide into three groups. The first, called "generics," are nearly always blends of two or more types, and are sold under European names such as "Burgundy," "Chablis," "Claret," "Rhine Wine," and "Sauterne" (the latter spelled in California without an "s" on the end). Just because these are

THE VINEYARDS OF
California

Morgan

Mendocino

SACRAMENTO VALLEY

Sacramento

Sonoma
Napa

San
Francisco
Livermore

Santa Clara

SAN JOAQUIN VALLEY

Santa Cruz
Monterey

Fresno

PACIFIC OCEAN

San Luis Obispo

Santa Barbara

Santa Ynez

San
Bernadino
Cucamonga
Los
Angeles

Temecula

0   25   50   75   100
MILES

blended wines it does not follow that, when made by a conscientious producer, they will not be of good value. Many of them are sold in sizes of more than a liter, and they are inexpensive : one can buy 1½ liters of good generic "Chablis" or "Claret" for $4 to $5. The important thing to bear in mind is that the wine will probably not even taste like a third cousin thrice removed of its European namesake.

The second, and qualitatively highest, category of California wines is known to the trade as "varietals." These are the wines in which the producers take the most pride. They are invariably sold in small bottles, meaning a "fifth" or a "tenth"—and they go by the name of the principal grape from which they are made. Although by law a varietal need only contain 51[1] per cent of the juice of the variety whose name appears on its label, in the case of the best producers it will usually be a pure product of that grape. Even so, it matters little. For shocking as this seemingly arbitrary *Appellation Contrôlée* might appear to some Europeans, it has its distinct advantages in an industry which is, after all, hardly a hundred and fifty years old. Innumerable producers of California varietals are by no means dedicated to the god of mass production, and granted that the law allows some producers to pass off poor and/or blended wines under a label indicative of high quality, it is a blessing to others who understand the need to experiment and improve their vintages.

The third (and often somewhat fuzzy) category of California wine names comprises the "proprietaries." These are wines which the producer, for reasons of his own, has chosen not to give generic or varietal names. An example would be *Blanc de Blancs* (originally a French Champagne term for white wine made from white grapes only). A *Blanc de Blancs* in California in all probability is a wine without one grape predominating sufficiently, or one which the producer does not wish to market as Chablis. Many a good California producer will explain the blend of a wine on his label; some even record the acid and sugar (Brix) content before and after fermentation (residual sugar).

The following are the most commonly seen California varietals.

RED WINES. *Cabernet Sauvignon.* Made from the principal red grape of Bordeaux. Unquestionably the most successful (according to Old World standards) of all California reds. Often an unblended prod-

---

[1]Due to be changed to 75 per cent in 1983.

uct; if not, it may be blended with Cabernet franc or Merlot, other Bordeaux grapes. The latter has a softening effect. Well-made Cabernet Sauvignons are almost never given enough age; the wineries release them too soon, and the public can't seem to wait to drink them. When made by a good producer, eight years of age is an ideal minimum.

Pinot Noir. The red grape of Burgundy's Côte d'Or. By no means as successful in the New World as the Cabernet Sauvignon; particularly those whose taste buds are experienced in red Burgundy will find it a bit insipid, light in color and body, with a weak middle taste and an unfamiliar aftertaste. Even when one or two of these faults are not present, some other will show. Wines labeled *Pinot St. George* are not made from a legitimate Pinot grape.

Zinfandel. Once thought to have been of Hungarian origin (though never found in Hungary), this grape may have been introduced into California in the last century by a flamboyant fortune seeker of the Hungarian nobility, Count Haraszthy, known in the industry as the "Father of California Wine." Recent oenological researchers have advanced evidence that it is actually the *Primativo di Gioia* from southern Italy; but no one as yet has advanced a plausible theory as to how it got from there to here in pre-Civil War years. Californians like to refer to it as their "mystery grape." At one time Zinfandel was talked about as the "Beaujolais of California"—a wine made in a light style, fruity and with a characteristic "bramble" flavor, ready to drink within a year or two. Of late some producers have been treating it very much as a "classic" Bordeaux, with heavy body and a high degree of tannin, requiring much age in the barrel and many ensuing years in the bottle. The question as to whether the Zinfandel was created for any such reverent treatment remains, so far, a moot one.

Gamay and *Gamay Beaujolais.* In California there are two grapes called Gamay, often confused. One—more seen in the past decade—is actually a clone (relative) of the Pinot Noir, but its wine is paradoxically known as Gamay Beaujolais. Also paradoxically, it is the one which far more resembles the jubilant red Beaujolais of southern Burgundy that the citizens of Lyon—and any other Frenchman who can get his hands on it—pass down their throats with such alacrity. In California it is light and charming, sometimes slightly astringent, and should always be drunk young. The other, legitimately named, is sometimes called the *Gamay Noir* or *Napa Gamay.* By comparison it makes a muddy-tasting, dull wine.

Barbera. The red grape used with such success in the Piedmont region of northern Italy. The wine is rather rough and coarse, like so many Italian reds. Good varietal Barberas are produced in the North Coast counties—notably Mendocino and Sonoma—as well as in the Central Valley and Cucamonga districts in the southern part of the state.

Petite Sirah and *Sirah.* The Petite Sirah is not the celebrated red Syrah of the Côte Roti and Hermitage on the Rhône, although for many years in California it was purported to be. It has now been identified as another Rhône grape, the Duriff, a lesser grape variety long since banished from all the *Appellations Contrôlées* vineyards of the Rhône. It actually does better on our West Coast than in its homeland: as a varietal, and with sufficient age (three or four years), it is a sturdy, deep-colored wine with a strong, attractive bouquet, gaining fast in popularity. Several California producers have recently planted and made wine from the real Syrah, a wine of much promise but whose still youthful bottles match a nineteenth-century description of Hermitage: "black and powerful."

Merlot. A common ingredient in many Bordeaux reds (used in Pomerol in its pure state), and a varietal in Switzerland, northern Italy, Yugoslavia and elsewhere. As a varietal in California it is mellow, quite comparable in taste and bouquet to a Cabernet Sauvignon, but lacking some of the latter's "tang" and virility.

WHITE WINES. *Chardonnay* or *Pinot Chardonnay.* California wine from this grape, the source of all the finest white wines from Chablis to Mâcon, is the opposite number to red Cabernet Sauvignon. Soft and dry, and at its very best showing a characteristic "beeswax" bouquet and flavor (a term used to describe it in Burgundy), it has no equal in quality and breeding. Here is one rare instance where emulation has paid off: California producers have meticulously studied French methods of producing it—especially as to types of European oaks used for ageing—and many a French expert at a "blind" tasting has been fooled into thinking the California wine came from his own land. Some producers today overdo the oak flavor; but the pendulum should swing the other way before long. Ironically a great quantity of French Chardonnay is not aged in oak at all, but in stainless steel or glass-lined tanks. The grape is a shy producer; well-made Chardonnay is an expensive drink.

Pinot Blanc. A grape used to good advantage in California for

"Champagne." Considerable confusion—not to say contention—rages in California as to what this particular grape really is. In Burgundy the term Pinot blanc is sometimes colloquially interchangeable with Pinot Chardonnay, or Chardonnay; but actually the relationship is nonexistent. Pinot Blanc varietal wine should be crisp, a bit sharp and clean-tasting.

Chenin Blanc. Responsible for Vouvray of the Loire, as well as the white wines of Anjou. The California version is often reminiscent of a Vouvray, and slightly on the sweet side. When fermented very dry, this wine is often called White Pinot or sometimes Pineau de la Loire.

Gewürztraminer. The Gewürztraminer, as the reader will remember, is the source of those beautifully spicy and highly perfumed white wines of Alsace, Austria and the Italian Alps. The California product is quite comparable to the European types—though distasteful, to this writer anyway, when made bone dry. A few producers make it as a sweet "Late Harvest" wine. (See Johannisberg Riesling below.)

Sylvaner. In California the "second" grape of Germany makes a wine that is dry and pleasant. It is often simply called Riesling, or Franken Riesling, distinguishing it from the Johannisberg (see below).

Johannisberg or *White Riesling.* The Californians have appropriated the name Johannisberg (from Schloβ Johannisberg) to indicate the true German Riesling. In the hands of good producers it has a nice, mild bouquet, and is neither too sweet nor too dry. (Bottles labeled "Grey Riesling" or "Emerald Riesling" are not made from the same grape. The former, as a varietal, is gaining in popularity. It is dry and mild, with a nice tang.) The Johannisberg Riesling, along with the Gewürztraminer and Sémillon (see below) is also made in California as a sweet "Late Harvest" wine, meaning the equivalent of a German *Beerenauslese* or a French Sauternes, utilizing the famous *pourriture noble* or "noble rot." Comparable to the California Chardonnays that nowadays often fool Frenchmen, "Late Harvest" Johannisberg Rieslings have been known to fool German experts. Curiously, it was not until well after the California wine industry's hundredth birthday that the state's vinicultural officialdom got around to distinguishing between the *pourriture noble* and others of the several common "rots" that attack grapes. All "rotten" grapes were banned for years, though a few "old time" wine makers with childhood memories of Germany and France made *Beerenauslesen* and botrytized Sauternes promiscuously for their own consumption.

Folle Blanche. In France, wine of the Folle blanche grape is atrocious—yet when distilled, it is responsible for French Cognac, universally accepted as the finest brandy on earth. (See Chapter 10.) Used in California largely as a blend for Chablis, "Champagne" and other sparkling wines, it is offered as a varietal by a few producers. Generally tart and rather high in acidity.

Colombard; French Colombard or *Colombard Blanc.* Another grape from the Cognac district of France. It makes a wine with a light body, dry (when made sweet it is repulsive!), with a strong, pronounced bouquet and taste—not always too attractive if met in an exaggerated degree. Largely because of extensive plantings years ago, French Colombard is prevalent as an element of many a Chablis, where it is disguised (or at least "let down") by the presence of other wines. As a varietal it is usually also blended to attain delicacy.

Sauvignon Blanc; Fumé Blanc or *Blanc Fumé.* Next to the Chardonnay probably the most distinguished dry white of California, made from one of the three grapes used for French Graves and Sauternes, also for Pouilly Fumé and Sancerre on the Loire. In California it resembles the Loire wines more than Graves: clean, subtly perfumed and piquant, though unfortunately without the celebrated "gun flint" flavor peculiar to the Pouilly area. Some producers who use the Loire terminology of their labels attempt to compensate for this by using variations and degrees of aging in oak.

Green Hungarian. A dull white wine made by some wineries. The grape is of unknown origin.

Sémillon. The name of another of the three white-wine grapes of Bordeaux. In its pure state, it is responsible for one of the most successful dry white varietals of California. A well-made Dry Sémillon (emphasis on the Dry) may be almost indistinguishable from a French Graves—sometimes even a little better—and without any trace of the metallic overtones common to some California whites.

OTHER WINES. *Grenache Rosé* and *other rosés.* The Grenache is responsible for the classic *rosé* wines of France—those of Tavel and Provence—and was the first grape to be widely used in California for *rosé* wines. The result is a light, pretty wine, usually dry but somehow a bit metallic and often slightly astringent. Better *rosés*, in our opinion, are made from the Gamay, the Cabernet Sauvignon and the Pinot Noir. These will be softer, though usually sweeter. The best come from the Coastal Counties.

Blanc de Noir(s). The public's current preference for white wine over red has resulted in many producers turning to their over-plentiful red grapes for white wines. This is accomplished by arresting the winepress before the red color on the inside of the skins becomes too apparent, and then fermenting the white juice by itself. (See Champagne, Chapter 8.) Even so, many of these Blancs de Noirs can carry a subtly pinkish color. Not to be compared in purity of tastes to *bona fide* whites, they are fruity and attractive, always with a faint haunting taste of a red wine. The best are made from the Gamay Beaujolais and the Pinot Noir.

Champagne. California "Champagnes," which we will deal with more fully in Chapter 8, are not strictly varietals, though a few producers sometimes make them from the Chardonnay, in which case they will be so labeled.

As we have so often witnessed in the case of the wine-growing countries of the world, once again it is to the Church—in this instance the Spanish missions—that credit must go for the introduction of the wine grape to California, where the first plantings of the *Vitis vinifera* appear to have taken place near San Diego about 1770. Later the Franciscans took the grape northward to the cooler climates of the Sonoma and Napa valleys, north of San Francisco Bay. These were grapes of Spanish origin—only one of which, the so-called Mission, is used to any extent in the industry today. The monastics did not sell their wines to the outside world, but kept them for their own use.

About the middle of the nineteenth century, California commenced to experience an invasion of vinous fortune seekers—Frenchmen, Germans and the famed Count Haraszthy from Hungary. Many of these Europeans were already conversant with the art of wine making, and they either imported or brought with them thousands of cuttings of European vines. The majority of them, to their dying day, labored under the fleeting hallucination that European wines could soon be duplicated—or perhaps even surpassed—on California soil. As we have seen so frequently, certain grapes excel—to make fine wines in their own right—on certain soils; but wines are almost never "duplicated."

By 1875 California was producing more than four million gallons of wine. Paralleling the experience of the Franciscans before them, it was discovered that the best areas for wine making lay in the Coastal Counties, in the vicinity of San Francisco Bay: Mendocino, the Napa and Sonoma valleys, Alameda (no relation to Almadén Vineyards), Santa Clara and Santa Cruz. In the other wine-growing regions of the state—the vast Central Valley between the coastal range and the Sierras, the Cucamonga district near Los Angeles (now the sources of nearly 75 per cent of all California vinous produce, and largely devoted to generics and fortified wines)—the climate was too hot, and the grapes reached maturity with more sugar and less acid than is requisite for good table wine. Today a few good varietals are raised in the Cucamonga district—notably from Barbera and Zinfandel grapes; but in general the inland regions of California are the lands of wine in the jug, of Chiantis, or Ports and Sherries and Vermouths that are akin to their European counterparts in name only.

Many vineyards of the Coastal Counties, where the *Vitis vinifera* truly flourish, are still carried on in the tradition of the founding families. Inglenook Vineyard, with its imposing ivy-covered winery reminiscent of the Old World, was for many years managed by the great-nephew of its founder. Similarly, Beaulieu Vineyard, of comparable fame and charm, even though now the property of a large liquor conglomerate, adheres to the standards of its original French owner, Georges de Latour. Another name hallowed by Californians is that of Louis M. Martini, a comparative newcomer to the group, from Italy, who succeeded in making some of the best varietals in the state, and whose cuttings are in great demand by other vineyard owners. The century-old firm of Charles Krug, a Prussian who pressed his first grapes in the Napa Valley with a cider press, is owned and managed by yet another old wine-making family, the Mondavis. One member of this family with his own independent winery, Robert Mondavi, an innovator with a paradoxical dedication to Old World wine types, has probably done more to put California on the wine map than anyone else of his generation. Southeast of San Francisco, in the Livermore Valley, a region most noted for its white wines, the grandsons of Carl Wente, another German, still operate the vineyards. It is impossible to describe them all, but the reader will find most of them in the listings that follow. Their company is continuously being joined by small vineyard owners—retired businessmen, former ambassadors, stage and screen people or just plain people who are intrigued with living on the soil and making good wine. All of these producers are ably aided by the Department of Viticulture and Oenology of the University of California, which, among other valuable services to one of California's most important industries, has mapped the state into zones or "microclimates" climatically suitable to the *Vitis vinifera*. In consequence, the past couple of decades have witnessed a rash of new plantings—and many good wines—in places where it was never before believed wine grapes would flourish. Most of these, reversing the trend of the last century, have been south of San Francisco, in elevated spots protected by the first range of coastal mountains: the Monterey Valley, Paso Robles, San Luis Obispo and the Santa Ynez Valley near Santa Barbara, and even so far afield as Riverside County south of Los Angeles.

Even though most California vintners, especially those who produce varietals, are impelled to make better and better wine, there are trends in the industry of which the consumer should be aware for his own protection. One of these is embodied in our perennial American emphasis on "marketing." Most large producers are forced by the competition to employ elaborate sales staffs, and to think that they must produce a full "line": that in order to compete one must make a Cabernet Sauvignon, a Sémillon, a Sauvignon Blanc, a Zinfandel, a Chardonnay—and many another. Some producers, for example, make as many as five or six Sparklings. One has to be dry, one sweet, one pink, one red (to compete with Sparkling Burgundy), another a "Crackling *Rosé*," yet another perhaps a Cold Duck.

Obviously nothing could be more ridiculous. Good wines and high-pressure salesmanship were not made for marriage, and the point we are making is that the consumer should soon learn that the California producers who make a *few* wines, those best suited to their soil, are the ones who best reflect quality and progress. The opposite philosophy is comparable to the old Hollywood boast that a film producer need not move out of the state to obtain any backdrop in the world—whether the scene be the Via Appia, the peaks of the Andes or the Bay of Bengal.

The highest allowable appellation in California is the words *Produced and Bottled by*.[2] Law forbids the use of this term for any wine made from less than 75 per cent of grapes crushed and fermented at the

---

[2]Another rarely seen (and often ambiguous) appellation embodies the words "estate-bottled"—meaning wine made in a winery adjacent to the vineyards where the grapes are grown.

vintner's winery, or from grapes of another district or county; otherwise the label may only bear the words *Made and Bottled by.* This is a distinction not generally known by the public, and perhaps not one to be emphasized: the proof is, after all, in the drinking. Some excellent wines can be *Cellared and Bottled by.*

In addition to finding the right grapes for the right soils, a lesson in European tradition from which many California producers—along with the wine-drinking public—might well profit, is the absurd bugaboo about sediment. Many of the larger California producers go to inordinate lengths to insure that there is neither sediment nor cloudiness, nor in fact anything but the vision of virginal purity in any of their wines. The tiniest speck floating in a limpid white, the slightest trace of a dreg in a red, destines any bottle on the production line to cruel oblivion. Yet no Frenchman or Italian would think twice about a few specks in a bottle of Pouilly-Fuissé or Soave—and as the reader should know by now, the presence of a teaspoonful or so of dregs in any European red wine is not only entirely allowable, but the mark of a well-made wine. There is no doubt but that many of the elaborate clarifying devices used in deference to this silly bugaboo are simply not good for the wine.

Finally, there is the matter of years for California—good and bad. One often hears that vintages in California are nonexistent—and this is, in general, true. The temperature and dependable climate, as compared with that of Chablis or the Moselle, say, renders vintage years of far less significance than those of northern Europe. But nearly every California vintner will tell you that such things as good and bad years do exist. As with the *Reservas* of Spain and Portugal, one vintner may have had good luck in 1960 with his Cabernet Sauvignon, whereas in the next valley some vineyards may have been subjected to quixotic rainfall, hail or early frost. Certain large California producers because they are afraid that a (good) year on a label will prevent the marketing of wines of a less good one, bridle at so much as the mention of the word "vintage." Others wish to blend the years and maintain a "type." But California definitely has its vintage years, and it is only fair to the consumer to mention them. Furthermore, a good California wine, especially a red, needs as much age in cask and bottle as any, and the public is entitled to know the age of the wine it buys, regardless of the marketing policies of the producer. In this respect, for a wine without a year on its label, the wine drinker is fortunate in having a handy—

though not infallible—little custom of the bottle industry on his side, although not everyone is aware of it. Most manufacturers of American wine bottles blow a record of the year in which the bottle was made into the bottle's base. This generally appears in two-digit form ('76, '77, '78) to the right of an easily spotted hallmark. Thus if one knows, in addition, that in the hands of the best producers of varietals, red wines usually stay a year or more in the barrel before bottling, and white wines and *rosés* rest in tank or barrel storage at least over the winter and sometimes longer—one is provided with a reasonably accurate index for gauging the age of the wine.

For California vintage years see page 234.

Summary

California wines are usually labeled either as "generics"—mostly blends, carrying European names such as "Burgundy," "Chablis," etc.—or as "varietals," these being named for the grape from which they are predominantly made—"Pinot Noir," "Cabernet Sauvignon," etc. The latter, usually sold in bottles instead of jugs, are the best, especially if they come from the Coastal Counties. The best reds are Cabernet Sauvignon, Pinot Noir, Gamay Beaujolais and Zinfandel; the best whites are Chardonnay, Sauvignon Blanc (or Fumé Blanc), Chenin Blanc, Johannisberg (White) Riesling and Gewürztraminer. Three good *rosés* are made from the Gamay Beaujolais, the Pinot Noir and the Grenache.

A third (and somewhat questionable) category of California names on labels are "proprietary names"—neither grape (varietal) nor generic names. Sometimes these are there because the producer does not choose to use the name of the predominant grape—more often because he thinks the wine will sell better if the lily is gilded a bit.

Vintage years in California are not as important as in Europe, although the best producers put them on labels so that the consumer will know how old the wine is. Should the label not have the year, one may *usually* learn when the wine was bottled by looking for a two-digit date ('76, '77, '78) that manufacturers blow into the bottle's base. To estimate the actual age of the wine, allow at least a year before bottling for the reds, and six months or a bit more for the whites and *rosés*.

There are more than 350 registered wineries in California, of which a large majority belong in the categories of medium or small production recommended in Table O. The reader should bear in mind that wines from these two smaller categories are bound to represent the best quality.

TABLE O
Leading California Vineyards

Large Production

Almadèn	Paul Masson
E. and J. Gallo	Sebastiani
Italian Swiss Colony	Taylor California Cellars

Medium Production

Beaulieu	Robert Mondavi
Charles Krug	Monterey
Fetzer	San Martín
Inglenook	Sonoma
Louis M. Martini	Souverain Cellars
Mirassou	Wente Brothers

Medium-to-Small Production

Alexander Valley	Hoffman Mountain Ranch
Burgess Cellars	Jordan
Calloway	Landmark
Chappellet	Joseph Phelps
Chateau Montelena	Ridge
Chateau St. Jean	Rutherford Hill
Clos du Val	St. Clement
Concannon	Simi
Dry Creek	Spring Mountain
Freemark Abbey	Stags Leap
Gundlach-Bundshu	Sterling
Hanzell	Stoney Hill
Heitz Cellars	Trefethen

The Pacific Northwest

During the past few decades wines have been appearing in the northwest corner of the U.S., specifically Washington State, Oregon and Idaho, which rival any made elsewhere on our continent. The latitude of these northwest states is almost identical to that of the northern vineyards of the European wine belt (Chablis, Champagne, Germany), and many growing conditions can be found in common: long summer days with lingering sunlight, cool nights to develop acids, comparable soils (with one notable exception), and in general, freedom from those deep winter frosts that so plague the vineyards of the East and Midwest.

The notable exception with soils is Washington's Yakima Valley, the growing area for all the state's finest wines. The valley lies beyond the Cascade Mountains, some two hundred miles east of Seattle. Its soil is rich, powdery volcanic ash, often reaching a depth of fifteen feet or more; but before irrigation came in the early 1900s, the Yakima was an unproductive desert. Today enormous crops are raised there, including grapes. In this respect the Yakima represents a paradox in traditional wine making: as we have observed so often in these pages, the *vinifera* or wine grape is a lover of adversity and poor soil; and irrigation, which tends to keep the roots near the surface and nurtures over-production, is frowned upon in nearly every other part of the world producing good or great wine.

It is not difficult, even for a novice, to spot dissimilarities and unique characteristics in Yakima wines, all of which are made from varietal grapes also found in California. The white Sémillon—one good example—is a soft, fruity and gentle wine, definitely distinguishable from a "rusty" French Graves or a typical steely California one. Unlike most dry white wines, it markedly improves with bottle age. Yakima's Johannisberg Riesling comes closest to a German Riesling; but its Chenin Blanc—a wine with much body and a honeyed fragrance—is far, far removed from any Vouvray or California Chenin Blanc. The Yakima is predominantly a "white wine country," but it also produces outstanding Merlots and Cabernet Sauvignons; and the Grenache *rosé*—once again, totally unlike a Tavel or some Grenache *rosé* from vineyards to the south—is in the opinion of many experts a wine any country can be proud of.

The pioneer in the Yakima was Château Ste. Michelle, the descen-

dant of a winery which once made fruit wines in western Washington.
Château Ste. Michelle picks and crushes its grapes in the valley, then
brings the *must* (the juice and skins) in hermetically sealed tanks across
the mountains to be fermented and aged in its plant near Seattle. Other
outstanding Yakima wineries include Preston Cellars (acclaimed for its
Chardonnay), Hinzerling Vineyards and Associated Vintners. To date,
however, the only one with extensive national distribution is Château
Ste. Michelle.

In terms of size and development, the vineyards of Oregon are still
considerably behind the Yakima. The best of them are to be found in
gentle foothills west and south of Portland, in a region known viticul-
turally as the Willamette Valley. It is not unusual for these Oregon
wineries—through quirks of nature, or pestilences, such as overwhelm-
ing visitations by birds just before the harvest—to be obliged to import
grapes from Washington or even nearby Idaho, but when the wines
are made from their own grapes they, too, are indicative of quality and
promise. In any event, their labels will inform you where the grapes
came from. One encouraging trend among Oregon vineyards points to
the possibility that nature has equipped this area to make a creditable
Pinot Noir—something which can come close to a *bona fide* red Burgundy. Oregon wineries are still youthful; and it takes longer, for some
reason, to perfect the art of producing red wines. Already, highly creditable Cabernet Sauvignon and Pinot Noir are made by Eyrie Vineyards; Tualatin Vineyards is best known for its Petite Sirah, Muscat
and *late-harvested* Riesling. Other Willamette wineries that have
earned recognition are Sokol Blosser (Sauvignon Blanc), Elk Cove
(Rieslings) and Knudsen-Erath (Chardonnay). Another wine-producing section of Oregon is the Umpqua Valley, south of the Willamette
near the California border. Formerly devoted to the making of excellent fruit wines, some of the Umpqua's vineyards have turned to the
production of *vinifera*, and should be heard from soon.

Idaho's bellwether vineyard is Ste. Chapelle, near Boise. Though
founded only in 1976, its Merlots, Gewüztraminers and Johannisberg
Rieslings have already captured many awards in Pacific Northwest
competitions. Other Idaho vineyards are bound to follow. This same
area also has many *vinifera* plantings (independent of any winery), a
source frequently drawn on by wineries in the neighboring states in
times of ill luck.

Eastern States Vineyards

As every American school child knows, the Nordic discoverers of North America called our country Vinland, or "Wineland." Vines in tremendous abundance, from Massachusetts to Georgia, greeted the settlers wherever they landed, and it was thought that only a little attention and proper pruning would turn the whole continent — or what was then known of it — into a bountiful vineyard. But our sanguine forebears suffered disappointment after disappointment. The native grape turned out not to be the wine grape, *Vitis vinifera*, but, instead, other varieties, such as the *Vitis labrusca*, one of the common non-wine grapes. And when these were cultivated, a mysterious sickness seized the vines that could neither be cured nor explained.

When all efforts to tame the wild grapes of Massachusetts, New York, Maryland, Virginia and elsewhere failed, attempts were made to plant European grapes. Lord Delaware imported French vines and vintners; the Huguenots made serious attempts at viniculture in the Carolinas; late in the eighteenth century cuttings from Portugal were brought to Georgia. In all cases the vines suffered from inexplicable plagues and withered away. From what we know now, this second failure was undoubtedly attributable to the dread *phylloxera*, to which all European *Vitis vinifera* vines fall prey. It was as tragic as a gold rush without gold.

Had it not been for a Swiss immigrant named Jean Dufour, who persisted with his European cuttings in Kentucky, the American wine industry might well have disappeared until revived in California years later. Dufour's Kentucky plantings were not exactly spectacular — only one survived. This was a vine bearing a hitherto unknown black grape, reputedly imported as a seed from the Cape of Good Hope and thought to be of *vinifera* origin (though authorities today are skeptical and tend to believe it was an accidental cross between a European and an indigenous vine). Called the Cape, or Alexander, in any event it made plausible wine, and its success gave American vintners the courage to experiment further and develop others. The first of these of any lasting importance were two distinctly native grapes, both from coastal North Carolina: the Catawba, whose still and sparkling wines, produced by the Longworth family in Ohio, were acknowledgedly the best of eastern wines previous to Prohibition days, and the Scuppernong. Somewhat later their numbers were augmented by the Delaware, the

Niagara, the "Missouri Riesling" and others—all of the woodland *Vitis* varieties.

Only about 10 per cent of all the wine made in the United States is produced outside of California, and although the greatest bulk of this derives from the New York State Finger Lakes district, a host of small vineyards making wine from hybrid and *vinifera* grapes has sprung up all the way from Connecticut to Arkansas. As we have already mentioned, wines from native American grapes have a flavor all their own—universally described by the word "foxy"—denoting a raw, musky or grapelike flavor that is anything but pleasing to the wine drinker who has been brought up on European or California wines. *Labrusca* and other indigenous grapes are also higher in acid than the *vinifera;* and inasmuch as it is the acid that largely carries the taste and the aroma we experience in wines, it is for this reason that the "Champagnes" and sparkling wines made from these grapes—by virtue of added sugar and often *vinifera* juices—are less "foxy" and more acceptable to European-trained palates.

Hybrid grapes, on the other hand—meaning a cross of a European variety with another variety having either better production or more hardiness, or both—make wines that are generally devoid of "foxiness" and taste more like European types. Hybrids are more suitable to eastern climes, where the frost runs deep. Some of the most successful with hybrid wines are Wagner Vineyards, Bully Hill, Heron Hill and Glenora in New York State. Haight Vineyards in Connecticut, Markko Vineyards in Ohio, Tabor Hill in Michigan and Wiederkehr Wine Cellars in Arkansas have made names for themselves with *vinifera*. Nor should one omit the Vinifera Wine Cellars of Konstantin Frank on the Finger Lakes, a Russian oenologist whose experimental vineyards have produced rootstock and cuttings for most of the *vinifera* vines east of the Rockies.

As with California brands, Eastern still wines have their generic names, such as New York State "Burgundy," American "Chablis," etc. These are probably the most misleading of all wine terms on earth: a New York State "Burgundy" is even less related to true Burgundy than a California blend of the same name—which is at least derived from European grapes, though they may not be the Pinot noir or the Gamay. The sole resemblance between a New York State "Chablis" and a French one is that of color. Eastern varietals follow the California pattern and are named after the grapes themselves. The most successful of the indigenous ones are Niagara (white), Delaware (both red and white), Isabella (red) and Catawba, Diana and Dutchess (white). The best hybrids are the Baco Noir, Chancellor and Maréchal Foch (all red), and Seyval, Ravat and Videl (white). But more and more, the small wineries are turning out *vinifera* wines.

Probably the best New York State still wines to be made from indigenous grapes are from the Widmer Wine Cellars at Naples, New York—though two other firms, Great Western Producers (Pleasant Valley) and Gold Seal Vineyards, along with the Taylor Wine Company (New York) and Meier Wine Cellars (Ohio), all have excellent reputations.

Summary

Eastern States wines, when made from indigenous grapes, taste different from wines of Europe and California. The best come from the Finger Lakes district of New York, the leading wineries being Great Western (Pleasant Valley), Gold Seal Vineyards, Widmer Wine Cellars, and Taylor Wine Company. The two most noted "Champagnes" are made by Great Western Producers and the Taylor Wine Company.

As with California wines, eastern wines are classified as generics (New York State "Burgundy," American "Chablis," etc.) and as varietals, named after the principal grape. They sometimes bear proprietary names. The most successful indigenous varietals are Niagara (white), Delaware (red and white), Isabella (red) and Catawba and Diana (both white). Good hybrids are Baco Noir (red) and Seyval Blanc (white).

South America (*Argentina and Chile*)

South American countries produce roughly one-tenth of the world's wine, and along with not inconsiderable imports from Europe, drink almost all of it. In fact, the per capita consumption of the Argentine is just behind that of Portugal, Italy and France. In terms of world production of table wines, country by country, the Argentine is third. Among South American countries, Chile comes next, making more than one hundred million gallons of what was, until recently, considered the best wine of the continent.

In recent years, with the acquisition of modern wine-making equipment and the use of techniques borrowed from California, Argentina has markedly improved the quality of its wines for export, and is on the point of establishing a healthy foreign market. *Vinifera* grapes (Cabernet Sauvignon, Merlot, Chardonnay, Chenin Blanc, etc.) are used predominantly, and the ensuing results are clean, uncomplicated wines of substantially more than just good quality, available in the U.S. at reasonable prices. So far the outstanding varietals are Cabernet Sauvignon and Chardonnay.

Argentina's best vineyards, with an elevation of three thousand feet or so, lie in the western extreme of the country, tucked behind the sharply chiseled peaks of the Andes, in the three provinces of Mendoza, San Juan and Rio Negro. Sequestered hundreds of miles from Buenos Aires and the South Atlantic, a high-flying bird could skirt the peaks and alight in the vineyards of Chile in a short day's journey. It is because of these protective mountains, blocking storms from the west, that the rainfall in Mendoza and its neighboring provinces is notably sparse, clouds in the sky are a rarity, and cool nights serve to create a healthy amount of acid in the grapes. The problem of sparse rainfall— once an inhibiting factor in making good wine here—has now been combatted by irrigation, drawn from the snowfields of the towering mountains nearby.

A unique aspect of all South American wines is that the grapes are harvested in February and March, hence it is not unusual to find a bottle of Argentine wine, of an early maturing type, on a U.S. retailer's shelf—of this year's vintage! The wine might have been aged and then bottled in June or July, and found its way to New York by December.

Most labels for Argentine exports are in English, resembling U.S. labels, without Spanish terms such as *Reservado* or *Gran Vino*, or complicated classifications. Two of the better vineyards shipping to foreign markets are *Andean* and *Trapiche*.

Eighty years or so ago the wines of Peru gained a certain popularity in England; today nearly the only wines found on export markets, besides those from the Argentine, are from Chile, that narrow little strip of a nation on the Pacific side of the continent, two hundred and fifty miles across at its widest, and more than two thousand miles long.

The northern section of Chile is arid desert, the southern part a storm-lashed forest. The important vineyard areas are in the central part of the country—all located between the 34th and 38th parallels, south latitude, the latter being the southernmost limit for the wine grape on the continent. The climate of the vineyard districts resembles northern California; the soil is volcanic and unusually fertile for the successful production of good wines. As in Mendoza on the opposite side of the Andes, the vineyards are irrigated by streams draining the snowfields of the mountains—some of whose peaks reach heights of more than twenty thousand feet—and it has been said that the land has never been invaded by the *phylloxera* or any other serious plague of the wine grape. Most of the wine is made in cooperatives.

Nearly every important European wine grape is grown in Chile, including the Pinot noir of Burgundy and the Cabernet sauvignon of Bordeaux for the reds, the Chardonnay, the Sylvaner and the Riesling for the whites. Labels usually bear the grape names, as with United States and Alsatian varietals, along with such qualitative words as *Reservado, Especial* and *Gran Vino* (the highest appellation). The best producers also add vineyard or area names on labels—names which, by dint of some curious promotional sleight of hand, nearly always seem to coincide with the names of the original producers themselves. The best of these are Carmen, Conchalí, Concha y Toro, Tocornal, Santa Rita, Linderose, San Pedro and Undurraga.

Chilean reds are light in color and tend to be rather muddy tasting, but the *rosés* are often excellent. The whites—especially the Rieslings—are very dry, with an appealing purity. In the United States these are inexpensive, and are particularly to be recommended. Chilean Rieslings and Rhine wines are usually sold in squat, dark-green *Bocksbeutels*, comparable to those used in Germany for Frankenwein. Chilean "Champagnes," rarely exported, are nearly as good as second-string French ones. Except for bottles labeled "Rhine Wine," the generic blends and imitations of European types (*Tipo*) are to be avoided. A bottle of blended wine that once came to our attention bore words supplying an unexpectedly candid story: *Chilean White Wine Tipo Chablis. Elaborated and bottled by. . . .*

Australia

Although Australia produces almost seventy million gallons of *vinifera* wines annually, nearly half of it is turned into distillates or fortified wines. Canada and Britain are its principal export markets, but this is a comparative trickle. The Australians are now working on the

United States and Japan. Nearly all the vineyards are in the southern section: New South Wales, Victoria and South Australia—scattered between Sydney and Adelaide. The best regions are the Hunter and Barossa valleys, and a tiny, isolated region of red soil and limestone noted for its "claret" called Coonawarra, a couple of hundred miles southeast of Adelaide. The most significant exporting firms are Glenloth, Hamilton, Gramps, Lindeman, Reynell (Château Reynella) and Seppelt. Most of these are very large firms, with properties in more than one district; and they are not above blending wines of two or more districts to attain their desired tastes.

Australian vineyards are filled with nearly all varieties of European grapes, which sometimes do strange things on their soils—and sometimes not so strange. Of the whites, the Gewürztraminer makes an outstanding typical wine; but an Australian Riesling *may* be made from the Riesling grape; it *may* taste like a Riesling and it may not; or it may simply be labeled Riesling and be a blend of Trebbiano and Sémillon, yet be an outstanding wine. In any event, many Australian whites are clean and crisp, even though their tastes may be unfamiliar. For the reds, the predominant grape for the best of them is usually the Shiraz, or Syrah of the Rhône. Australian reds need much aging, and the best of them—as with the whites—are called "Bin Wines," comparable to *Reservas* in Spain. Bin wines are always numbered. Travelers from New York State are always surprised to learn that Australia's best and most popular "Champagne" is called Great Western—just as Californians are sometimes piqued to find that Australia makes a more than just excellent Sherry.

To European ears many Australian labels have a cacophonous ring: Chardonnay Sauternes, Hermitage Claret or Shiraz (Syrah) Burgundy. Some other names are more alarming yet: we have seen a bottle labeled Urgundy (definitely not a printer's mistake) and another labeled "Claret No. O."

Summary

South American countries make (and drink) large quantities of wine, but the only countries to export them in any quantity are Chile and Argentina. Chilean reds (named varietally after the grapes) include wines from the Pinot noir and the Cabernet; but Chile excels in its dry whites and *rosés*. Among the best producers are Undurraga, Carmen,

Conchalí, Concha y Toro, Tocornal, Santa Rita and Linderose. Wines made from the Chardonnay, the Sylvaner and especially the Riesling are all excellent. Labels bear qualitative terms such as *Reservado, Especial* and *Gran Vino*—the latter being the highest. Except for bottles specifically labeled "Rhine Wine," Chilean generic wines—whose labels often carry the word *Tipo* (type)—are to be avoided.

Argentina exports cleanly made varietals of nearly all the types found on our West Coast. Its red wines (unlike Chilean ones) are at least equal in quality to the whites, and all are reasonably priced. Labels on most exported Argentine wines are printed in English.

Australia produces European-type (*vinifera*) wines, many of which are excellent. The reds possess interesting bouquets and need age; the whites are usually clean and crisp. Some rare whites are almost duplicates of European tastes; others can be startlingly unfamiliar.

CHAPTER 8

Champagne and Sparkling Wines

French Champagne: The "King of Wines"

Although the name is borrowed the world over, there is no true Champagne but French Champagne—the "King of Wines." This is made in a strictly demarcated area of northern France, south of the city of Reims on the Marne River, by more than one hundred and fifty firms, each of which uses its own particular secret formula. The grapes used for Champagne are two we have already met in the Côte d'Or and elsewhere: the red Pinot noir and the white Chardonnay. But Champagne is never made from the grapes of one vineyard alone—and, in most instances, it is not even the product of a single year. Grapes from all over the district are purchased by the individual firms; the wines themselves are in turn blended according to the manufacturer's formula, and may derive from several years.

Vintage Champagnes (those bearing a year on the bottle) are blends of wines from that particular year. Traditionally they are only made in the best years, as selected by their respective producers. But as the demand gradually exceeds the supply, the "best years" seem to occur more and more frequently. They constitute only a small part of the total production; but they are the acknowledged best and, needless to say, the most expensive. Champagnes—and, for that matter, all imported sparkling wines—are a luxury. To begin with, they are taxed as though they were jewelry; the United States duty on sparkling wine is around ten times that placed on still wine. Again, because sparkling wines are universally considered to be a rich man's drink, or something to embellish a special occasion, restaurants and retail stores feel privileged to charge a mountainous mark-up.

Another factor that renders Champagne so expensive is the basic cost of making it. The process known in France as the *méthode champenoise* is long and complicated. Since the wine is usually made in part from the red-skinned Pinot noir, a very careful pressing (involving considerable waste) is necessary to insure that no pink tinge appears in the juice.[1] After fermentation, the wine is kept in casks through the winter, to be bottled in the spring. At this time its sugar content is carefully measured, and when the wine is bottled it is infused with more sugar yet and a culture of yeast, in order to bring about a second fermentation. The bottle is then securely capped to prevent any gases from escaping, and now begins a long period of storage in the bottle (which with the best Champagnes may last two or more years), during which time the wine both matures and builds up its carbonation.

When the product is adequately aged, the bottles are placed in racks, their necks slanting downward, to begin the very specialized treatment which so contributes to the wine's ultimate cost. For weeks or even months each downward-pointing bottle is twisted by hand, part of a turn each day, allowing the sediment to settle on top of the cork. Now the wine is ready for its final processing. With the cork still downward, a skilled worker uncorks the bottle to allow only the sediment to escape, quickly turns it right side up, injects more sugar to sweeten the wine if necessary, a bit of brandy to arrest any further fermentation, and recorks and wires the bottle. When done by an experienced worker, the whole process is accomplished in the space of a few seconds, and none of the valuable natural carbonation is lost. Many Champagne makers nowadays freeze the bottle necks, so that the sediment pops out as a frozen plug.

In recent years another process, never used for superior French

---

[1]Pink (*Rosé*) Champagne, sometimes called *oeil-de-perdrix*, once much more popular than it is nowadays, is made by continuing with the pressing until a pink tinge is obtained.

Champagnes, has been employed by the makers of sparkling wines and so-called "Champagnes" as a time- and labor-saving device. Called the bulk method, it became possible only with the invention of high-pressure glass-lined tanks. The bulk method involves a rapid second fermentation in the tank, from which the wine is siphoned off from the top, eliminating the protracted hand labor of rotating and disgorging. Many inexpensive sparkling wines, including most German *Sekt* and much California "Champagne," are made in this way. Obviously this is a cheaper procedure than the *méthode champenoise*, but with wines carbonated by the bulk method there is almost always an unpleasant trace of residual yeast; nor does it necessarily require the palate of an expert to detect that the wine has usually not been properly aged. Only with the best and most conscientious bulk-method producers are the two processes combined: the wine is actually aged in the bottle and then transferred to the tank for settling. Even so, a certain taint always remains.

No one quite knows how the evolution of making natural sparkling wines came about. As we have mentioned, many wines—the whites of Alsace, Vouvray and the Moselle are examples—oftentimes undergo of their own accord a repetitive, seasonal secondary fermentation in the bottle, unintended by their makers. Even the experts can be at a loss to explain certain of its phenomena; and many an expert whose wine drinking should have taught him otherwise refuses to face all the evidence. Usually occurring in the warm spring—beginning about the time the sap is rising in vineyards, and lasting only a few months—the wine takes on a gentle fizziness, producing a slight prickle on the tongue. Other wines stay fizzy in this way the year round, and one may observe minuscule bubbles; and many wines today are made this way purposefully.

Wines with this faint effervescence are called *pétillants* or *crémants* in France as opposed to *mousseux*, the latter term being used for Champagnes and sparkling wines in which larger bubbles have been induced by a purposeful second fermentation in the bottle, or by direct carbonation. It is apparent that the wines of the Champagne district—which until several hundred years ago were always marketed as still wines—must have also contained a potential for the sparkling characteristics. Dim as history is on the subject, we do know that these French sparklings were first popular in England, and that in those days the French had neither strong bottles nor proper, airtight corks. The English, on the other hand, had both; and everything points to the fact that it was

Champagne shipped as still wine in casks to England, and bottled there in the spring of the year, that was responsible for the innovation. Only some years later did the French themselves commence to imitate this "sparkly," as the English called it.[2]

Legendarily the invention of Champagne is attributed to a certain Dom Pérignon, a monk and the cellarer of a Benedictine abbey near Hautvilliers in the Champagne district. But there is no evidence that Dom Pérignon—whose chief contribution to Champagne apparently was to perfect the art of blending—put sugar and yeast cultures into his bottles to supplement natural effervescence. This procedure apparently came later. Nor did Champagne—today's most fashionable drink among the French themselves—come into its own in its native land until comparatively recently. Ignored for almost two centuries in France, elsewhere in Europe, especially across the Channel, its popularity grew by leaps and bounds. This is no doubt why a bottle today labeled *English Cuvée* or *English Market* almost invariably represents the cream of the crop from any one of the many firms of the Champagne district.

The Champagne district operates under regulations laid down by the *Appellations Contrôlées* laws, but these words—so important a guarantee of quality with most French wines—do not appear on labels. Nor are there any classifications for Champagnes except those arbitrarily placed on the labels by the manufacturers themselves: the words *Premier Cru* or *Grand Cru* on a bottle, for example, mean nothing official. Champagnes are graded by the manufacturing firms according to their degree of dryness—the driest and best of which is generally known as a *Brut*. Next comes *Extra Sec* (extra dry), followed by *Sec* (a French word essentially meaning dry, but in the case of Champagnes and other *mousseux* wines it indicates something moderately sweet). Bottles labeled *Demi-Sec* and *Demi-Doux*, like those bearing the mysterious terms *Goût Américain* or *Drâpeau Américain*, are usually made for South American and Slavic countries, where the sweetest Champagnes are much appreciated. Other terms on Champagne labels—*Réserve, Privat, Spéciale* and *Première Cuvée*—are all relatively pointless, with the exception of the last, which is a guarantee that the wine has come

---

[2]Thomas Jefferson, visiting Champagne about this time, reported that "while the sparklings are little drunk in France ... they are endeavoring to make all they can. This is done by bottling in the spring, from March till June. If it succeeds, they lose an abundance of bottles. This is another cause for increasing the price."

from the first (always the best) run of the juice. A Champagne labeled *Blanc de Blancs* means that only the white Chardonnay grape has been used, without an admixture of the Pinot noir. A *Blanc de Blancs* of a named vintage year will be ultradry, and a superlative light product. A Blanc de Noirs tends to have more body. Still wines from Champagne—white and red—are labeled Coteaux Champenois. The best red is from the village of Bouzy.

Champagne is one wine that fits with almost any food, and may be served throughout a meal. Another use for it, about which we shall have more to say in Chapter 11, is in place of a cocktail, as an *apéritif* before a meal planned to show off the qualities of good wines. One is often asked what are the best Champagnes. Unfortunately the answer is not easy to come by—for Champagnes are blends that do not spring from any particular piece of soil, and their quality and particular character are dependent upon the formulas of their producers. Furthermore, each one of us generally has his own favorite, the result of long experimentation. One may commence by saying, however, that a vintage Champagne, one with a year on the label, is invariably better than a non-vintage one—though not perhaps always really worth the appreciable difference in price. One of the most expensive (and considered by many the best) brands is produced by the firm of Moët et Chandon, and named after the fallaciously traditional "Father of Champagne," the Benedictine Dom Pérignon. Dom Pérignon is always "vintage." The other superb Champagnes, manufactured in several degrees of sweetness, are made by the firms of Krug, Bollinger and Taittinger. Salon is another—the favorite of the late Duke of Windsor, who appreciated the good life. For the balance we have appended a list (Table P) of a dozen or so others, with which the wine drinker cannot go far wrong—though he may wish to experiment with several before he has found one truly to his liking.

Vintage Champagnes often live ten years or more in the bottle; non-vintage ones hardly improve after a year. As is the case with almost all wines, Champagne is better when it comes from a larger bottle than from a smaller. Champagne bottle sizes have a wide range: they include the split (quarter bottle), the half-bottle and the bottle, the magnum (double bottle), the jeroboam (four bottles). Of these, perhaps the magnum is the most practicable, provided as much as two bottles is to be served. Actually, there are four yet larger traditional ones: the Methuselah, the Salmanasar, the Balthazar and the Nebuchadnezzar (the last

TABLE P
Recommended French Champagne Manufacturers

Ayala	Mumms
Bollinger	Perrier-Jouet
Goulet	Piper-Heidsieck
Charles Heidsieck	Pommery et Greno
Heidsieck Monopole	Pol Roger
Irroy	Louis Roederer
Krug	Ruinart
Lanson	Salon
Laurent-Perrier	Taittinger
Moët et Chandon (Dom Pérignon)	Veuve Clicquot

containing the equivalent of twenty bottles). Although theoretically Champagne from one of these would be preferable, it requires little stretch of the imagination to realize that as they progress in size they become increasingly difficult to cool and to pass around the dinner table. Perhaps they serve their best purposes today in show windows.

"Champagnes" and Sparkling Wines

Under French law no *mousseux* or sparkling wine, unless it be made in the Champagne district itself, may be called Champagne. Sparkling Vouvray, for example, is "Vouvray *Mousseux*," not "Vouvray Champagne." Although the United States is not one, many nations—at the request of the French—refrain from calling their sparkling products Champagnes. The Germans call theirs *Sekt;* the Portuguese and Spanish use their own terms (and for export purposes often add the words "Sparkling Wine"); the Italians also have terms of their own, such as *Spumante* and *Frizzante.*[3]

Though there is no sparkling wine that duplicates the special quality given by the sun, the chalky soil and the grapes of Champagne, there are many substitutes, and good ones. We have already mentioned Sparkling Vouvray and Saumur of the Loire Valley, semisweet wines that

[3]Portuguese "Champagnes" are called *Espumantes;* Spanish, *Xampâns* or *Gran Cremants.* Chilean "Champagnes" are of excellent value but never exported.

correspond to the Champagne grading of *Sec*. Made from the Chenin blanc grape, they have a slightly different flavor—but they are considerably less expensive than the "King of Wines" and are frequently a practical substitute. Good sparkling wines also come from Savoie, specifically from around the town of Seyssel. The only other important sparkling wine of France is Sparkling (red) Burgundy, which of course has its California and New York State namesakes. What the reader should know, simply put, is that Sparkling Burgundy—not usually made by the true *méthode champenoise*—was conceived for the sole purpose of disposing of poor, surplus wine. French Sparkling Burgundy rarely comes from the little royal ribbon of vineyards on the Côte d'Or; it is only infrequently made with the unadulterated juice of the Pinot noir. It is always, perforce, heavily sugared. No Burgundian would drink it himself; in fact, it is never seen on any wine list in the Côte d'Or, and rarely on any French one, except in the expensive dives of Montmartre. The only thing to recommend it, as opposed to its California or New York State cousins, is that it is at least made of Old World grapes on Old World soils—and thus its taste carries a certain hint of Old World *terroir*. In effect, U.S. Sparkling Burgundies are purer products and more fairly priced.

Again, there are many good substitutes for true Champagne that are not even necessarily French *mousseux*. An experimenting wine drinker may find that one of the most satisfactory, in terms of taste and price, is the classic Italian "Champagne," Asti Spumante. This wine, or its Portuguese and Spanish equivalents mentioned below, may be substituted at weddings or other festive occasions: their costs range from one-half to two-thirds the price of French Champagne and, especially after the first glass or so, few of the guests will know the difference.

German "Champagne," *Sekt*, is logically not made from superior wine, for it is usually the product of the poorest years, when good still wines cannot be made. A quantity of sugar must be added to *Sekt* to blanket its extreme acidity—and no amount of dosing or blending can ever serve to disguise an inferior or basically overly acidic product. By contrast, both Spain and Portugal make excellent, if somewhat bland, sparkling wines. The best of the Portuguese are Raposeira and Messias, both *Brut*. Two other good ones are Borges and Royal *Brut*. The finest Spanish sparklings are the *Extra Bruts* of the firms Castellblanch and Cordorniú.

If one is not hypnotized by a foreign label, several California brands compete most favorably with the imports (see Table P). Cheap California "Champagnes" made by the bulk method are of little value. But one may choose with good reward among the better and more expensive California producers, such as Schramsberg, Kornell, Korbel, Sonoma and Domaine Chandon, the latter not labeled "Champagne," but "Napa Sparkling." United States "Champagne" terms, following the European pattern, are *Brut*, *Extra Dry*, *Dry* and *Sec* in that order. Pink "Champagne" tends to be of the *Extra Dry* grading. The best guide to quality in "Champagnes" is the phrase "Bottle-fermented" or *méthode champenoise*.

Most New York "Champagne" is labeled *Brut* or *Extra Dry* (which usually indicates more sweetness than its California counterpart). The Gold Seal Vineyards of the Finger Lakes produce a Charles Fournier *Brut* "Champagne *Blanc de Blancs*" which—if one does not object to its slight foxiness—one will acknowledge to be of good quality. Great Western "Champagne" has been the "Standard of the East" for years. There is no denying that its quality and taste are greatly enhanced by a certain amount of California *vinifera* juice. Taylor and Widmer are the other two leading New York State houses.

Summary

Most French Champagnes are blends, sometimes containing wines of two or more years, made by private formulas of the individual manufacturers. Vintage Champagnes—those with a year on the label—are the best, but also the most expensive and sometimes not worth the price. They are made only in the best years, but owing to increasing demand, there seem to be more "best" years than formerly.

French Champagnes are graded in order of dryness: *Brut* (the driest), *Extra Sec* (extra dry), *Sec* (sweetish), *Demi-Sec* and *Demi-Doux* (very sweet). The only other terms on a label with any real meaning are: *Blanc de Blancs* (indicating that the wine is made exclusively from white grapes and very dry), *Première Cuvée* (meaning from the first and best pressing of the grapes), and *English Cuvée* or *English Market* (usually indicative of the producer's best quality).

Other "Sparkling Wines"—French, Italian, Portuguese and Spanish—may be good, inexpensive substitutes for French Champagne. Of these the best are Italian Asti Spumante; Portuguese Raposeira *Brut*, Messias *Brut* and Royal *Brut*; Spanish Castellblanch *Extra Brut* and

Codorniú *Extra Brut*. German "Champagne" (*Sekt*) is usually a doctored wine of a poor year.

The best California "Champagnes" nowadays compete quite favorably with imported ones. Among the better producers are Schramsberg, Kornell, Korbel, Domaine Chandon and Sonoma. Among New York State producers look for Great Western, Widmer, Taylor and Gold Seal Vineyards.

CHAPTER 9

Fortified Wines

Port, Sherry and Madeira, together with Sicilian Marsala, certain European Muscats, variously labeled, Californian Angelica and many others are known as fortified wines—meaning that they are all basically table wine, either red or white, to which a certain amount of brandy or alcohol (and sometimes sweetening) has been added. In Portugal and Spain, they are called, respectively, *vinhos* or *vinos generosos* (noble wines); in Italy, *vinos di lusso* (*lusso* is also the Italian term for "luxurious" or "lush"); in France *vins de liqueur* (sweet or luscious).

The practice that began in earnest in the eighteenth century, of "spiking" or fortifying something that we must assume to have been a good table wine in its own right, appears in all instances to have had its roots in economic rather than gastronomic ground. One of these springs from the simple biological fact that wine with 18 per cent alcohol or more is all but immune to the hordes of harmful yeasts ever-present in the air. Thus brandy was added to the wine as a preservative. Another reason is that wine low in alcohol does not travel as well—or at least didn't in the days of long, hot voyages. By contrast, some fortified wines—Madeira, in particular—are even improved by travel.

A perhaps more significant reason yet for fortification is the fact that, in countries not in the wine belt, there has always been more of a predilection for the alcohol in wine than for wine itself. This applies alike to the British Isles, Scandinavia and the former Portuguese African colonies, to name only a few. Here is certainly the true explanation for the original popularity of Sherry and Port, and many other fortified wines (either extant or extinct). It is significant that—as a nation—the Spanish drink comparatively very little Sherry; virtually the only Portuguese who drink Port or Madeira are ones in the Port or Madeira trade, or those who have learned to drink and appreciate them in foreign lands.

Many a fine table wine in history has had its reputation ruined—or at least temporarily eclipsed—by vintners who gave in to the temptation of making it (for export) a stronger wine than nature intended it to be. Among dozens of them we may count Portuguese Colares and Bucelas, the wines from Tarragona in Spain (Tarragona Port) and the once reputedly excellent Constantia from South Africa—with the result that the first-named, two of Portugal's traditional best, temporarily lost favor on the export market, and the latter two have sunk into a worse state of oblivion.

The fact remains, however, that wines of certain parts of the world—the forbidding Douro Valley in Portugal, the chalky little triangular area surrounding Jerez de la Frontera in southern Spain, the volcanic island of Madeira off the African coast—are ones that time has shown to be better suited to fortification than not, and these have been the classic survivors. Though the vogue for fortified wines can hardly be said to be increasing, one hopes that the pendulum may once again swing the other way: there is still a place for dry and semi-sweet fortified wines in the civilized world. Port (especially dry white Port), dry Sherry and crisp Madeira are all excellent as *apéritifs*, and far better for the human race than the habitual strong cocktail. And there is no doubt whatsoever but that—like Champagne—they are better suited to precede wine, a true appreciation of which is never enhanced by spirituous liquors. The sweeter ones make delicious, satisfying after-dinner drinks.

Port

Port—red Port, that is—is a dessert wine; Sherry, the best of which is very dry, is an *apéritif*; in terms of uses, Madeira falls between the two—it may be either.

Of all the fortified wines, Port is made and comes to maturity by the simplest processes, and therefore may be said to be the purest. A prophet without much honor in its own land, Port has for generations been known as the Englishman's drink. Its origin is typically commercial—as opposed to gastronomic. During the eighteenth century, as a result of a ban on French wines, Portuguese natural table wines had gained considerable popularity in the British Isles. History does not record the name or names of the Portuguese merchants who, shipping their wines from the little fishing town of Viana do Castelo on the river Lima, chose in poor years to adulterate table wines destined for England with a little alcohol, adding the juice of elderberries "to improve the color." The use of elderberry juice met with understandable disfavor and was shortly abandoned; but the taste for stronger and stronger wine (not called "Port" until the industry was later centralized in the city of Oporto) caught on so indelibly that numbers of Englishmen were soon journeying to Portugal to take part in the production of this new British quasi-national drink. Some of these Englishmen stayed on to enter the trade: hence many of the names found on Port labels—Cockburn, Graham, Robertson, Sandeman, Dow and Yeatman, all shipping firms at Vila Nova de Gaia, the "Port" town opposite the city of Oporto at the mouth of the Douro River.

The birthplace of Port is the steep and narrow Douro Valley in central Portugal—a veritable furnace where high mountains shut off any possible moisture or coolness from the ocean, and where during the growing season the temperature in the depths of the valley may rise to 110 degrees in the shade. For five months of the year the Douro River dries to a mere trickle; at the bottom of the valley one sleeps at night on the bare earth to benefit from any coolness it might afford; high on the steep mountainsides, where the best vineyards lie, the peasants are often short of sufficient water in which to cook their vegetables. Somehow the vines miraculously acquire enough moisture from the rocky granite and schistose soil of the precipitous, man-made terraces to produce grapes that come to quick maturity, with an exceptionally high sugar content. Unlike most other fortified wines, no sugar need ever be added to Port; in fact, it is forbidden by law.

Although Port is born a thousand feet above the Douro amid these humanly burdensome conditions, the wine remains there only during its infancy. Shortly after fermentation has taken place in the *quintas* (wine houses) situated on the valley floor far below the vineyards, it is taken in small casks or "pipes" down the river to the "wine lodges" at Vila Nova de Gaia to complete its adolescence in aging and blending. In days gone by the journey was made in the late fall or early winter, when the river comes in flood, carried by shallow-draft boats with flaring square sails and rudders uniquely designed to pass the dangerous rapids. Nowadays Port is carried down to its second home less romantically, by truck and railroad.

Port is made almost entirely from grapes strictly indigenous to the Douro, sometimes from an admixture of several dozens of them. During the fermentation process, in the case of red Port, the grape's natural sugar is allowed to convert to alcohol only until such time as the wine's sugar content is reduced to the particular degree desired by the producer—at which point all further fermentation is arrested by the addition of brandy or grape alcohol. The result is a wine with an alcoholic content ranging from 18 to 23 per cent, and 8 to 10 degrees of sugar. White Port, actually preferred by the Portuguese themselves, is made of white grapes, and is usually drier as a result of having been allowed to ferment to roughly 15 per cent alcohol before the brandy is added. For this reason white Ports make such excellent *apéritifs*.

White Ports are rarely blended in the wine houses of Vila Nova de Gaia. The legitimate ones are a product of their own "pipe." In this sense they are much like the type known as Vintage Port—the most highly prized abroad, especially in England. Vintage Port, though it may be a blend, is always one of a single year, a year that the shippers' organization at Vila Nova has decided on as outstanding. As opposed to other types—"Ports from the wood," which mature in the cask and are ready to drink when bottled—Vintage Port remains in the cask for only two years, and grows up in the bottle. This is a slow process: many a Vintage Port does not come into its own until it has rested in the bottle for forty years or more.

Port is classified by its producers into six general categories: Full, Red, Ruby, Light, Tawny and White—although labels now rarely carry more than a brand name or some company's special promotional invention, accompanied by one of the three classifications of Ruby, Tawny or White. Of these the first, Ruby Port, is a deep, rich color— as its name implies—a blend of new and old wines that may be consumed relatively young, say at the age of ten years or less. Tawny Port, more expensive, is lighter, with a brownish tinge, and has simply received more blending and more age than Ruby (although some inferior Tawnys, called "shortcuts" in the trade, are made from a blend of red and white wines). Like Sherry, Port is usually at its best when slightly chilled, and since its aroma is definitely an integral part of its charm, it should never be served in a small glass—but, instead, in one which is large enough to allow sufficient evaporation. Very old Ports— Vintage Ports—cast a heavy sediment, a "crust," and should in all cases be decanted. Some Port shippers nowadays produce what is termed a "late-bottled" Vintage Port: the "crust" has been allowed to accumulate in the barrel and the wine is then bottled clear. For obvious reasons, a "late-bottled" Vintage Port will not have the same quality as one which has been aged in the traditional manner.

Sherry

The name Sherry is an Anglicization of Jerez de la Frontera, the Andalusian town that is the epicenter of Sherry making, in the province of Cádiz in the southeastern corner of Spain. Like Port, Sherry is as often spoken of as a British drink as a Spanish one.

Although Sherry is made principally from two sweet white-wine grapes, the Palomino and the Pedro Ximénez (thought to be a cousin of the Riesling), and is a *vino generoso*, even its sweetest version is hardly a dessert wine. In fact, until the last century the English name for Sherry as we know it was Sack or Sherris-Sack, terms deriving from *wyne sec* or *seck*, meaning dry.[1]

The history of Sherry as a fortified wine closely parallels that of Port. The wines of Cádiz were introduced into England as early as the twelfth century, probably by returning Crusaders, at the time when Jerez de la Frontera—as well as most of southern Spain and Portugal— was under Moorish domination. It was not until comparatively recently that it became a fortified wine. As with Port, it was the proclivity of the Dutch and the British for wine strong in alcohol that appears to have established the type.

Sherry is raised under almost ideal climatic conditions for growing the wine grapes. On the Cádiz peninsula, rains abound in winter, and the spring and summer are extremely hot and dry. The chalky soil on which the Sherry grapes thrive—almost as dazzlingly white as the

---

[1]A well-known contemporary brand name is Dry Sack, its bottle incongruously wrapped in sackcloth.

whitewashed seaport city of Cádiz itself—is too poor for anything else. If one digs a well among the inland vineyards, one comes across roots of the vines that have probed thirty feet or more through lime and rock in their search for moisture. Yet much of the Cádiz peninsula is a beautiful part of the world: near the coast, olives and chestnuts and oaks, grains and citrus fruits and even cotton and sugar cane all flourish.

The making of Sherry differs from that of Port in two distinct ways. The first is the utilization of what is called the *flor* yeast, a yeast presumably native to Jerez (although it is successfully cultured elsewhere) that gluts itself on both oxygen and alcohol and, as it grows, spreads a thick, protective crust or white film over the aging wine. *Flor* means flower in Spanish, but the resemblance is slight; in actuality the sight of the *flor* crust floating on top of the wine is all but repulsive. Its useful purposes with Sherry are to shut out harmful yeasts and to give the wine the individualistic "nutty" flavor and aroma that differentiates it from other fortified wines.

The other unique factor in making Sherry is the blending process known as the *solera* system. Sherry is always a blend, and the *solera* system entails rows or tiers of casks, sometimes five, six or more lines of them arranged above each other and interconnected, through which the wine passes slowly from the top tier to the bottom one in the course of its aging. Each year new wine is put into the top of the system, and in the best tradition of Sherry making, it may require nine years before it graduates, mixed little by little with more mature wines. Fine Sherries that bear dates on their labels should never be thought to derive entirely from that year. A year on a Sherry label means the year the oldest cask of the *solera* was put down—and it might be added that if any one Sherry were left in its cask for fifty years or so, unblended with new wines, it would be totally undrinkable, even with the benefit of fortification. Unlike Port, fortified at the finish of its fermentation, Sherry acquires its brandy at the end of the *solera* process. At this time it may be colored with evaporated grape juice, and sweetened. More sweetening goes into Sherry intended for export than for that made for home consumption, since Spaniards prefer their Sherry absolutely bone dry.

The best Sherries, as we have said, are dry, and for this reason useful as *apéritifs*. They are generally classified as Fino, which is moderately dry and rarely acidic, perhaps the *ordinaires* of the field; Manzanilla (also the Spanish name for camomile tea), which—although not technically a Sherry—is made in the same district on sandy soil and is likewise dry, though apt to be somewhat bitter; Amontillado (mountain Sherry), which reaches an even more desirable degree of dryness, with a top alcoholic content of 24 per cent; and Oloroso (the word denotes perfume), which has the greatest body and the deepest color, and is relatively sweet. Nearly all other names on Sherry labels are individual brand names or manufacturers' terms, except for Montilla, a wine from the inland city of Córdoba, often confused with Sherry. Montilla is a totally unfortified wine, slightly lighter than Sherry. Usually found in tall bottles the shape of German bottles, at its best it is dry and elegant, and not too alcoholic.

Among the more frequently seen brand names of Sherry are Cream Sherry, Brown Sherry and Cocktail Sherry. The first two are basically Oloroso—sweetened and colored accordingly. Cocktail Sherry is apt to be somewhat akin to Amontillado. Table Q lists the brands and manufacturers which are particularly recommended.

TABLE Q
Recommended Spanish Sherries

Fino

Brand	Shipper
La Ina	Domecq
San Patricio	Garvey
Tio Pepe ("Uncle Joe")	Gonzalez Byass

Manzanilla

Brand	Shipper
Prodigio	Domecq
Villamarta	Rivero

Amontillado

Brand	Shipper
Amontillado	Duff Gordon
Amontillado Botaniz	Domecq
Amontillado Vina AB	Gonzalez Byass

TABLE Q Continued
Recommended Spanish Sherries

Oloroso

Brand	Shipper
Anniversary	Duff Gordon
La Raza	Domecq
(and any others by Domecq or Gonzalez Byass)	

Montilla

Brand	Shipper
Flor de Montilla	Carbonell

Other excellent Sherry shippers include Williams and Humbert, Sandeman and Harveys.

Madeira, Malaga and Marsala

Whereas Port is a simple fortified wine, aged and blended in an almost elementary way, and Sherry is to be distinguished from it by the use of the *flor* yeast and *solera* system of blending the old wines with the new, Madeira is characterized by what is called the *estufado* method, a treatment which amounts literally to cooking the wine during the aging process.

The volcanic island of Madeira, which lies six hundred miles southwest of Lisbon off the African coast and is administered as part of continental Portugal, was first discovered by Portuguese fishermen early in the fifteenth century. Breathtakingly beautiful, extremely mountainous, ribbed with deep ravines and valleys, at the time of its discovery it was entirely covered by dense forests. Almost the first act of its colonizers was to burn them off—the fires lasted seven years—and plant great sections of the island with vines. The soil of Madeira was well suited to the wine grape, however coarse the basic wine; the island has a hot growing season and plentiful rainfall twice a year, in October and March. It was not long before Madeira became known as one of the principal vineyard areas of Europe. Its trade in that day—once again—was in table wine. Madeira wines were not fortified until later.

The individualistically bitter and peculiar burnt taste that Madeira has today—contrasted with the sharp, "nutty" flavor of Sherry and the candid fullness or "winyness" of Port—is attributable to the special treatment it receives while aging, or cooking, in the cask. There is no reason to believe that Madeira, as originally fortified, tasted like this at all. After it became the practice to fortify the wine, it was found that Madeira (supposed to be the only wine that will live almost indefinitely in the bottle) was tremendously improved by long voyages. To the amazement of nearly everyone, when subjected to severe climatic changes, to the hot, putrid holds and constant rolling motion of ships, it became an entirely different (and far better) wine. A voyage between continents vastly improved it; a voyage around the world doubled—or sometimes trebled—its monetary value. Traveled Madeira, or *vinho do roda* (wine of the road, as it came to be called), gained such favoritism among connoisseurs that its producers set out purposely to devise a process to duplicate the effects of a long sea voyage. This is the origin of the *estufado* method used today, in which the casks of aging fortified wine are either left in the hot sun to bake or else stored, sometimes for as long as six months, in heated rooms with temperatures as high as 140 degrees Fahrenheit. Unfortunately much Madeira today is turned out by use of an approximation of the *solera* system. A true vintage Madeira with a date on it is a scarce item—but usually well worth any price.

Madeira was once enormously popular in England, as well as in the United States in the early days of its history. But this vogue has greatly fallen off in recent years, and Madeira today, despite all promotional efforts of the Portuguese, retains a really profitable market only in Scandinavian countries. The decline may be attributed to several factors, one of which dates back to the last century, when these island vineyards were first heavily attacked by the mildew disease known as *oidium*, and then hit harder yet, some twenty years later, by *phylloxera*. Thus, for many years good Madeira was almost unavailable—and the vacuum was filled by other fortified wines. Another factor, of course, is the worldwide flagging taste for fortified dessert wines and *apéritifs*.

As with Ports, most of the best shippers of Madeira are of British origin, and such names as Blandy, Leacock, Cossart and Gordon are entirely typical on labels. With a few exceptions, such as "Rainwater Madeira" and a few created brand names, the wines take their nomenclature from grapes, of which there are four chief traditional varieties, three red and one white: Sercial Madeira is dry and tangy; Bual (or

Boal) is rich and fruity, perhaps the closest of all to a red Port; Verdelho, from a white grape, is medium dry, with a pronounced tang; Malvasia (Malmsey) is rich and luscious, and considered the finest. "Rainwater Madeira" is something else again. Lighter both in color and in texture than the average, it purportedly gained its name in the days when the wine was so universally popular in colonial America. It is said that a certain Savannah importer, knowing that Madeira always improves by extremes of heat and cold, stored his casks or "pipes" under the eaves. The tapped casks were drawn off by a pipe leading down to his shop—the wine always slyly referred to as "rainwater." The term was later adopted by the Madeira producers themselves.

It is unfortunate that Madeiras, especially the dry ones (which show themselves to best advantage when slightly chilled), are now largely thought of in many civilized countries simply as "the best cooking wines." More true than false—they are excellent for this purpose, especially to add zest to brown sauces or soups. But their uses as *apéritifs* to wine drinkers should not be overlooked.

Two other European fortified wines, less well known, are Spanish Málaga and Sicilian Marsala. The former is made principally from Muscat and Pedro Ximénez (Sherry) grapes, and comes from around the port of Málaga on Spain's southern coast. A dark-colored wine made from raisined grapes, with a taste faintly reminiscent of molasses, it has an unusually strong bouquet, and is the favorite sweet *vino generoso* of the Spanish nation. Likewise Marsala is the Italian's most desirable *vino di lusso*. Dark and usually very sweet (it is sweetened with cooked-down essence of grape juice mixed with alcohol), it is mainly used away from home as the perfect ingredient for veal scaloppini. One of the best Marsalas is *Florio*. In other parts of Italy they make a strong, sweetish Sherry-like wine called Vin Santo, considered a great delicacy, especially in rural areas.

None of these European fortified wines, with the possible exception of Sherry, are ever really duplicated or equaled by their imitators in other lands. Certain South African and Australian Sherries have gained much favor among adherents of the wines from Jerez—but these are perhaps the sole exceptions. California and New York State Sherry, when made with the *flor* yeast and an abbreviated version of the *solera* system, is sometimes a good approximation—and a good drink. But much American Sherry is *cooked* like Madeira and *called* Sherry. Nor

could anything be more of a double-barreled misnomer than "California Solera Port." Most domestic Port is simply sweetened and fortified
wine that is released to the consumer in its youthful state—a concoc-
tion which has usually been fermented from grapes, such as the Zinfandel, never heard of on the precipitous slopes or sizzling terraces of
the Douro, much less benefited by even an approximation of the loving
and prolonged care afforded genuine Port in the great wine houses of
Vila Nova de Gaia. As with all imitations—good, innocuous or bad—
they would all probably stand up better under other labels. We are not
agitating against them. Just let us not have anyone ask us, with a straight
face, "Will you have a Sherry?"

Few domestic Ports or Sherries of any intrinsic value are bargains.
Among the best U.S. Sherries are Widmer's from New York State, and
Louis M. Martini's Dry Sherry from California. Ficklin's California
Port is one that has earned a worthy name for itself; we also recom-
mend the highest-priced Ports of Paul Masson.

Summary

Fortified wines—table wines that have had brandy or alcohol added
to bring their content to between 18 and 24 per cent—are useful both
as dessert wines and as *apéritifs* before a meal with wine. Of the latter,
the best are dry white (cocktail) Port (also excellent on the rocks),
Sherry and dry Madeira.

Dessert Ports (reds) are generally called Ruby (quite sweet) and
Tawny (less sweet). The most expensive Ports are Vintage Ports (to
be distinguished from "late-bottled" Vintage Ports), which require
many years in the bottle.

Traditionally, the best Sherries are the driest. One labeled Oloroso
or Cream Sherry will probably be the sweetest available. Dry ones are
Fino, Manzanilla, Montilla (actually an unfortified wine made by the
Sherry process) and Amontillado. Many producers today make a
medium dry "Cocktail" Sherry. Some of the best manufacturers are:
Domecq, Duff Gordon, Garvey and Gonzalez Byass. Sherries are
always blends. A date on a label will simply indicate the age of the
oldest Sherry in the blend—it may be only a few drops.

Madeiras are both dry and sweet, but never as sweet as red Port. Of
the four principal types, named after grapes, Sercial and Verdelho are

dry, Bual (Boal) and Malvasia (Malmsey) are sweet. "Rainwater Madeira," an invented name, is light and medium dry.

Most American Sherries are only approximations of imported ones; domestic Ports are usually simply sweetened and fortified raw wines, lacking in age. There are no "bargains" in domestic fortified wines: stick to the more expensive ones in your initial experimentations.

Fortified wines are better when slightly chilled and served in generous-sized glasses, to allow their bouquets to assert themselves.

CHAPTER 10

Brandies

Fine Champagne, Cognac and Armagnac

Brandies, properly speaking, are spirits distilled from wine—and the two best are French. The first and finest are known generically as Cognacs; and the superlatives of these are called, somewhat confusingly, *Champagnes*. The Cognac district, which surrounds the little town of the same name, is to be found northeast of Bordeaux, close by the ancient fortress port of La Rochelle. At its very epicenter are two little areas known as Grande Champagne and Petite Champagne. When Cognacs from these two areas are blended—the ideal blend— they are entitled to the name *Grande Fine Champagne*,[1] the highest appellation of all. Progressing farther afield, as it is produced on less appropriate soil, the liquor is known as Cognac, Borderies, Fins Bois and Bons Bois, in that order. All these are usually generically called Cognac.

The white wines of the Cognac district are actually so mediocre that they are all but undrinkable. An unusually chalky soil produces wines

[1]Often abbreviated and referred to as *Fine Champagne*. In a French café one simply asks for a *Fine*.

[212]

so high in acid and proportionately low in alcohol that even the natives don't seem to enjoy them. Curiously enough, this appears to have been anything but the case four hundred years ago, when white wines from the Charentais (as that part of France is called) were in demand both in England and in Holland. No one seems to know exactly what happened to this trade. One often-accepted version, incongruous as it sounds, is that certain canny French vintners, seeking to save on transportation costs, concluded that "condensed" wines — that is, distilled — could be shipped abroad more economically, watered upon arrival, and neither the Dutch nor the English would know the difference. Another more plausible explanation is that each farmhouse of the Charentais of that day had its own little illicit still, the products of which eventually reached various ports on the coast and became understandably popular with sailors from visiting ships. The production of brandy thus turned out to be more profitable than wine. Whatever the explanation, brandy — known originally in France as *vin brûlé* (burnt wine) — in its unadulterated state was avidly taken up first in Holland and then in England, and replaced Charentais table wines. The Dutch called it *brandewijn* (again meaning burnt wine); the British translated this to brandywine, and later simply to brandy.

The best evidence that Cognac originated as a product of small farms of the Charentais is the crude machinery by which brandy is distilled throughout this part of France. To this day even the biggest firms use primitive copper "pot stills," of a design appreciably unchanged from five or six centuries ago. The wine is first fermented in the usual way, the principal grape nowadays being the St.-Émilion (no connection with the Bordeaux wine region) or Ugni blanc (a blending grape one meets in California). After several months in casks it is then subjected to two progressive distillations, the final result being a totally colorless and almost tasteless liquor with an alcoholic content of approximately 70 per cent. This liquor is then stored in charred casks wrought from oak of the nearby forests of Limousin and, depending upon the desired quality, aged from three to twenty-five years. The best unblended and undoctored Cognacs derive their color and flavor from the cask; and it is well to know, too, that after bottling, Cognac ceases to improve. This is a fact that pulls the props out from beneath the "Brandy of Napoleon," which — were it even to exist nowadays — would not be any better than the day it was bottled. "Napoleon Brandy" ranks high among some of the more transparent promotional tricks of the liquor industry.

True richness, mellowness and color come to all brandies only with many years in the cask, but because of a demand far exceeding the supply of good Cognacs, even the best firms blend and dilute with water, and color and sweeten the mixture with caramel—to cut the rawness and instill the proper "aged" hue and flavor. Thus the stars or symbols on a bottle of brandy, supposedly indicating age, may mean far less than one would think. One star is supposed to indicate that the Cognac has spent three years in the cask; each additional star theoretically means an added year—but a clever blending of spirits from several years, plus the requisite amount of caramel, can do wonders for a relatively newborn product. For the *Champagnes* (one should remember that *Grande Fine Champagne* is the best) the producers have yet another series of symbolisms: *V.O.* (Very Old) stands for ten years or more in the cask; *V.S.O.* (Very Superior Old) for fifteen; *E.* or *X.* (for Extra) are usually entirely superfluous. The highest appellation, *V.S.O.P.* (*P.* for Pale), is something else again. It should mean a liquor which is a better blend.

It is not without significance that all these letter symbols—most significantly *P.* for Pale—stand for English words instead of French ones. Obviously, at some time in the annals of Cognac, the producers of the Charentais, in too much of a hurry to age their products long enough in the cask to give them the traditional color and softness, must have sold someone on the idea that raw, pale brandy was the best. Genuine, well-aged *Grande Fine Champagne*, dark in color, strong-flavored and aromatic, is suited only to sipping and sniffing in small quantities. In fact, it is all but repulsive when diluted with water or soda—which is not the case with a brandy that is light and young. Knowing the proclivity of the French for promotion, one doesn't wonder long over why the Englishman came to drink his Very Superior Old Pale—which if taken straight would have removed the lining of his stomach—with soda.

Today, most of the large brandy houses in Cognac, because of the inordinate demand for their products, have had to abandon the *Champagne* terms on their labels, and simply use Cognac, oftentimes embellished with brand names to imply quality. Among the best of these houses are Courvoisier, Hine, Hennessey, Rémy Martin, Martell and Delamain.

The other celebrated brandy of France, made in the *département* of the Gers in the Pyrénées, is Armagnac. This also is a twice-distilled liquid, from native Picpoul and Jurançon grapes, made in the same way as Cognac—except that much Armagnac is still the direct product of small farms, bought and blended by the firms that bottle it after aging. By virtue of the loving care which Armagnac often receives from its individual producers, together with the fact that the name is not as widely known throughout the world as that of Cognac—one will sometimes find it of excellent quality, and relatively inexpensive. After a long life in the cask, a fine Armagnac will have a deliciously indivi-dualistic, fruity bouquet—reminiscent of prunes. Armagnac, inciden-tally, is never selected by taste—but by smell. In the cafés of its home ground, the Béarn, it is not unusual to see the farmer sitting with his little flask over a coffee with the buyer, shaking out a few drops on the latter's palm, to be rubbed around, sniffed, assessed and bargained for.

Surprisingly, there are no large or universally known Armagnac houses that ship recommendable Armagnacs; and most importers seem to view it as a second-rate Cognac. Thus the best rule of thumb for the consumer is to be wary of brand names and large shippers or importers, and to seek out Armagnacs from the smallest and most personalized producers. We warrant one will be amply rewarded.

A year on a bottle of *Fine Champagne* or Armagnac may occasion-ally be seen—as with *solera* Sherry, but with a difference. It does not indicate the year of the oldest few drops in the blend. Certain small producers in the Cognac district continue to turn out unblended and undoctored *Champagnes*, known as *Naturs* or "Single Cask" brandy. Brandy produced in this fashion is almost prohibitively expensive—and to the average brandy drinker, accustomed to the tastes and flavors of the standard, doctored blends, the *Naturs* may well be disappointing. Aging without any interference or treatment, except for the final addi-tion of a certain amount of water to reduce its strength, results in a liquor that is unusually dry and sharp, and though appreciated by con-noisseurs, is definitely an acquired taste.

Other Brandies

The reader should beware of anything simply marked *French Brandy*,[2] and try an import from some other country instead. Brandies

---

[2]The terms *Cognac,* (*Grande*) *Fine Champagne* or *Armagnac* should at least appear on the label; without them, the liquor will not even approach a comparative value.

from wine are made in almost every other wine-producing country in the world—and though they vary enormously, many of them are good. Both Portugal and Spain manufacture considerable amounts of brandy, much of which is used to fortify Port, Sherry and Madeira. To a certain degree all brandies are acquired tastes, and Spanish brandy in particular has many enthusiasts, acquired during the last war, when French brandy was unavailable. Unfortunately, the Spanish conception of the term "brandy" is a rather loose one: it may simply mean a highly fortified wine. Thus the reader is advised to stick religiously to the best. These are almost invariably produced by the most reputable Sherry houses: Carlos III (by Domecq), Carabella Santa Maria (by Osborne) and Insuperable (by Gonzalez Byass) are three of the best. Perhaps the most popular Spanish brandy is Fundador, though its quality leaves much to be desired. Fundador's Portuguese equivalent is known as Constantino. Italian brandy, among the two most popular of which are Stock and Sarti, is by comparison mediocre. California makes far more "brandy" than France—liquor which, were it ever properly aged, might well be comparable in quality, anyway, to European (not French) brandy. But this never seems to happen, and most California products are young, strong and sweetish in taste, and give the impression of being overpoweringly alcoholic. California producers pride themselves on this "purity," and certainly sales speak for themselves. Only the rarest and driest of California brandies can be consumed as one would Cognac. Most of it is in another ball park—best suited for use in mixed drinks.

In many countries of Europe a bastard type of brandy is distilled from the *marc* or leftover "must" of the grapes, watered and refermented after the juice for the wine has been pressed out. Known specifically in France as *eaux-de-vie* (waters of life),[3] it is colorless, coarse and medicinal-tasting, a common drink with peasants and low-income groups for the simple purpose of inducing a quick state of intoxication—as a nocturnal stroll around any French port will speedily bear out. In certain parts of France, however, one will find superior *marcs* carefully made from certain grapes or combinations—*Marc de Traminer, Marc de Bourgogne*, etc. With these, the delicate aroma of the grape greatly enhances the distillation; they are much sought after by con-

---

[3] Also often called *marc* in France, in Germany it is *Trestebranntwein* or *Trinkbranntwein*, in Italy *grappa*. The Spanish equivalent is called *aguardiente* (burning water), the Portuguese equivalent *agurdente*.

noisseurs. Calvados, a French "brandy" made from cider, can be delicious with sufficient age, carrying a delightful, haunting aroma of apples. Other excellent European fruit brandies include those made from cherries (Kirsch), from wild raspberries (Framboise), from strawberries (Fraise)—not to mention Swiss pear brandy (Poire), and France's Prunelle and Poland's Slivovitz, distilled from fermented plums to produce firewater with the power of an atomic submarine. The finest fruit brandies derive from Alsace, Switzerland's Valais and Germany's Black Forest.

Summary

The best brandies are French Cognacs, the superlative of which is called *Grande Fine Champagne*. Almost all brandies are blends, and one should not be shocked to learn that even the best liked are generally doctored with caramel to give the color, richness and flavor that the public demands. A year on a French brandy label usually means nothing unless it be a pure unblended product also labeled *Natur* (or "Single Cask"). It will be expensive and probably disappointing to those who are used to sweetened and otherwise doctored blends.

Brandy improves only in the oaken cask, never in the bottle; anything named "Napoleon Brandy," implying great age, smacks of a marketing hoax.

The second-finest brandy of France, less well known, is called Armagnac, from the Pyrénées. Good Armagnac is softer than Cognac. The only truly recommendable ones are those from very small producers—bottles rarely seen away from France.

One should be wary of something simply labeled *French Brandy*. Imports from other countries—notably Spain, Portugal, Italy—are better. Most California brandy has a taste and strength of flavor all its own.

The best fruit brandies, always colorless, include Kirsch (cherries), Fraise (strawberries), Framboise (raspberries), and Poire (pears). Calvados is a French brandy, somewhat resembling Cognac, made from cider.

CHAPTER 11

The Service and Uses of Wines

Serving Wines

Wine is, after all, primarily for enjoyment—only secondarily is it for show. Yet serving wine presents so many perplexing problems to so many people that it often precludes the enjoyment and use of wine at all. Many of these perplexities may be solved by following a simple rule: given the facilities at hand, do the best you can.

The matter of glasses is as good a case in point as any. One of the pleasantest things about wine is its bouquet—the sensation one receives as the glass is being brought to the lips. The sense of smell, with all of us, is very closely allied to taste, and bouquet is thus the forerunner of taste. So the larger the glass (within obvious limits), the more ample the exposed surface of wine for evaporation and the more bouquet. One often hears that wine should be "allowed to breathe." Of equal importance is the reverse: the wine drinker should be allowed to inhale the bouquet of the wine. Hence wine is logically at better advantage when served in a tumbler than in a thimble. In Burgundy, for example, where great stress is laid on the bouquet of a wine, the traditional glass is the size of a small finger bowl.

If one does not own the exactly appropriate wineglasses, one will certainly have tumblers or water goblets. Their size will at least provide the surface for adequate evaporation. Save the decorous little long-stemmed glass thimbles someone gave you for a wedding present; they may make the dinner table pretty, but their true function is for *apéritifs* or after-dinner liqueurs. No wine will ever really be enjoyable in them; in fact, many a wine will not even taste like itself in one of them.

Eventually everyone who becomes a lover of wine wishes to serve it at its best advantage. This does not involve expensive glasses. There are excellent, moderately priced glasses to be had which will cover all contingencies. The ideal all-purpose wineglass—suitable for any still or sparkling wine, or even brandy—is tulip-shaped, made of clear glass, and its bowl between four and five inches high. The length of the stem is immaterial (though this has its practical breakage problems in the washing of it), and can be left to one's own personal esthetic taste. But the glass itself should be wide-brimmed (two inches or more across) and large enough so that, if filled to the brim, it would hold at least seven or eight ounces, preferably more. In Alsace and Germany, where the white wines often approach the paleness of water, the traditional glasses are elaborately cut or decorated. But the all-purpose wineglass should be clear glass, so that along with the bouquet and the taste, one may have the added enjoyment of the wine's color. The tints and hues of wines are pretty.

The corollary to the rule of making the best of what's available is that no wineglass—whether it be the perfect one or the water goblet—should ever be filled more than half full. Many people who do not understand the reason for this take it to be an affectation—or lay it to the miserliness of the host. But the custom has a very practical basis. The basic principle is that the unfilled top half of the glass channels and concentrates the wine's bouquet to the nose—whereas with a glass filled to the brim, the bouquet obviously floats off in all directions and most of it is lost. This is why the tulip-shaped glass has become the traditional best: very much as with the flue rising from a fireplace, its inward-slanting brim concentrates the evaporation, and the bouquet rises in a single column.

How many wines to serve at a meal? Nowadays, customarily one—the one that fits best with the main course. But there may be occasions when one will wish to serve two or more wines at the same meal—and here there are certain pertinent conventions which, if known, may save embarrassment or needless expense. If one perchance owns glasses of different sizes and is serving two or more wines, a white wine is more appropriate in the smaller glass—whereas red wine benefits from having a larger surface for evaporation. Different glasses are certainly not necessary, but the dinner table always has a gayer and more festive appearance with a variation of glassware than with two or more similar glasses set at each place. For those with a closetful of glassware, use your largest, widest-brimmed, balloon-shaped glasses for red Burgundies, your slightly narrower and smaller ones for white wines and other reds (including Bordeaux) and the longest-stemmed goblet types for the Rhine, Moselle and Alsatian wines. The smallest of all will serve for after-dinner brandies and liqueurs, or Sherries and Ports—although, as we have mentioned, fortified wines also are best when there is plenty of surface for evaporation.

Brandy is traditionally served (always in small quantity) in squat, balloon-shaped "snifters," though an ordinary all-purpose wineglass does nearly as well. The finer and more aromatic the brandy, the less one should serve. For Champagnes and sparkling wines, the all-purpose glass also does as well as any. Shallow, broad-brimmed "coupe" glasses customarily used by caterers and others for Champagnes—attributed by some wit to have been modeled after the breasts of Helen of Troy— are to be avoided. As with the totally filled wineglass, Champagne loses much of its charm—as well as its effervescence—by being afforded too much surface for evaporation. Traditional wineglasses are illustrated on p. 221, but few households can boast the whole assortment.

No wineglass should ever be chilled—this inhibits proper evaporation; nor, incidentally, should any glass ever be heated, even for brandy. But whites and *rosés*, Champagnes and sparkling wines are all considerably enhanced by a certain amount of cooling in the bottle. We use the term "cooling" instead of "chilling" advisedly. A wine which is too cold is never itself—though in this connection it may be useful to know that the faults of many a white or *rosé* wine, sparkling or otherwise, may be concealed by a good sound chilling (a favorite trick of wine waiters to cover up a poor vintage). By the same token, the frequently seen advice on the labels of a producer or bottler should serve as a danger signal. Unless it is a wine he knows well, the reader is advised to be wary of the quality of any white or *rosé* bearing on its label the words: *Serve very well chilled.*

Opinions vary, but the approximate temperature for a cooled wine is in general between 45 and 50 degrees. Champagnes and sparkling

Traditional Wineglasses

Burgundy

Champagne

Bordeaux

Rhine Wine

Brandy

wines should be even cooler. This may be achieved in several ways: by putting the wine in a bucket of ice and water—or even better yet, snow and water!—for half an hour or so; or in the refrigerator for about two hours; or in the freezing compartment for approximately half an hour. In dealing with ice or snow, the following is important: Be sure the bottle is immersed up to its neck. The use of the water, too, is all-important.

One should remember, furthermore, that any wine, once it has been overcooled or chilled, never really regains its original power and charm. Such is especially the case with wine that has been frozen—one of the main worries of importers who are oftentimes forced to bring wines across the Atlantic in winter. Occasionally one will come across a white wine with minute crystals—or whitish flakes. These generally are the result of precipitation—from too much prolonged cold—of the natural cream of tartar or tartaric acid in the wine. There is no harm to them, and no permanent damage has been done the wine, other than the slight degeneration from too much cold. If one finds them esthetically objectionable, a few days in a warm room and a bit of periodic agitation of the bottle will usually dissolve them.

With a few minor exceptions (Beaujolais and some domestic reds are the principal ones), red wine should not be cool—but not *warmed* or heated, either. If it is practical to do so, the red wine one intends to drink should be allowed to remain for at least two hours in the room in which it will be consumed. But it should not be left next to the stove, warmed with hot water or put before an open fire. Wine brought suddenly to room temperature loses much of its vigor—as does wine served at a temperature appreciably higher than room temperature. Under ideal conditions, the wine should actually be a little cooler than the room itself. This may perhaps be accomplished by leaving it in the coolest part of the room—on the floor, say, away from heating units.

Should red wine be opened ahead of time? All red wines are improved by having been opened an hour or so before the meal and allowed to breathe. This, of course, is never done in restaurants—unless one orders it so beforehand—and is often overlooked in the home. In our opinion, the practice is by no means as important as it is made out to be. Many lovers of wine, especially those who enjoy lingering over their glasses, experience much pleasure in all the different and intriguing stages of aeration which wine poured directly from the newly opened bottle undergoes in the glass. A possible exception might be a very old wine—for which more aeration could be necessary than for a younger one. White wines should never be opened until just before serving.

Well-made red wines—especially aged ones—often have a sediment, which is unpleasant if mixed with the contents of the bottle. Obviously, if one has bought a bottle at the corner liquor store and brought it home to drink that evening, there is nothing much to be done about it. But ideally one should have bought it a few days, or preferably a week or so, ahead of drinking, to let the wine rest, with the bottle standing upright to allow the sediment to collect at the bottom. Well before drinking, one may—if one wishes—ease the bottle gently onto its side and lay it in a wine basket. The important point is not to joggle an aged wine any more than possible in pouring—whether it be in an upright position or in a basket. Or else one may decant it, a recommended practice for very old wine containing a great deal of sediment. The conventional way to decant is to pour the wine slowly, several hours before serving, into another receptacle—preferably a glass decanter—with a bright light or a candle behind the neck of the bottle. The decanting is stopped when the first sign of dregs appears. A simple glass decanter is always a useful accessory to any wine-drinking household.

This leads us to the by no means unimportant matter of corkscrews and uncorking. If one has gone to all the trouble to allow the dregs of the red wine to settle, obviously a battle between the bottle and the wine drinker using an inefficient corkscrew will negate all one's previous good intentions. Happily, the best corkscrews are both the simplest and the cheapest: those which resemble a fat pocketknife, with a small curved blade that folds into one end and a corkscrew into the other. Most liquor dealers or wine merchants will present you with one of these with their compliments. With the knife take away the foil around the lip of the bottle, and thoroughly wipe (or lightly wash) the exposed surface of the cork and the neck of the bottle. The corkscrew is then inserted directly down the middle of the cork—as far as possible, but not so far as to lose leverage for pulling. Most corks break or shatter not as a result of being faulty, but because the corkscrew has not penetrated deeply enough, or not been driven down the middle. Pull gently and evenly—and firmly. In the case of an extra-long cork, one may have to pause midway to drive the corkscrew further, to gain more leverage.

One should remember that just because a cork breaks, or part of it appears to be rotten, it does not follow that the wine is spoiled. An almost invariable rule of thumb for knowing if a wine has been "corked," or spoiled, is to smell the wet end of the cork: if it smells of clean wine, the bottle probably is good. On the other hand, if it smells of musty cork, there are grounds for investigation.

Champagne and sparkling wines should never be opened with a corkscrew. After removing the wire and the foil, hold the bottle a little on its side (in your right hand), grasp the cork in your left hand and twist the bottle itself — *not* the cork. Use a towel or a cloth for a better grip and for your own protection in case the bottle contains a flaw and should explode. As the bottle is thus twisted, ease the cork out gently. The pressure within the bottle usually does the job itself. After the cork is out, continue to hold the bottle at the same angle for a few short seconds before pouring, to deter foaming.

Well-cooled Champagne will open with a discreet pop and a faint whiff of the blue smoke; but, if one *must* open a bottle of insufficiently cooled or warm Champagne, it is a part of wisdom not to aim the cork at a guest's eye — and one should count on a considerable wastage.

Champagne, and even wines, are sometimes served encased in a towel. This is, at best, an affectation. It is also an insult to one's guests, who deserve the courtesy of inspecting the label.

Although it is traditional for the host to pour — or to have poured — a small amount of wine into his own glass, this can often turn out to be an awkward and embarrassing practice, in which case it should be skipped — with the wine simply passing around the table from place to place. The reason for this custom, of course, is to ensure that the host's glass will receive any little fragments of cork floating in the bottle; also so that he may taste the wine and reject it, if necessary, before it is served to his guests. A far more gracious procedure, we think, is one by which the host tastes the wine when it is opened, away from his guests.

Purists shudder at the thought — but an opened bottle of wine may be kept over for an ensuing meal or until the next day. White and *rosé* wine should be stored in the refrigerator, red wine in a cool place — both tightly corked. It should not be forgotten, however, that wine is a living thing, containing a minuscule number of residual live yeasts, and always prey to the vinegar-making yeast, which feeds on the alcohol in the wine. It will never keep longer than unpasteurized milk.

Many white wines—especially the older and sweeter ones—also stand a chance of becoming *maderizé* (turning the color of Sherry and developing a bitter taste) when kept over; occasionally one even runs across a bottle of white wine that becomes *maderizé* within a few minutes after being opened. Should it be a wine you particularly like, remember to open the next bottle at the very last minute, and to consume it without delay. One's wine merchant should be informed of any such development, so that he may warn his other customers and his supplier.

Finally, although the average person today will want to serve only one wine with a meal, there do exist certain customs having to do with sequences in serving wines—something that often has a bearing on the menu one plans for a meal. In the ensuing pages the reader will find suggestions as to what wines go best with certain foods; but leaving aside, for the moment, the matter of appropriate fare, the following are the two traditional rules covering the serving of more than one wine at a meal. The first is best summarized as "youth before beauty." A less distinguished wine—meaning a lighter or a younger one, or one with a less pronounced taste, bouquet or body—precedes an older or heavier or stronger one. In this way one avoids what may turn out to be a disappointing anticlimax. The second rule is that a white wine always asserts its character and charm better when served before a red. The principal exception would be a sweet white wine, such as a French Sauternes or a German *Beerenauslese*—suited to desserts and fruits or consumed with coffee as a *liqueur*.

Wines with Foods

There are no inalterable rules about foods with wines, but there are highways and byways to guide the reader toward a better enjoyment of wine with meals. Of one thing the wine drinker may be entirely certain: "hard liquors" never really mix with wine. Cocktails and strong alcoholic liquors served before a meal with wine tend to destroy one's taste, and this applies particularly to cocktails or drinks laden with sugar or fruit juices, such as a rum cocktail. A dry martini, on the other hand (in essence a doubly or sometimes astronomically fortified Vermouth), is for some people less burdensome to the palate. Others can get away with a whiskey. But the ideal is dry Sherry or dry white Port, or a Vermouth or, if one can afford it, a glass of Champagne. This is not to say that there is something criminal in having a strong drink before a meal with wine: only a warning that good wine does not bloom on the palate after hard liquor, and that it is therefore foolhardy to serve an expensive or choice wine at a meal which has been preceded by cocktails. Better to serve a modest Beaujolais or a humble *rosé*, and leave the Chambertin or Bernkasteler Doktor for another day.

Certain foods, too, definitely cloud the vision of a wine's beauty. These are principally overseasoned or spicy dishes, using curry, horse-radish, mint, chutney, cloves—and even garlic. A Chablis, a Pouilly-Fuissé and a dry German Riesling are notably excellent companions for oysters, clams and many other seafoods—but if one insists on Worcestershire, Tabasco or a strong cocktail sauce with seafood, it will be expedient to skip the wine with that course. Another incompatible with wine is vinegar and all foods which contain it, such as pickles. One may successfully substitute lemon juice for the vinegar in salad dressing—but pickled foods are an insurmountable problem. Not only do they contain vinegar, but also sugar, both enemies of most wines. As one will soon discover, only sweet dessert wines ever seem to go well with sweet or sugar dishes. A Sauternes enhances ice cream and sherbert, puddings and sweet soufflés; but a red Bordeaux, a Chianti *Classico* or a Californian Pinot Noir have the opposite effect. Perhaps the sole exception is that sweet wines are oftentimes the most suitable for Chinese and Polynesian cookery. Most vegetables are in general enhanced by wine—the exception being, perhaps, artichokes, whose mysterious chemical qualities even change the taste of water.

The best friend at the table of all wines is cheese—especially delicious with red and *rosé*, though we think the wine drinker will eventually discover that the stronger the cheese, the redder and heavier he will want the wine. For very strong cheeses, one of the fortified wines (Port, Madeira or Marsala) is probably the best accompaniment. Yet cheese can also be a false friend of wine: it so enhances wine that even a bad wine tastes delicious. This is the reason we always see cheese at promotional wine tastings. If one really wants to assess the wines, nibble on the bread and resist the cheese!

Many people overlook the natural affinity that wines of one nation have with that nation's native foods. Italian dishes, for example, so often enhanced by strong tomato and meat sauces, cheeses and herbs, are gastronomic bedfellows of those relatively coarse and rough reds of Italy, whereas a delicate Médoc is hopelessly lost in their company. By the same token, an Italian Soave or a Chablis from California taste bland and inadequate with a rich, complicated French sauce. Yet a Swiss cheese *fondue* attains its true glory only when washed down by a white Neuchâtel. When serving dishes of a distinctly nationalistic character, the wine drinker will do well to keep this affinity in mind. Also, a wine always tastes just a little better in the place of its birth.

There is, of course, the age-old saying that white wine is for white meat, red wine for red meat—"St.-Émilion with fur, Médoc with feathers!" is another classic gastronomic adage. These are all very well as general guides—yet there are notable exceptions, including several classic French fish dishes with red-wine sauces, and some celebrated Germanic creations of venison or beef embellished with Riesling. In Germany it is customary to drink white wine with everything. Cynics say this is because Germany makes no good red wine, but the proof is in the pudding—the combination is anything but disharmonious. But the tradition of taste has it that whites are for fish; white, red (St.-Émilion *or* Médoc) or *rosé* wine go well with any white-meat dish— whether it be chicken (feathers) or veal or rabbit (fur); and red wine is, of course, better with beef and game. Pork (a borderline white meat) and ham never seem to lend themselves to any still wine. As an accompaniment to baked or broiled ham, most people settle for a sparkling white or a Champagne, or skip the wine entirely. Champagne and *rosé* wines, in the last analysis, are always common denominators: even though they do not blend ideally with all foods, they are rarely offensive or out of place, and one may be sure that they will at least taste like wine. Champagnes and sparkling wines go with desserts, but take care that your Champagne is not too dry.

Cooking with Wine

The French, whose wonderful culinary skills are sometimes debasingly characterized as the "art of cooking with leftovers," are masters of cooking with wine. Sauces and stews and marinades made with wine, fruits with cooked (or uncooked) wine, fish poached in wine are all recipes that abound in their cookbooks. The bibles of *Haute Cuisine*, such as Brillat-Savarin and Escoffier, often go several steps further. Here you will find *Sole au Champagne* or *Turbot au Chambertin*, *Poires Château Lafite* and many another dish which in this day and age of high prices constitute near-blasphemy.

Yet the unwritten rules of *Haute Cuisine*, however impractical they may be to follow to the letter, are valid principles, wisdom to be heeded in any kitchen. The first is: "Cook with your best and drink the rest!" Its corollary is more flexible. "Make the dish with the wine you plan to drink." In other words, a wine unfit to drink is not fit to cook with. Also, don't build the steak's sauce around a Médoc and wash it down with Chianti, or poach a fish in Soave and drink a Moselle. The sole exceptions to the second maxim (but *not* the first) are cooking with Sherry or Madeira, always used sparsely and for flavoring at the end; or burning off excess fat or butter with brandy, which adds flavor too.

So-called cooking wines, usually non-alcoholic or else adulterated with salt and other ingredients, or low-grade Sherry or Madeira or brandy have no true place in the kitchen. Wine adds zest and flavor to the food, but since it is usually reduced or concentrated in the cooking to at least a half or a third, and sometimes to almost nothing, its qualities (or faults) are proportionately exaggerated. Cooking with a poor or inappropriate wine may ruin the entire meal. If you do not have enough of the good wine you plan to drink to cook with as well, at least use a comparable type for cooking—perhaps a Californian made from the same or a kindred grape.

Dry white and red wines are best for cooking, except in rare instances where the residual sugar of a sweet or semi-sweet wine can be counted on to harmonize with the sugar of a sauce or a dish. Sauces for game, which often include Madeira and currant jelly, fall in this category; as does a celebrated French chicken dish, *Poulet Cintra*, the sauce for which calls for brandy, white wine, Port and cream. Some white Bordeaux, incidentally, turn inexplicably blue when used to poach fish. It doesn't matter.

Cooking with wine or reducing it boils out the alcohol, so banish the idea that a "winey" dish contributes so much as one tiny drop to your inebriation. However, the residual liquid sometimes requires painful waste on the part of the chef. Enough wine to cover and poach a fish a few brief minutes, for example, even if mixed with water or *court-bouillon*, often leaves too much liquid for a subtle sauce. Pull yourself up by your bootstraps and throw part of it out. Reduced wine is flavorsomely strong. It should be thought of somewhat as herbs, for which one fatuous little proverb goes: "A sprig of thyme lasts a long time; a leaf of bay goes a long way."

Summary

Wine is primarily for enjoyment—only secondarily for show: just because one does not have the perfect glassware and the know-how of a connoisseur is no reason for not serving it. There are certain simple rules to heed: wine profits by evaporation in the glass, thus it is better served in a tumbler or a water goblet than in a thimble. It is not necessary to purchase a different type of wineglass for every different type of wine. All-purpose wineglasses—suitable for red, white, *rosé* and sparkling wines—are not expensive. They should be tulip-shaped, at least two inches wide at the brim, and hold seven or eight ounces or more.

In serving wine, the glass should never be much more than half filled. This concentrates the bouquet.

If one serves two or more wines, a white is more effective if served before a red; similarly, a young or "lesser" wine before an older and "greater" one. White and *rosé* wines should be cooled (but not heavily "chilled"); red wine, except for Beaujolais and comparable types, is best at slightly below room temperature.

The maxim that red wine goes with red meat, white wine with white meat, is a sound rule—but not infallible. Chicken tastes well with both. Pork and ham present problems; they are probably best with a not-too-dry sparkling white. *Rosé* or sparkling wines are often the most practical, harmonizing with almost any dish.

Beware of highly seasoned food with wines: curry, pickles and vinegar do not mix with any wine.

The best drinks before wine are dry Sherry, dry white Port, dry Vermouth, and Champagne. Cocktails containing sugar or fruit juices kill a wine's taste: to serve an expensive wine after any of them is foolhardy. If one must serve spirits, the universally acknowledged cocktail is a martini, which, in the last analysis, is a fortified Vermouth.

Wine used judiciously in cooking enhances flavors of certain foods. One may not be able to follow the traditional maxim of French *Haute Cuisine*—"Cook with your best, drink the rest!"—but cooking with good wine pays off. If possible, cook with the wine (or at least the type of wine) you intend to drink with the dish served. And remember that except for wines with fruits, the wine of a sauce or a stew is generally reduced to at least a half or a third of its original volume, exaggerating its flavor, as well as its faults.

CHAPTER 12

The Storage of Wines

A wine dealer may be of much value in storing a quantity of wine until one needs it. Nowadays only a few of us live where we may have a wine cellar or satisfactory storage facilities. A dark closet accomplishes the purpose in the case of a dozen or so bottles, especially a red wine that should settle for a while after joggling on its journey from the store—provided one intends to consume the wines within a month or two. But over a period of time wine ages prematurely and deteriorates rapidly when not stored at a reasonably constant temperature, ideally ranging between 50 and 55 degrees. Furthermore, it should be stored on its side; otherwise the cork dries and air, carrying vinegar-making and other harmful yeasts with it, enters to spoil the wine.

One's storage space should be neither too damp nor too dry. It should be free of bright light, especially daylight—and vibration. Consequently, if one is without these facilities—or even with them, if one lives near a subway or an express parkway or on a busy street—the ideal solution is to have wines stored by one's local dealer at a nominal fee, bringing them home a few at a time. For large quantities, some use air-conditioned public warehouses.

Those of us who live where we may store our own wines properly are in luck. Wine is almost always cheaper when bought comparatively young and by the case, and waiting to purchase properly aged red wines from merchants is an expensive affair. Given all the above ideal conditions (correct temperature, no light or vibration, etc.), the following additional advice may be of value to the wine drinker contemplating a wine cellar of his own. One's bins should be square, but tipped to a diamond shape so that a corner is at the bottom—thus a single bottle constitutes the first tier. Additionally, bins should be large enough (at least fourteen inches square) to hold a full case of Burgundy or Champagne, the thickest bottles extant in the "fifth" size. Since white wines mature faster, lay them (on their sides) in the bins closest to the cool floor, with the reds on the top tiers. Fortified wines (Sherries, Ports, etc.) are traditionally stored upright, as are brandies and other spirits. A slight seasonal variation of temperature in your wine closet or cellar—one of 5 degrees, say—will do no appreciable harm, even though it is not ideal. The rule of thumb regarding temperature is that the warmer the storage area, the sooner the wine matures. But no wine profits by being forced to maturity. Thus a temperature of more than 70 degrees over a protracted length of time will be ruinous.

Many wise wine drinkers, with or without their own cellars, supplement their memories and greatly add to their pleasure in wine by maintaining a cellar book, or even a scrapbook of labels, in which they record the wine's cost, where it was purchased, notations on importers and the bottlers—as well as notes on the progress toward maturity of successive bottles of wines that have been bought in quantity and laid down. For those who wish to acquire a knowledge of the subtleties of wines, such a practice cannot be recommended too highly. It will soon be noted, too, that all wines, most especially reds, pass through inexplicable and alarming stages in the process of reaching their maturity—periodic setbacks of taste and character. Statistics or notes on this and many other developments in the cellar are invaluable.

When buying quantities of wine, it should not be overlooked that although half-bottles are a great convenience, especially for a small family or for purposes of tasting and experimentation, the smaller the bottle the faster the wine matures. This is why one sometimes finds stores having sales or "specials" on half-bottles several years or so ahead of the logical time for a wine's maturity. The ideal size bottle for almost any wine is the magnum—equal to two full bottles or "fifths." Today this translates to the 1.5-liter size. Unfortunately, magnums are impractical except for large functions or parties, though the farsighted master of his cellar will do well to have a few around for special occasions.

One comes to the touchy matter of summarizing the rules of age and maturity. As a rule, white wines may be consumed between one and four years of age; most red wines—at least those made within the last decade—between three and eight. A fine red Bordeaux, especially a Médoc or a Graves, will have twice the life of a comparable Burgundy, the best of which are usually starting their prime at the age of ten. Well-made red Rhône wines, especially from recognized vineyards, improve in the bottle over many years, as do the superior (*Reserva*) reds of Spain, Portugal and Italy. But these latter must be of superlative quality. And one will be amazed at the improvement and change in character of a California red from one of the classic grapes, such as a Cabernet Sauvignon, that takes place after five or even ten years in the cellar.

Few dry white wines—Californian, French, German, Italian, Spanish or Portuguese—improve in the bottle after a year or so, when they have lost their "greenness"; thus there is no valid reason not to drink them young. But the sweetest ones from French and German vineyards do indeed mellow and grow with time. For immediate drinking, a Beaujolais or a *rosé* from any country may always be relied on.

Vintages should be heeded, of course. That is why the charts are prepared by experts. But it must be borne in mind that vintage years for California (even though we give them, for what they are worth) and for any European vineyard south of Bordeaux or any but the classic Rhône regions, are of no great or intrinsic importance. As one works northward, however, vintage years become of increasing significance— their greatest value being, of course, as a guide to the proper selection of an old wine, or a young wine one wishes to buy and lay down. Yet even so, at the risk of repetition, it cannot be emphasized too strongly that vintage charts and statistics must be regarded with a well-cocked eye: like all statistics, they have their outstanding exceptions. Through some freak of nature or some particular skill on the part of a grower, fine wines—even in the northernmost climes—are sometimes made in poor years. Only personal experimentation or a tip from a friend or one's wine merchant will find them. Abject slavery to any vintage chart is simple idiocy, enabling the other fellow to get the real bargains and sometimes the best wines.

Summary

Unless one has almost perfect facilities—a relatively dry storage area with an ideal constant temperature of between 50 and 55 degrees, without bright light and free from vibration—one should try to get a local dealer to store any wine one wants to buy by the case; a good red wine of a fine year can be expensive if one waits for the importer or dealer to age it for sale.

In storing one's own wines, lay the bottles on their sides. White wines mature faster than reds and should be closer to the floor, where it is cooler.

Wine in half-bottles matures faster than in full bottles; magnums of red (1.5-liter size) age ideally, but are not always practical. In any complete cellar, one or two magnums, however, should be available for occasions.

Vintage charts have their uses, especially for the wines of France and Germany: but people who keep their noses glued to them often lose out. Some wines from poor years may be excellent bargains. One should consult one's dealers and keep one's ears open.

In general, white wines may be consumed between the ages of one and four; red wines between three and eight. The finest of France, Spain, Portugal and Italy need more age. *Rosés* are ready to drink when young. None of them—and only a few whites—ever improves appreciably in the bottle. The notable exceptions are French white Hermitages, Sauternes and Barsacs, and German *Beerenauslesen* and *Trockenbeerenauslesen*.

APPENDIX A

General Evaluations of Recent Vintage Years

	1966	1967	1968	1969	1970	1971	1972	1973	1974	1975	1976	1977	1978
BORDEAUX RED	(E)	F	P	P	(E)	F	P	F	(G)	(E)	(G)	F	(G)
BORDEAUX WHITE	F	G	P	G	E	F	F	G	F	E	G	P	F
BURGUNDY RED	E	F	P	E	(E)	(E)	F	F	P	P	(E)	P	(E)
BURGUNDY WHITE	E	G	F	E	G	G	G	G	G	G	(G)	F	(G)
RHÔNE	E	F	P	F	E	(E)	F	F	P	P	(E)	(F)	(E)
LOIRE	G	G	P	G	E	E	P	F	G	G	E	G	G
GERMANY	G	E	P	G	G	E	P	G	P	E	E	F	F
ITALY	P	G	F	G	F	F	F	G	E	(E)	G	(G)	(G)
CALIFORNIA	G	P	E	G	E	F	F	G	E	G	(E)	G	G

P = POOR   F = FAIR   G = GOOD   E = EXCELLENT   ◯ = LAY DOWN (EXCEPT BEAUJOLAIS)

Bibliography

ADAMS, LEON. D. *Wines of America,* 2nd ed. McGraw Hill Book Co., 1978.

ALLEN, H. WARNER. *Natural Red Wines.* London: Constable, 1951.

——. *A Contemplation of Wine.* London: Michael Joseph, 1951.

AMERINE, M. A., and M. A. JOSLYN. *Table Wines: The Technology of Their Production.* 2d rev. ed. Berkeley: University of California Press, 1970.

BESPALOFF, ALEXIS. *The First Book of Wine.* New York: World Publishing Co., 1972.

BROADBENT, J. M. *Wine Tasting.* London: Wine and Spirit Publications, Ltd., 1968.

CHURCHILL, CREIGHTON. *A Notebook for the Wines of France.* New York: Alfred A. Knopf, 1961.

——. *The Great Wine Rivers.* New York: The Macmillan Company, 1971.

COCKS, C., and E. FERET. *Bordeaux et ses Vins.* Bordeaux: Feret & Fils, 1969.

CROFT-CROOKE, RUPERT. *Sherry.* New York: Alfred A. Knopf, 1956.

DALLAS, PHILLIP. *The Great Wines of Italy.* New York: Doubleday, 1974.

DION, ROGER. *Histoire de la Vigne et de Vin de France.* Paris: Dion, 1959.

HALÁSZ, ZOLTÁN. *Hungarian Wine Through the Ages.* Budapest: Covina Press, 1962.

HALLGARTEN, S. F. *Alsace: Its Wine Gardens, Cellars and Cuisine.* London: Wine and Spirit Publications, 1978.

——, and ANDRÉ L. SIMON. *The Great Wines of Germany.* New York: McGraw-Hill Book Co., 1963.

[235]

HYAMS, EDWARD. *The Wine Country of France.* Philadelphia: J. B. Lippincott, 1960.

——. *Dionysus: A Social History of the Wine Vine.* New York: The Macmillan Company, 1965.

JACQUELIN, LOUIS, and RENÉ POULAIN. *The Wines and Vineyards of France.* New York: G. P. Putnam's Sons, 1962.

JOHNSON, HUGH. *Wine.* rev. ed. New York: Simon and Schuster, 1975.

——. *Wine Atlas of the World.* rev. ed. New York: Simon and Schuster, 1978.

LANGENBACH, ALFRED. *German Wines and Vines.* London: Vista Books, 1962.

LARMAT, L. *Atlas de la France vinicole.* Paris: L. Larmat, 1949 *et seq.*

——. *Les Vins de Bordeaux.*

——. *Les Vins de Bourgogne.*

——. *Les Vins de Champagne.*

——. *Les Vins des Côtes du Rhône.*

——. *Les Vins des Coteaux de la Loire.*

——. *Les Eaux-de-Vie de France: Le Cognac.*

LICHINE, ALEXIS. *Guide to the Wines and Vineyards of France.* New York: Alfred A. Knopf, Inc., 1979.

——. *Encyclopedia of Wines and Spirits.* New York: Alfred A. Knopf, 1967.

LUCIA, S. P. *Wine as Food and Medicine.* New York: Blakiston, 1954.

MARRISON, L. W. *Wine and Spirits.* London: Penguin, 1962.

MELVILLE, JOHN. *Guide to California Wines* (paperback). San Carlos, Calif.: Nourse Publishing Co., 1972.

POUPON, PIERRE, and PIERRE FORGEOT. *A Book of Burgundy.* New York: Hastings House, 1958.

——. *The Wines of Burgundy.* Paris: Presses Universitaires de France, 1971.

QUIMME, PETER. *The Signet Book of American Wine.* 3rd rev. ed. New York: New American Library, 1980.

RAY, CYRIL. *Lafite: The Story of Ch. Lafite-Rothschild.* New York: Stein & Day, 1969.

RODIER, CAMILLE. *Le Vin de Bourgogne.* Dijon: L. Damidot, 1948.

——. *Le Clos de Vougeot.* Dijon: L. Damidot, 1959.

ROGER, J. R. *The Wines of Bordeaux.* New York: E. P. Dutton, 1960.

ROWSELL, EDMUND PENNING. *The Wines of Bordeaux.* London: The International Wine and Food Society—Michael Joseph, 1969.

SAINTSBURY, GEORGE. *Notes on a Cellar-Book.* 1920. Reprint. New York: Mayflower Books, 1978.

SCHOONMAKER, FRANK. *Encyclopedia of Wine.* rev. ed. New York: Hastings House, 1980.

SICHEL, PETER. *The Wines of Germany: Completely Revised Edition of Frank Schoonmaker's Classic.* New York: Hastings House, 1980.

SHAND, P. MORTON. *A Book of French Wines.* 2nd rev. ed. New York: Alfred
. A. Knopf, 1960.

SIMON, ANDRÉ L. *A Wine Primer.* London: Michael Joseph, 1962.

——. *The Noble Grapes and the Great Wines of France.* New York: McGraw-
Hill Book Co., 1957.

——. *Guide to Good Food and Wines.* London: Collins, 1960.

——. *Wines of the World.* New York: McGraw-Hill Book Co., 1967.

STREET, JULIAN. *Wines.* rev. ed. New York: Alfred A. Knopf, 1948.

——. *The Common Sense of Wine.* New York: World Publishing Co., 1966.

VALENTE-PERFITO, J. D. *Let's Talk About Port.* Oporto: Instituto do Vinho do
Porto, 1948.

WAGNER, PHILIP M. *American Wines and Wine-Making.* New York: Alfred A.
Knopf, 1961.

YOUNGER, WILLIAM. *Gods, Men & Wine.* New York: World Publishing Co.,
1966.

YOXALL, H. W. *The Wines of Burgundy.* rev. ed. New York: Stein & Day, 1979.

Pronouncing Glossary of Wine Terms and Names

Abbreviations

Fr. French   *Ger.* German   *Port.* Portuguese
It. Italian   *Hun.* Hungarian   *Sp.* Spanish

abboccato (ah-bo-*kaht*-oh) (*It.*): Sweet; sweetish.

Abfüllung (Ahb-*fuel*-lung) (*Ger.*): Bottled by; *eigene A.:* own bottling; *A. Weingut* (*Vine*-goot): Estate bottled by ... ; *A. Weinkellerie* (*Vine*-kel-ler-*ree*): bottled in the cellars of ... ; *A. Winzer* (*Vin*-tser): bottled by grower.

adamado (ah-dam-*ad*-oh) (*Port.*): Sweet; literally: "for ladies."

adegas (eh-*day*-gash): Portuguese wine house; producer's cellars.

Alella (Al-*aye*-ya): Spanish wine, made near Barcelona.

Alavesa (Al-ah-*vay-sah*): Section of

Spanish Rioja region, east of Ebro River.

Aligoté (Al-ee-*got*-ay): White (and inferior) Burgundy grape.

Aloxe-Corton (Al-*laws*-Kor-*taw*): Burgundy commune (Côte de Beaune).

alta (*al*-tah) (*Sp.*): High; upper: as in Rioja Alta.

Amontillado (Ah-mont-ee-*ah*-doe): Popular type of dry Sherry.

Anbaugebeit (An-*bau*-ge-bite) (*Ger.*): Region (new German wine law). See Rheingau, etc.

Anjou (Anh-*zhoo*): Wine (and region) of lower Loire (France).

apéritif (a-pair-ee-*teef*) (*Fr.*): Before-meal drink, usually fortified wine.

Appellations Contrôlées (Ap-pell-ass-see-*yaw* Kon-troll-*ay*): Regulations pertaining to principal vineyards and wines (France).

Arbois (Arr-*bwa*): Wine (and commune) of Jura (France).

Arinto (Ar-*reen*-too): Portuguese white-wine grape, kin of Riesling.

Armagnac (Ar-man-*nyack*): Brandy (and region) of Pyrénées (France).

Asti Spumante (*Ahs*-tee Spoo-*man*-tay): Popular Italian sparkling wine, Piedmont region.

Aus dem Lesegut (*Layz*-ay-goot) (*Ger.*): Harvested by. . . .

Aus eigenem Lesegut (Ows *eye*-gen-em *Lay*-say-goot) (*Ger.*): Grower's own harvest.

Auslese (*Ows*-lay-seh) (*Ger.*): Wine from specially selected ripe grapes.

Ausone (Oh-*sohne*): (Château) "1st Growth" St.-Émilion (Bordeaux).

Badacsonyi Kéknyelü (*Bahd*-ac-cho-ny *Kek*-en-ay-loo): Hungarian white wine.

baja (*ba*-hah) (*Sp.*): Lower: as in Rioja Baja.

Barbaresco (Bar-bar-*ess*-co): Italian red wine, Piedmont region.

Barbera (Bar-*bair*-ah): Italian grape and generic red wine; also Californian.

Bardolino (Bar-doe-*leen*-oh): Italian red wine, made near Verona.

Barolo (Bar-*oh*-lo): Italian red wine, Piedmont region.

Barsac (*Bar*-sack): Subdivision of Sauternes region (Bordeaux).

Bâtard-Montrachet (Bah-*tar*-Maw-rahsh-*ay*): Burgundy vineyard, part of Montrachet "group" (Côte de Beaune).

Beaujolais (Bo-zho-*lay*): Southern Burgundy red wine (and region).

Beaune (Bone): Principal town of Côte d'Or (Burgundy); (Côte de) southern half of Côte d'Or.

Beerenauslese (Beer-en-*ows*-lay-seh) (*Ger.*): Wine from individually picked, overripe grapes.

Bereich (Bare-*ikhe*) (*Ger.*): District (under new German wine law).

Berg (Bairg) (*Ger.*): Hill or mountain; steep hillside.

Bergerac (Bair-zhair-*ack*): Wine (and wine town), Dordogne (France).

Beugnon(s) (Burr-*nyaw*): "2nd Growth" Chablis vineyard.

Beychevelle (Bay-sheh-*vell*): (Château) "4th Growth" Médoc (Bordeaux). Unofficially considered a "2nd."

Bèze (Clos de) (Klo deh Baihz): Classic Burgundy vineyard of Chambertin "group."

Blanc de Blancs (Blahw deh Blahw) (*Fr.*): Predominantly a Champagne term, indicating wine made from white grapes only.

Blanchots (Blahw-*show*): "1st Growth" Chablis vineyard.

blanco (*blan*-koe) (*Sp.*): White (wine).

Blaye (Côtes de) (Coat deh Bly): Wine region of Bordeaux.

Bocksbeutel (*Box*-boy-tell) (*Ger.*): Squat, flagon-shaped bottle, used for Frankenwein and Steinwein.

bodega (bo-*day*-ga) (*Sp.*): Wine house; producer's cellars.

Bonnes-Mares (Bohn-*Mar*): Famous Burgundy vineyard (Côte de Nuits).

Bordeaux (Boar-*doh*): French port; wine from Bordeaux district.

Bourg (Côtes de) (Coat deh Boorg): Wine region of Bordeaux.

Bourgogne (Bur-*goyn*) (*Fr.*): Burgundy; (*vin de*) wine thereof.

Bourgros (Boor-*grow*): "1st Growth" Chablis vineyard.

bouteille(s) (boo-tay) (*Fr.*): Bottle(s).

Boxbeutel: See *Bocksbeutel.*

Brouilly (also Côte de Brouilly) (Bru-*ee*): Two of the nine principal (superior) subdivisions of Beaujolais (France).

brut (*broo*-t): Champagne or sparkling-wine term: very dry.

Bual (Boo-*al*): Madeira type most comparable to red Port.

Bucelas (Boo-*sell*-ush): Wine (and region) of central Portugal.

Cabernet sauvignon (Kab-err-*nay*): Red-wine grape, basically of Bordeaux; Cabernet franc: related grape, less used, also Bordeaux.

Cabinett (*Ger.*): See *Kabinett.*

Calvados (Kal-va-*dohs*) (*Fr.*): Spirits distilled from cider.

Carcavelos (Kar-kar-*vell*-oush): Portuguese sweet wine.

Cassis (Kah-*see*): Currant liqueur (Burgundy); Mediterranean wine town (and wine).

caves (kahv) (*Fr.*): Cellars; wine storehouses.

Cérons (Sair-*ahw*): White-wine region of Bordeaux.

Certan (Sair-*tanh*): (Château) "1st Growth" Pomerol (Bordeaux).

Chablis (Shab-*lee*): Northern Burgundy white-wine region.

Châlon (Shall-*onh*): Vineyard (Château) of Jura (France); Chalon: wine town, Southern Burgundy.

Chalonnaise (Shall-awn-*ays*): Southern Burgundy wine region.

Chambertin (Shawm-bair-*tanh*): Classic Burgundy red-wine vineyard.

Chambolle-Musigny (Sham-*bowl*-Mew-seen-*yee*): Burgundy commune (Côte de Nuits).

Champagne (Shawm-*pahn*) (*Fr.*): Sparkling wine from French Champagne district (or foreign imitations); brandy from superior part of Cognac.

Chardonnay (Shar-dawn-*ay*): Burgundy white grape, sometimes called Pinot Chardonnay; commune of Southern Burgundy.

Charlemagne: See Corton-Charlemagne.

Chassagne-Montrachet (Shass-*ahn*-Maw-rahsh-*ay*): Burgundy commune sharing (with Puligny) the great Montrachet vineyard.

Chasselas (*Shas*-sel-ah): Common white-wine grape, used in Germany, Switzerland and France.

château(x) (shat-*oh*) (*Fr.*): Wine-producing estate(s) or vineyard(s).

Châteauneuf-du-Pape (Shato-nuhf-duh-*Papp*): French Rhône wine.

Chenin blanc (Shen-*anh* Blahw): White-wine grape, basically of the Loire (France); also used in California.

Cheval Blanc (Shev-*al* Blahw): (Château) "1st Growth" St.-Émilion (Bordeaux).

Chevalier-Montrachet (Shev-al-*yay*-Maw-rahsh-*ay*): Burgundy vineyard, part of Montrachet "group."

Chianti (Key-*an*-ti): Italian wine and region (central Italy).

Chinon (Sheen-*anh*): Wine town of central Loire (France).

classé (class-*say*) (*Fr.*): Officially classified: as in *Cru Classé.*

clairet (*klair*-ay) (*Fr.*): Original term for claret; light-colored red wine.

claret: Red Bordeaux wine.

clos (klo) (*Fr.*): Vineyard; literally: "yard."

Cognac (Ko-*nyack*): French brandy from district of same name.

Colares (Koe-*lar*'sh): Wine (and region) of central Portugal.

colheita (kool-*yea*-tah) (Port.): Vintage year; vintage.

consumos (kanh-soom-*oush*) (*Port.*): Common wines: *ordinaires.*

Cornas (Kor-*nar*): Wine commune of Rhône district (France).

Corton-Charlemagne (Kaw-*taw*-Schar-leh-*man*): Classic (red and white wines) Burgundy vineyard.

cosecha (ko-*say*-chah) (*Sp.*): Vintage; vintage year. *cosechado* (ko-say-*char*-doh): "of the vintage of"

côte(s) (coat) (*Fr.*): Hillside; winegrowing area.

Côte d'Or (Coat *dohr*): Traditional (central) Burgundy region.

Côte Rôtie (Coat Roat-*ee*): Rhône red-wine region (France).

crémant (cray-maw) (*Fr.*) fizzy.

cru (krew) (*Fr.*): Growth, crop; wine from a specific vineyard.

crust: Stringy sediment (dregs) in old bottles of Port.

cuvée (*Fr.*): See *Têtes de Cuvée.*

Dão (Downh): Portuguese wine (and region) of central Portugal.

doce (dohs) (*Port.*): Sweet.

Dolcetto (Dol-*chett*-oh): Italian redwine grape; generic wine.

Dôle (*Doe*-l): Swiss red wine, canton of Valais (Val-*ay*).

Dom Pérignon (Dom Par-ee-*nyaw*): Benedictine monk, often called the "inventor of Champagne"; Champagne brand name.

domaine (doe-*mane*) (*Fr.*): Vineyard; control or management of several vineyards.

Dordogne (Door-*doyn*): River of Bordeaux district; wine region.

Douro (*Door*-roe): River and wine region of central Portugal, principally producing Port.

doux (doo) (*Fr.*): Predominantly a Champagne or sparkling-wine term: usually denotes sweet or sweetish.

d'Yquem (dee-*kem*): (Château) "1st Growth" Sauternes (Bordeaux).

eaux-de-vie (oh-deh-*vee*) (*Fr.*): Spirits distilled from crushed grape leavings; distilled spirits in general.

Échézeaux (also Grands Échézeaux) (Esh-ay-*zo*): Famous Burgundy vineyards (Côte de Nuits).

Echt (Ekt) (*Ger.*): Unsugared wine; genuine; "natural."

Edelfaüle (*Aye*-dell-*foy*-leh) (*Ger.*): "Noble rot"—equivalent to French *pourriture noble.*

Edelzwicker (*Aye*-del-*swick*-er): Alsatian blended wine from "noble" (superior) grapes.

êggrapoir (aye-grapp-*pwar*): Revolving cylindrical machine separating grapes from stems and stalks.

Egri Bikavér (*Egg*-ree Bee-kah-*vare*):

Hungarian red wine ("Bull's Blood").

Einsellage (*Ine*-zell-*lag*-ger) (*Ger.*): Individual vineyard; smallest geographical vineyard name allowed under new German wine law.

Eiswein (*Ice*-vine) (*Ger.*): Sweet wine from frostbitten grapes.

Entre-Deux-Mers (Awn-trer-Deh-*Mair*): Wine region (Bordeaux).

Ermitage (Air-mee-*tahge*): Swiss white wine.

escogida (ess-co-*hee*-dah) (*Sp.*): Specially selected.

especial (ess-spay-see-*al*) (*Sp.*): Special (Chilean).

espumantes (es-poo-*mant*-esh) (*Port.*): Sparkling wines.

estufado (esh-too-*fah*-dou) (*Port.*): Method of heating Madeira during aging process.

Étoile (Aye-*twall*): Wine (and commune) of Jura (France).

exceptionnelle (ess-sep-tyon-*el*) (*Fr.*): Special; exceptional; as in *Cru Exceptionnelle.*

Fass (Fahss) (*Ger.*): Cask or barrel.

feine (fine) (*Ger.*): Fine or excellent.

feinste (*fine*'st) (*Ger.*): Finest, most excellent.

Fendant de Sion (Fawn-*daw* der *See*-anh): Swiss white wine.

fiaschi (fee-*as*-kee) (*It.*): Straw-wrapped, flagon-shaped bottles, usually used for Chianti.

finesse: Delicacy or elegance (of a wine).

Fino (*Fee*-no): Type of common Sherry: very dry.

Fixin (Fee-*sanh*): Commune of Côte de Nuits (Burgundy).

Flasche (*Flash*-eh): Typical tall, slim German wine bottle.

Fleurie (Flur-*ee*): One of nine principal (superior) subdivisions of Beaujolais (France).

flor (flor) (*Sp.*): Yeast or bacteria producing a whitish crust on wine's surface; encouraged in production of Sherry.

Folle blanche (Foll blawnch): White grape of Cognac (France); also Californian.

Frankenwein (*Fran*-ken-vine): Wine from Franconia (Germany).

Frascati (Frahs-*kaht*-ee): Italian wine from vicinity of Rome.

Freisa (*Fray*-sa): Italian red-wine grape; generic wine.

frizzante (free-*zhan*-tee) (*It.*): Slightly sparkling; *pétillant.*

Fronsac (Côtes de) (Coat deh Fron-*sack*): Wine region (Bordeaux).

Fuder (*Foo*-der) (*Ger.*): cask or barrel.

Furmint (*Foor*-mint): Hungarian grape, principally used for Tokay.

Gamay (Gam-*may*): Red-wine grape of Beaujolais (France).

garrafeira (garr-ah-*fay*-ra) (*Port.*) Selected; specially chosen.

Gattinara (Got-ee-*nahr*-ah): Italian red wine, Piedmont region.

generic: Wine term meaning "type" (deriving from a well-known area); often borrowed: as with "California Burgundy," "Chilean Chablis," etc.

Gevrey-Chambertin (Zhev-*ray*-Shawm-bair-*tanh*): Burgundy commune containing the famous Chambertin vineyard.

Gewürztraminer (Ger-*veutz*-trah-min-*er*): White-wine grape, version of Traminer (*q.v.*), used principally in France, Germany and California.

Gran Vino (Gran *Vee*-no) (*Sp.*): Fine or "great" (Chilean).

grand (Grahw) (*Fr.*): Large; superior or "great," usually unofficial.

grappa (*gra*-pa) (*It.*): Distilled grape spirits. See also *marc; eaux-de-vie.*

Graves (Grahv): Red- and white-wine region (Bordeaux); also the wine from this region.

Grenache (Gren-*ahsh*): Wine grape, principally a source of *rosés.*

Grenouilles (gren-*wee*): "1st Growth" Chablis vineyard.

Grignolino (Grin-nyo-*leen*-no): Italian red grape; generic wine.

Grillet (Gree-*yay*): (Château) white-wine Rhône vineyard (France).

Grosslage (*Gross*-lag-ger) (*Ger.*): Collective vineyard; name for several traditional vineyards lumped together under the system of the new German wine law.

Gruaud-Larose (*Grew*-oud-La-*rose*): (Château) "2nd Growth" Médoc (Bordeaux).

Grünlack (*Groin*-lahk) (*Ger.*): "Green seal." See Johannisberg (Schloß).

Halbtrocken (Halb-*tra*-ken) (*Ger.*): Slightly sweet; not bone dry.

Haro (*Ah*-roe): Principal wine town of the Rioja region (Spain).

Haut-Brion (Oh-bree-*yohw*): (Château) "1st Growth" Graves (Bordeaux).

Haut-Médoc (Oh-May-*dock*): Superior wine region (Bordeaux).

Hermitage (Air-mee-*tahge*): Region of Rhône district (France).

hochfeinste (hock-*fine*'st) (*Ger.*): Finest; most superior.

Hochheim (*Hock*-hyme): Famous wine town of German Rheingau.

hospice (aw-*spees*) (*Fr.*): Hospital, almshouse; in France frequently supported by income from vineyards (Hospice de Beaune, etc.).

Hunawihr (Hun-a-*veer*): Wine town of Alsace (France).

Jerez de la Frontera (Hair-*eth* day lah Fron-*tair*-ah): Sherry town: region of southwestern Spain.

Johannisberg (Schloß) (Schlohs Yo-*hann*-is-bairg): A universally famous vineyard, Rheingau region (Germany).

Josephhof (*Yo*-sef-hoef): German vineyard, Moselle region.

Jurançon (Jur-anh-*saw*): Wine (and region) of Pyrénées (France).

Kabinett (once *Cabinett*) (Ka-bin-*et*) (*Ger.*): Formerly "specially reserved or selected"; under new German wine law, lowest (driest) grading of *Qualitätswein mit Prädikat*, q.v.

Keller-Abfülling (*Kell*-er-Ahb-*fuel*-ung) (*Ger.*): Estate-bottled.

konsumwein (kon-*sume*-vine) (*Ger.*): Formerly common wine; *ordinaire.*

Lacryma Christi (*La*-cream-ah *Krees*-tee): Wine from slopes of Vesuvius; term for generic Italian sparkling wine.

Lafite-Rothschild   (La-*feet*-Raw-

sheeld): (Château) "1st Growth" Médoc (Bordeaux).

Lage (*Lahg*-eh) (*Ger.*): Vineyard (plural: *Lagen*).

Lagrein Rosato (La-*grain* Rose-*ah*-toe): *Rosé* wine, Italian Tyrol.

Lascombes (Lass-*kawmb*): (Château) "2nd Growth" Médoc (Bordeaux).

Latour (La-*toor*): (Château) "1st Growth" Médoc (Bordeaux).

Latricières (La-tree-see-*air*): Burgundy vineyard of Chambertin "group" (Côte de Nuits).

Léoville-Las-Cases (Lay-oh-*veel*-Las-*Cass*): (Château) "2nd Growth" Médoc (Bordeaux).

Lesegut (*Lay*-say-goot) (*Ger.*): Harvest, crop.

Liebfraumilch (*Leeb*-frow-milch): Popular generic Rhine wine.

liqueur (lee-*ker*): Sweet cordial or after-dinner drink.

liquoreux (lee-ker-*err*) (*Fr.*): Sweet; "luscious"; dessert wine.

Lirac (Lee-*rack*): Rhône commune, principally noted for *rosés*.

Listrac (Lees-*track*): Subdivision of Médoc (Bordeaux).

Lussac (Lew-*sack*): Subdivision of St.-Émilion (Bordeaux).

Mâconnais (Mack-awn-*ay*): Southern Burgundy wine region.

Madeira (Mad-*air*-ah): *Apéritif* or desert wine (Portuguese).

maderizé (mad-air-ee-*zay*) (*Fr.*): Oxidized white wine, dark and bitter. Literally: like Madeira.

Magnum: Two-bottle size.

Manzanilla (*Man*-tha-*nee*-yah): Sherry-like wine (Spanish).

marc (maa) (*Fr.*): Spirits distilled from the "must" or leavings of pressed grapes.

Marcobrunn(er) (*Mark*-o-*bruhn*): German vineyard, Rheingau region.

Margaux (Mar-*go*): Subdivision of (and "1st Growth" Château in) Médoc (Bordeaux).

marque déposée (mark *day*-poe-*say*) (*Fr.*): Registered brand name.

Marsala (Mar-*sah*-la): Italian fortified sweetish wine from Sicily.

Mateus (Mat-*ay*-osh; English alternate: Mat-*toose*): Portuguese *rosé* from Douro region.

Mazoyères (Mah-zoy-*air*): Famous Burgundy vineyard in Chambertin "group" (Côte de Nuits).

Médoc (May-*dock*): Bordeaux wine region: technically includes both Médoc and Haut-Médoc.

méthode champenoise (may-*tohd* shaw-pan-*warhz*) (*Fr.*) Traditional French process of making Champagne.

Meursault (mair-*so*): Burgundy commune (Côte de Beaune).

mise (meeze) (*Fr.*): Literally: put or placed. *Mise en bouteilles au Château:* bottled at the château; estate-bottled.

Mittelwihr (Mit-el-*veer*): Wine town of Alsace (France).

Monbazillac (More-baz-ee-*ack*): Wine (and region) of Dordogne (France).

monopole (mon-o-*pole*) (*Fr.*): Monopoly on a wine, vineyard or brand name.

Mont de Milieu (Maw deh Meel-*yehr*): "2nd Growth" Chablis vineyard.

Montilla (Mawn-*tee*-yah): Unfortified Sherry-type wine (Spain).

Montrachet (Maw-rahsh-*ay*): Classic white-wine Burgundy vineyard.

Moscatel (Moosh-kah-*tel*): Portuguese dessert wine; region (Setúbal) south of Lisbon.

Mosel (*Mos'l*): Moselle, German wine region.

Moselblümchen (Mos'l-*bloom*-shen): Generic term for Moselle wine, usually a blend.

Moulin-à-Vent (Moo-*lanh*-a-*Vaw*): One of nine principal (superior) subdivisions of Beaujolais; name of outstanding vineyard of same area.

Moulis (Moo-*lee*): Subdivision of Médoc (Bordeaux).

mousseux (moo-*sir*) (*Fr.*): Sparkling wine.

Mouton-Rothschild (Moo-*taw*-Raw-*sheeld*): (Château) now a "1st Growth" Médoc (Bordeaux).

Moutonne (La) (Moo-*tawn*): "1st Growth" Chablis vineyard.

Muscadet (Moos-kah-*day*): White wine (and region) of lower Loire.

Musigny (Mew-seen-*yee*): Burgundy vineyard (Côte de Nuits).

Nahe (Narh): German wine region, west of the Rhine.

Natur (*Nature*) (Nat-*tour*) (*Fr.*): Brandy (*Champagne*) term, denoting unblended or from a single cask; sparkling wine (Champagne) term, usually meaning unsugared or "natural."

Naturwein (Na-*toor*-vine) (or *Naturrein*) (Na-*toor*-rine) (*Ger.*): Unsugared or unsweetened; "natural" wine (see *Kabinett*).

Néac (Nay-*ack*): Minor wine region (Bordeaux).

Nebbiolo (Nebb-ee-*oh*-lo): Italian grape; generic red wine; Nebbiolo *Spumante:* sparkling Nebbiolo.

Neckar (*Neck*-er): Small German wine region, east of the Rhine.

négociants (nay-go-see-*aw*) (*Fr.*): Producer, bottler, shipper: "middleman."

Nemeskadar (*Nem*-esh-*kah*-dar): Hungarian red wine.

Nierstein (*Neer*-styne): Wine town, Rheinheβen region (Germany).

Nozet (Château de) (No-zay): Vineyard (Pouilly-Fumé), upper Loire.

Nuits (Côte de) (Coat-deh-Nwee): Northern section of Côte d'Or (Burgundy).

Nuits-St.-Georges (Nwee-San-*Zhorge*): Burgundy commune (Côte de Nuits).

oeil-de-perdrix (oye-der-pair-*dree*) (*Fr.*): traditional term for *rosé*.

Oloroso (Oh-lo-*ro*-so): Sweet Sherry type.

Original-Abfüllung (Or-*ig*-in-al-Ahb-*fuel*-ung) (*Ger.*): Estate-bottled; not used with new German wine law.

Orvieto (Or-vee-*ate*-oh): White wine (and region) of central Italy.

Palomino (*Pahl*-oh-*mean*-oh): White-wine grape, used for Sherry.

Parsac (Par-*sack*): Subdivision of St.-Émilion (Bordeaux).

pasado (pas-*sah*-doe) (*Sp.*): "Old" (wine); generally invalid term.

Passe-Tous-Grains (Pass-Too-*Granh*)

(*Fr.*): Inferior type of Burgundy, a blend from two red grapes.

pastos (*pass*-tose) (*Sp.*): Common wines; *ordinaires*.

Pauillac (Poy-*yack*): Subdivision of Médoc (Bordeaux).

Pedro Ximénez (*Pay*-droe *Hee*-may-neth): White grape, used for Sherry.

Periquita (Pair-ee-*kee*-tah): Portuguese red grape; varietal wine.

pétillant (pet-ee-*anh*) (*Fr.*): Slightly sparkling; fizzy.

petit (p'tee) (*Fr.*): Minor, secondary; *Petit Chablis:* "3rd Growth" Chablis.

Pétrus (Pay-*troos*): (Château) "1st Growth" Pomerol (Bordeaux).

phylloxera (fill-*ox*-era): Vine louse of North American origin.

Pichon-Longueville (Pee-*shaw*-Long-eh-*veel*): (Château) "2nd Growth" Médoc (Bordeaux).

Pinot blanc (Pee-*no* blahw): French white grape; Californian varietal wine.

Pinot noir (Pee-*no* nwar): Principal Burgundy red grape; Californian wine.

Pomerol (Pom-air-*oll*): Wine district (Bordeaux).

Pommard (Po-*mar*): Burgundy commune (Côte de Beaune).

Pouilly-Fuissé (Poo-*ee*-Foo-ee-*say*): White wine (and region) of Southern Burgundy.

Pouilly-Fumé (Poo-*ee*-Foo-*may*): White wine (and region), upper Loire (France).

pourriture noble (pur-it-*ur* nob'*l*) (*Fr.*): "Noble rot" or mold that set-

tles on ripe grapes, responsible for sweet wines.

Prädikat (*Prey*-dee-kart) (*Ger.*): See *Qualitätswein*.

premier (prem-*yay*) (*Fr.*): First, foremost: as in *Premier Cru*.

Puligny-Montrachet (Pooh-leen-*ye*-Maw-rahsh-*ay*): Burgundy commune (Côte de Beaune).

puttony (*put*-on-yu) (*Hun.*): Term used to indicate degree of sweetness of Tokay wine.

Qualitätswein (*Kval*-i-tays-vine) (*Ger.*): Q.b.A.: second (middle) quality classification under the new German wine law; *Q. mit Prädikat* (*Pray*-dee-kaht): top classification.

Quarts-de-Chaume (Kah-deh-*Shome*): Famous sweet-wine vineyards of Anjou (Loire).

Quincy (Kan-*see*): White-wine region of upper Loire (France).

quinta (*keen*-tah) (*Port.*): Wine house; producer's cellars.

Reserva (Ray-*ser*-vah) (*Sp.*): "Reserve"; specially aged.

Reservado (Ray-sehr-*vah*-doe) (*Sp.*): Reserve; selected (Chilean).

Réserve (Ray-*zerv*) (*Fr.*): Special; specially selected.

Rheingau (*Rine*-gow): Most celebrated German wine region.

Rheinheβen (*Rine*-hessen): German wine region, west bank of Rhine.

Rheinpfalz (*Rine*-falz): German wine region, adjoining Alsace.

Rhône (Rohn): River of south-central France; wine from its valley.

Ribeauvillé (Ree-bo-veel-*ay*): Wine town of Alsace (France).

Ribero (Ree-*bair*-oh) or Ribeiro (Ree-*bay*-oh): Wine from province of Galacia (northwestern Spain).

Richebourg (Reech-*boor*): Burgundy vineyard, part of Romanée "group" (Côte de Nuits).

Riesling (*Rees*-ling): White-wine grape, basically German; varietal wine.

Rioja (Ree-*oh*-ha): Superior wine region of northern Spain.

Riquewihr (Reek-*veer*): Wine town of Alsace (France).

Riserva (Ree-*sair*-vah) (*It.*): "Reserve"; specially selected.

Roche (Clos de la) (*Clo*-deh-la-*Rawsh*): Burgundy vineyard (Côte de Nuits).

Romanée-Conti (Ro-man-*ee*-Kawn-*tee*): Celebrated Burgundy vineyard (Côte de Nuits).

Romanée-St.-Vivant (Ro-man-*ee*-Vee-*vaw*): Burgundy vineyard (Côte de Nuits).

rosé (rose-*aye*) (*Fr.*): Pink or rose-colored wine.

Roslack (*Rose*-lahk) (*Ger.*): "Rose" or "pink seal." See Johannisberg (Schloβ).

Rotlack (*Roht*-lahk) (*Ger.*): "Red seal." See Johannisberg (Schloβ).

Ruwer (*Rue*-ver): Wine-producing tributary of the Mosel (Germany).

Saar (Tsar): Wine-producing tributary of the Mosel (Germany).

St.-Amour (Sann-tah-*moor*): One of nine principal (superior) subdivisions of Beaujolais (France).

St.-Émilion (Sant-Ay-meel-*yaw*): Wine region (Bordeaux).

St.-Estèphe (San-Ay-*steff*): Subdivision of Médoc (Bordeaux).

St.-Georges (San-Z*horge*): Subdivision of St.-Émilion (Bordeaux); Burgundy vineyard (Côte de Nuits).

St.-Julien (San-Zhool-*yanh*): Subdivision of Médoc (Bordeaux).

Ste.-Croix-du-Mont (Sant-*Kwa*-deh-*Maw*): Wine region (Bordeaux).

Sancerre (Saw-*sayr*): White wine (and region) of upper Loire.

Saumur (So-*muyr*): Wine (and region) of central Loire.

Sauvignon (So-veey-*naw*): White grape, basically of Bordeaux.

Savennières (Sa-veh-*nyair*): Famous wine commune of lower Loire.

Schloβabzug (*Schlohs*-ab-*zug*) (*Ger.*): Estate-bottled formerly, nowadays *Abfüllung Weingut.*

sec (sek) (*Fr.*): Dry; Champagne or sparkling-wine term: usually denotes moderately dry, sweeter than *brut.*

secco (*sek*-ko) (*It.*): Dry.

Sekt (Sekt): Generic term for German sparkling wine.

Sémillon (Sem-ee-*yaw*): White grape, basically of Bordeaux.

Sercial (*Sir*-seal): Dry type of Madeira.

Šipon (Chi-pon): Yugoslavian grape (and white wine).

Soave (*Swa*-vay): Italian white wine from vicinity of Verona.

solera (sol-*air*-ah) (*Sp.*): System of casks arranged in tiers for blending and aging Sherry.

Spätlese   (*Sphate*-lay-*seh*)   (*Ger.*):
Wine from late-picked grapes.

spritzig (*shprit*-zig) (*Ger.*): Slightly
sparkling; *pétillant.*

spumante (spoo-*man*-tay) (*It.*):
Sparkling.

Steinberg (*Shtyne*-bairg): Celebrated
German Rheingau vineyard.

Steinwein (*Shtyne*-vine): German generic term for wine from the
Würzburg section of Franconia.

Stück (Shtyouk) (*Ger.*): Cask or
barrel.

Supérieur(e) (soo-pair-ee-*yur*) (*Fr.*):
Usually denotes wine of higher alcoholic content.

Sylvaner (sil-*vahn*-er): White-wine
grape, basically German.

Szamarodni (Sah-moor-*od*-nee): dry
Tokay (Hungary).

Tâche (La) (La-*Tash*): Burgundy
vineyard,   part   of   Romanée
"group."

Tafelwein (*Taf*-fell-vine) (*Ger.*):
"table wine"; lowest classification
under new German wine law; see
konsumwein.

Tart (Clos de) (Clo deh *Tar*): Burgundy vineyard (Côte de Nuits).

Tavel (Tav-*ell*): Rhône commune,
traditional source of best French
rosés.

terroir (tear-*wahr*) (*Fr.*): Special, individualistic quality of wine, attributable chiefly to soil type.

Tête(s) de Cuvée (*Tayt*-deh-Koo-
vay): Traditional Burgundian term
for finest vineyard(s).

Tokay (Tow-*kai*): Celebrated Hungarian white wine.

Tokay Aszú (Tow-*kai* Ah-*shu*):
Sweet Tokay.

Traminer (Trah-min-*er*): White-
wine grape; excels in Alsace and
Germany.

Trocken (*Tra*-ken) (*Ger.*): Absolutely dry.

Trockenbeerenauslese (*Tra-ken-beer-
en-ows*-lay-seh) (*Ger.*): Wine from
late-picked, raisin-sweet grapes.

Valdepeñas (*Val*-day-*pain*-yas): Wine
(and region) of central Spain.

Valmur (Vawl-*meeur*): "1st Growth"
Chablis vineyard.

Valpantena (Val-pant-*ain*-ah): Italian
red wine from near Verona.

Valpolicella   (Val-po-lee-*chell*-ah):
Italian red wine (Verona).

varietal: Wine named after predominant grape: Alsatian "Traminer,"
Californian "Riesling," etc.

Vaudesir   (Vo-day-*zeer*):   "1st
Growth" Chablis vineyard.

velho (*ver*-lyou) (*Port.*): Old; aged.

vendange (vawn-*dawj*) (*Fr.*): Harvest,
harvest time.

Verdelho (Ver-*dell*-you): Madeira
grape (and wine: medium dry).

Verdicchio (di Jesi) (Ver-*dee*-kee-oh):
Italian white wine made near
Venice.

Verdiso (Vair-*dees*-zo): Italian white-
wine grape; wine of the same name.

viejo (vee-*ay*-ho) (*Sp.*): "Old" (wine);
generally meaningless.

vieux (vyeh) (*Fr.*): Old.

village(s) (veel-*ahzh*) (*Fr.*): Vil-
lage(s); when hyphenated with another name, usually denotes a more
extensive   geographical   source

(area) (e.g., *Beaune* is classified higher than *Beaune-Villages*).

vin (vanh) (*Fr.*): Wine; *v. gris* (gree): a *rosé* of usually inferior quality; *v. jaune* (joan): yellow Sherry-type wine of Jura; *v. de paille* (deh *pie*): Sweet wine from raisined grapes; *v. de pay* (deh *pay*), country wine, generically not a great wine; *v. du pays* (due pay-*ee*): local wine, meaning of a given locality.

vino (*vee*-no) (*Sp.*): Wine; *v. de pasto* (*pas*-toe): common wine, *ordinaire; v. del pais* (dell-pie-*ess*) or *v. de la tierra* (day lah tee-*air*-ah): regional or country wine.

vinho (*veen*-you) (*Port.*): Wine; *v. branco* (*brank*-ou): white wine; *v. de consumo* (deh kanh-*soom*-ou): common wine, *ordinaire; v. generoso* (jeh-neh-*rah*-zou): fortified wine; *v. maduro* (mad-*oor*-ou): *rosé; v. de mesa* (deh *may*-zer): table wine as opposed to fortified wine; *v. tinto* (*teen*-tou): red wine.

Vinho Verde (*Veen*-you *Ver*-der): "New wine"; wine region of northern Portugal.

Vitis labrusca (*Wee*-tiss la-*brus*-ka): North American wild grape; also bred for wine.

Vitis vinifera (*Wee*-tiss weenie-*fair*-ah): Middle Eastern and European wine grape.

V.O.: Brandy term: "Very Old"; *V.S.O.:* "Very Old Superior"; *V.S.O.P.:* "Very Old Superior Pale."

Vollrads (Schloß) (Schlohs *Fawl*-rads): Famous German Rheingau vineyard.

Volnay (Voll-*nay*): Burgundy commune (Côte de Beaune).

Vosne-Romanée (*Vohn*-Ro-man-*ay*): Burgundy commune, containing the celebrated Romanée vineyards.

Vougeot (Clos de) (Klo deh Vou-zhow): Classic Burgundy vineyard.

Vouvray (Voo-*vray*): White wine (and region), central Loire (France).

Weinstraße (Vine-straß-eh): Principal group of wine-producing villages of Rheinpfalz (Germany).

Xampâns (*Sham*-pong) (*Sp.*): "Champagne."

Zwicker (*Zwick*-er): Alsatian common wine or *ordinaire.*

Index

Index

ABBREVIATIONS

ch.—château
class.—classification
com.—commune, village
dist.—district
gr.—grape
riv.—river
vyd.—vineyard
Aus.—Austria
Fr.—France, French
Ger.—Germany, German

Gr.—Greece, Greek
Hun.—Hungary, Hungarian
It.—Italy, Italian
Port.—Portugal, Portuguese
Rom.—Romania, Romanian
Sp.—Spain, Spanish
Switz.—Switzerland, Swiss
U.S.—United States
Yugo.—Yugoslavia, Yugoslavian

[253]